TO THE WATCH TOWER

Awake!
TO THE
WATCH
TOWER

VOLUME 1

DOUG HARRIS

Twickenham, England

ISBN 0 9513632 0 4

Production and printing in Great Britain for
REACHOUT TRUST
PO Box 43, Twickenham TW2 7EG by
Nuprint Ltd, Harpenden, Herts AL5 4SE

INDEX

NOTES

Many of the books, tracts etc about Jehovah's Witnesses mentioned in the text are available from Reachout Trust. An order form is provided at the back of the book.

Any emphasis in quotations by SMALL CAPITAL LETTERS is added to the original, unless indicated otherwise, whereas *italics* are to be found in the original. **Bold print** is always used to put back into the quotation what the Watchtower have replaced by '...'.

To save space the following abbreviations have been used throughout:

ABU - *Aid To Bible Understanding*, WBTS, 1971
EB - *Encyclopaedia Britannica*, various editions
KIT - Kingdom Interlinear Translation, WBTS, 1985
NCE - *New Catholic Encyclopaedia*, various editions
NWT - New World Translation, WBTS, various editions
Reasoning - *Reasoning From The Scriptures*, WBTS, 1985
SS - *Studies In The Scriptures*, WBTS, Vols 1-7
VINE - *Expository Dictionary of New Testament Words*, W E Vine, 1966
WBTS - The Watchtower Bible and Tract Society of Jehovah's Witnesses
WT - *The Watchtower*
WTR - *The Watch Tower Reprints*
ZWTR - *Zion's Watch Tower Reprints*

INTRODUCTION

This edition marks a complete revision, resetting and expansion of *Awake! To the Watchtower*.

I especially want to thank Bill Browning for his fellowship over the past years. His understanding of the Jehovah's Witness mind seems to blend well with the Christian point of view which I have. There is material in many chapters that has either come direct from Bill or been inspired by him. In addition Sections 9 and 10 are largely based on his work. I also wish to thank George and Anne Buck in Birmingham who spent much time researching the various quotes found in *Reasoning From The Scriptures*.

You may have noticed that this is Volume 1. Bill is in the process of preparing Volume 2 which will major on the false prophecies of the Society.

We praise God for the encouragement we continue to receive from those who have used the first edition and we trust that many more will see that they can share confidently with the next Jehovah's Witness that calls. Regularly we hear of good contacts with Witnesses, some of whom eventually leave the Society. It appears, however, that many are staying in the Society, even though unhappy and discouraged, because of the fear of being called 'apostate', or 'of the Devil' if they leave. What an opportunity for the Christian when that Witness calls!

Through teaching and encouragement we have seen churches become aware of this opportunity. As a result some towns in Britain are becoming very hard for the Witnesses to work in—yours could be another one. We will be happy to arrange a seminar in your area to show how you can witness with confidence. Please write for details. On the other hand, we find it sad that some churches feel we must, 'leave them alone'. We will reply to this attitude in the first two Sections. But just to set the scene, please note we have the Watchtower's blessing for what we are doing:

> It is not a form of religious persecution for anyone to *say* or *show* that another religion is false. IT IS NOT RELIGIOUS PERSECUTION FOR AN INFORMED PERSON TO EXPOSE PUBLICLY A CERTAIN RELIGION AS BEING FALSE, thus allowing persons to see the difference between false religion and true religion... it is a PUBLIC SERVICE instead of religious persecution... (WT, 15 November 1963, p. 688.)

Often we are asked questions concerning 2 John 9–10. You will find our understanding of these verses mentioned in different Sections.

Apart from sharing with the Jehovah's Witnesses we need to be aware of our responsibility to all people. We are the 'light of the world' and the 'salt of the earth'. The question is how bright do we shine and how much effect do we have on our area? We need to warn the people around us of the danger of false prophets and at the same time share the truth. Write for sample tracts especially designed for this purpose. I believe the only way this world will really see that the cults are wrong is when Christians live in the power and love of Jesus Christ.

At all times we need to be ready to witness but when we meet a Jehovah's Witness it is essential we are prepared. The first step is undoubtedly to know our God. It is of little value knowing where the Watchtower is false if we do not have a personal experience of Jesus Christ. Spend time with Him praying, reading and meditating on His Word. Don't look for Scriptures to 'zap' the Witness but aim to know the Lord. Next we need to know the basic doctrines of our faith. Christians are sometimes stumped by the Witnesses because we do not know the Bible and its doctrines. Of course we are always, or at least should be, growing in the Lord but we need to have spent some time knowing God and have some idea of our own doctrines before we launch into the Witness doctrines.

Read through this book and find the Sections you are at home with. Photostats of material mentioned are available from Reachout Trust, at reasonable cost. Sometimes spare copies of Watchtower literature are also available.

In your witnessing do show *love*. Remember the average Witness comes to the door because they believe they are serving Jehovah God. Persecution only convinces them they are right, but love and understanding confuses them and often makes them open to receive. Don't 'nit-pick' but seek the Holy Spirit's help as to what you should share. Then without accusation ask questions that will lead the Witness to the right conclusion. In other words don't say, 'You are of the Devil because you teach Jesus isn't God!' but 'Could we read Colossians 2:9 please. What does this say about Jesus?'

One thing you will often hear, once Witnesses know you are a Christian, is 'We are the only ones going from door to door preaching the Good News.' Some might quote events that show a wrong attitude by some clergy to war, sex etc. Don't be drawn into retaliation and tell them about the nasty happenings in the local Kingdom Hall. Admit that some people who call themselves Christians are not serving God but then tell them about the good things: how the Spirit of God is moving in the churches and what the Christians in your area are doing to reach the unsaved with the gospel. Never waffle. If you cannot answer a question admit it and arrange another meeting to give yourself time to study and find the answer.

You might sometimes feel drained after spending time with a Jehovah's Witness. Don't be alarmed, remember we are in a spiritual battle. Encourage yourself by meditating on Ephesians 6:10–20 and ask the Holy Spirit to bring you to the reality of protection in Christ. It will help to meet regularly with other Christians and pray for each other and the Witnesses. There are already some groups active in this way but we need more. Please remember that we are here to serve and so please contact us if we can help in any way.

Finally, we pray that the Lord will richly bless you and use you to share His light with those in darkness.

Douglas Harris
February 1988

REACHOUT TRUST
PO Box 43
Twickenham
TW2 7EG

SECTION 1

Why Should I?

One conclusion we've reached travelling around the country is that many Christians do not realize how much the Lord longs for Jehovah's Witnesses to be saved. If it were possible for God to love one group more than another, I believe He would choose Witnesses, and others like them, who often have reached out for God and spiritual things but have been misled and deceived into a man-made religion.

Christians have a God-given commission to share the gospel with Jehovah's Witnesses but often because of fear or ignorance we turn a 'deaf ear' and hope they go away. Our desire is that this manual will help overcome these and any other negative feelings you may have towards the Witnesses. The Jehovah's Witness comes with a false gospel and in so doing asks, 'Why do you believe differently?' The worse thing we can do is 'persecute' them by setting free the dog or slamming the door in their face. All that does is confirm to them that they are 'in the truth'! Anyway, 1 Peter 3:15 tells of Christ's promise to help us give an effective answer if He has the central place in our lives. It may not be a theological discourse, probably better not, but it will be a clear word of testimony.

You may not be able to grasp all the arguments presented here but you *can* share your personal relationship with Jesus and then politely excuse yourself from further discussion. If you can grasp some simple presentation, great, but remember, *Jesus alone can save*.

Motivation

Three words sum up our motivation, love, love and love! The desire of the Lord's heart is to rescue these ones and to this we should willingly sacrifice our time and talents. Meditate on John 3:16–17; Romans 9:1–3, 10:1–3; 2 Peter 3:8–9. See the motivation of those mentioned. Christ came to this world because of love; Paul reached out to those who hated him because of love; Christ has not returned to this world yet because He loves all and wants all to be saved.

This alone should be our motivation: *I love the Jehovah's Witnesses as Jesus loves them and I want to see them free in Christ.*

Preparation

Murphy's law (if that's not superstition!) tells us that the Witness will always call at the wrong time. You'll have hundreds of reasons not to talk, but didn't the Lord have reason not to talk to the Samaritan woman or Nicodemus? Sacrificial giving up of our favourite TV programme or the gourmet meal will take care of 99 per cent of our reasons and the other 1 per cent are overcome by fixing a return visit. However, you can prepare now for the next visit in three simple ways.

Prayer

We are at war, not with the Jehovah's Witness but with the spiritual forces behind the Society (2 Cor 4:1–4). May we learn more and more to be in the spiritual battle (see 2 Corinthians 10:3–5 and Mark 3:27).

Know the Lord and His Word

There is no substitute for this. We need a basic grasp of our own doctrines, salvation, justification, sanctification, hell, eternal life etc. The reason the Witness often stumps us is that we don't know what we believe and therefore we cannot argue that they are wrong! Let's get stuck in or as one brother says, 'Thou shalt bash on!' (see John 5:39, 17:3; Matthew 16:13–16).

Know the Jehovah's Witnesses

To talk at depth with a Witness you will need to know something about them. This is what this book is about. We need to know what are sensitive subjects and how to deal with them. We are to build bridges, not make a kamikaze run! In your first contact it is usually best to avoid areas that act as the proverbial 'red rag to the bull', e.g. the Trinity, blood, the cross or stake, Christmas. All these subjects can be dealt with later but they are not the best for bridge building.

Execution

This is where you get your head chopped off if you fail! Seriously, when time permits, two basic areas should be presented to the Witness. First, present facts that show the Watchtower organization to be false, and not, as they claim, the *only* channel of God. Second, present clearly the person of Jesus Christ. Never discuss the first area without the second. What is the point of cataloguing the faults of a sinking ship? Throw a lifebelt! If you do not have time to do both then simply share Jesus.

When you sow doubts about the organization do so in a loving way; never be vindictive or spiteful. Where possible have Watchtower literature or at least the date and page of statements you wish to quote so that the matter can be established.

The following pages will provide material for you to come to know the errors of the organization, (see especially Sections 2A and 2B) and how to share positively the gospel of our Lord Jesus (see especially Section 4). Happy Reading!

SECTION 2

Are Jehovah's Witnesses a Cult?

Some may feel that this Section is not necessary but our experience has shown otherwise. There are church-goers, regrettably leaders among them, who feel that we should leave the Jehovah's Witnesses alone and let them preach in their own way. We do not believe this to be so.

There are many good man-made definitions of a cult but I prefer to use a biblical one that should be acceptable to all. In the Witnesses own Bible we read:

> However, even if we or an angel out of heaven were to declare to you as good news something beyond what we declared to you as good news, let him be accursed. As we have said above, I also now say again, whoever it is that is declaring to you as good news something beyond what you accepted, let him be accursed. (Gal 1:8-9, NWT.)

When a matter is repeated in Scripture we must take note of it. Is the gospel that Jehovah's Witnesses preach the same as the one Paul preached? If not they are condemned by their own Bible. We will investigate several aspects of the gospel found in Galatians.

Revelation of Jesus Christ (Galatians 1:2)

The gospel originates with Jesus Christ. Do the WBTS believe this or are man's teachings put on a par with biblical revelation? The following quotes give the answer:

> Thus the Bible is an organizational book and belongs to the Christian congregation as an organization, not to individuals, regardless of how sincerely they may believe that they can interpret the Bible. For this reason the BIBLE CANNOT BE PROPERLY UNDERSTOOD WITHOUT JEHOVAH'S VISIBLE ORGANIZATION IN MIND. (WT, 1 October 1967, p. 587.)

> We all need help to understand the Bible, and WE CANNOT FIND THE SCRIPTURAL GUIDANCE WE NEED OUTSIDE the 'faithful and discreet slave' organization. (WT, 15 February 1981, p. 19.)

> To turn away from Jehovah AND HIS ORGANIZATION, TO SPURN THE DIRECTION OF THE 'FAITHFUL AND DISCREET SLAVE,' AND TO RELY SIMPLY ON PERSONAL BIBLE READING and interpretation is to become like a solitary tree in a parched land. (WT, 1 June 1985, p. 20.)

The evidence shows that the WBTS place their teaching and 'revelation' above or at least on a par with Scripture. This is not the true gospel.

Straightforward (Galatians 2:14)

There is no deception in the good news; no twisting or turning. Sections 2A and 2B will show that this is not true of the Witnesses' gospel. There is also one classic quote:

> While malicious lying is definitely condemned in the Bible, THIS DOES NOT MEAN THAT A PERSON IS UNDER OBLIGATION TO DIVULGE TRUTHFUL INFORMATION TO PEOPLE WHO ARE NOT ENTITLED TO IT... Jehovah God allows an 'OPERATION OF ERROR' to go to persons who prefer falsehood... (ABU, p. 1061.)

The gospel of the Jehovah's Witness is not straightforward.

Privileged Classes (Galatians 3:26–29)

The gospel has no privileged classes—all are equal before the Lord. Unfortunately the gospel of the Jehovah's Witness has a two-tier 'salvation' with only 144,000 ever being born again and seeing Jesus (see Section 6F). The rest live on earth clearing up the mess after Armageddon. They are not in the new covenant but may benefit from it. What a different gospel to the truth!

A Right Freedom (Galatians 5:1,13)

The gospel proclaims liberty to the captives: not a fleshly freedom but freedom to be ourselves in Christ. What freedom does the Watchtower gospel have?

> AVOID INDEPENDENT THINKING...Satan...promoted independent thinking... How is such independent thinking manifested? A common way is by questioning the counsel that is provided by God's visible organization...there are some who point out that the organization has had to make adjustments before, and so they argue: 'This shows that we have to make up our own mind on what we believe.' This is independent thinking. (WT, 15 January 1983, pp. 22,27.)

Quite clearly, even from this brief look, we conclude that the WBTS are a cult because they preach a different gospel to the one recorded in the New Testament. This is why we need to share the true gospel with them and our neighbours so that as few people as possible are led astray.

The Watchtower's False Prophecies

The second volume of *Awake! To The Watchtower* will cover this subject more fully but here are just a few of the Society's major false prophecies, taken from our booklet, *The Truth Revealed*. (An order form for publications mentioned is found at the end of the book.)

ARMAGEDDON

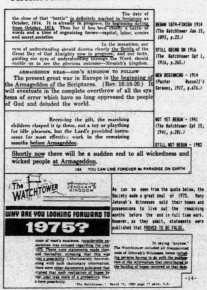

The date of the close of that "battle" is definitely marked in Scripture as October, 1914. It is already in progress, its beginning dating from October, 1874. Thus far it has been chiefly a battle of words and a time of organizing forces—capital, labor, armies and secret societies.

BEGAN 1874—FINISH 1914
(The Watchtower Jan 15, 1892, p.22.)

In the meantime, our eyes of understanding should discern clearly the Battle of the Great Day of God Almighty now in progress; and our faith, guiding our eyes of understanding through the Word, should enable us to see the glorious outcome—Messiah's kingdom.

STILL GOING ON 1916
(The Watchtower Spt 1, 1916, p.265.)

ARMAGEDDON NEAR—GOD'S KINGDOM TO FOLLOW
The present great war in Europe is the beginning of the Armageddon of the Scriptures. (Rev. 16:16-20.) It will eventuate in the complete overthrow of all the systems of error which have so long oppressed the people of God and deluded the world.

NEW BEGINNING - 1914
(Pastor Russell's Sermons, 1917, p.676.)

Receiving the gift, the marching children clasped it to them, not a toy or plaything for idle pleasure, but the Lord's provided instrument for most effective work in the remaining months before Armageddon.

NOT YET BEGUN - 1941
(The Watchtower Spt 15, 1941, p.281.)

Shortly now there will be a sudden end to all wickedness and wicked people at Armageddon.

STILL NOT BEGUN - 1982

154   YOU CAN LIVE FOREVER IN PARADISE ON EARTH

WHY ARE YOU LOOKING FORWARD TO 1975?

As can be seen from the quote below, the Society made a great deal of 1975. Many Jehovah's Witnesses sold their homes and possessions to live out the remaining months before the end in full time work. However, as they admit, statements were published that PROVED TO BE FALSE.

nium of man's existence, considerable expectation was aroused regarding the year 1975. There were statements made then, and thereafter, stressing that this was only a possibility. Unfortunately, however, along with such cautionary information, there were other statements published that implied that such realization of hopes by that year was more of a probability than a mere possibility.

In saying "anyone," *The Watchtower* included all disappointed ones of Jehovah's Witnesses, hence including persons having to do with the publication of the information that contributed to the buildup of hopes centered on that date.

'The Watchtower,' March 15, 1980 page 17 para. 5,6.

-14-

OLD TESTAMENT PROPHETS WILL COME BACK TO LIFE!

The SCRIPTURES fix the date as 1925. *(Millions Now Living Will Never Die, 1920, pp.88-90.)*

The chief thing to be restored is the human race to life; and since other Scriptures definitely fix the fact that there will be a resurrection of Abraham, Isaac, Jacob and other faithful ones of old, and that these will have the first favour, we may expect 1925 to witness the return of these faithful men of Israel from the condition of death, being resurrected and fully restored to perfect humanity and made the visible, legal representatives of the new order of things on earth.

Therefore we may confidently expect that 1925 will mark the return of Abraham, Isaac, Jacob and the faithful prophets of old, particularly those named by the Apostle in Hebrews chapter eleven, to the condition of human perfection.

Expected anyday! - ITS NOW 1942!

...those faithful men of old may be expected back from the dead any day now. The Scriptures give good reason to believe that it shall be shortly before Armageddon breaks.

We've even built a house for them!

(The New World, 1942, p.67.)

In this expectation the house at San Diego, California, which house has been much publicized with malicious intent by the religious enemy, was built, in 1930, and named "Beth-Sarim", meaning "House of the Princes". It is now held in trust for the occupancy of those princes on their return.

-15-

'THEY REALLY BELIEVED THEY WERE COMING'

Here is the Watchtower view from an OFFICIAL history Book of the Society.

JEHOVAH'S WITNESSES IN THE DIVINE PURPOSE
252

THE TIME FOR "THE PRINCES" TO APPEAR

For many years it had been the view of *The Watchtower* that the faithful men of old who served God faithfully before Jesus' time would be raised from the dead even before Armageddon to join in organizing Jehovah's modern-day people and to share in shouldering the remnant's responsibility of representing the Lord Jesus Christ in the capacity of overseers of the flock of God on earth." These men were variously referred to as "ancient worthies," "faithful men of old," and "the princes" in the light of Psalm 45:16.

Expected at EVERY Convention.

Because of the understanding of this text that had prevailed for so long, many of Jehovah's witnesses expected at every convention to greet Abraham, Isaac, Jacob, David and the others, welcoming them back from the dead.

FAILED PROPHECY, forced the Society to make a new claim about 'Beth-Sarim'. As we've seen already the house was actually for the princes but the Society's 1975 Year Book, p.194 (below), says it was built for their second president Rutherford. This is to cover-up failed prophecy because according to Watchtower teaching only people like David, who will live on earth, are called 'Princes', not heavenly beings like Rutherford. So who would live in 'The House of Princes'?

In time, a direct contribution was made for the purpose of constructing a house in San Diego for Brother Rutherford's use. It was not built at the expense of the Watch Tower Society. Concerning this property, the 1939 book *Salvation* stated: "At San Diego, California, there is a small piece of land on which in the year 1929 there was built a house, which is called and known as Beth-Sarim.

A testimony to Jehovah's Name?

The house has served as a testimony to many persons throughout the earth, and while the unbelievers have mocked concerning it and spoken contemptuously of it, yet it stands there as a testimony to Jehovah's name; ...—*Salvation*, p. 311

No! The house, now sold is a testimony of FAILED PROPHECY!

-16-

Oh No We Didn't!

When this type of information is presented to a Witness you will get various excuses as to why it shouldn't be called false prophecy. To overcome this you can use the Witnesses' own 'apologetics' book, *Reasoning*, pp. 132–37, in which they talk about false prophets.

Use two statements, the first from p. 133:

> True prophets speak in the name of God ... If any individuals or organizations claim to represent God but decline to use God's personal name, and make it a practice to express their own opinions on matters, are they measuring up to this important qualification of a true prophet?

Ask the Witness, 'Do you believe from this statement that the Society is a true prophet, because they speak in the name of God and uphold his personal name?' The answer has to be yes!

Second, from p. 134:

> What true prophets foretell comes to pass, but they may not understand just when and how it will be.

Again ask, 'You must also believe then that even though you don't understand the "when" or the "how", what the Society says must come to pass because they are true prophets?' The answer must be yes!

Finally ask, 'Please then, can you explain why these words of the prophet, spoken in the name of the Lord, did not come to pass? That means they are a false prophet, doesn't it?' With this in mind use the information firmly but lovingly and make a note of this quote:

> True, there have been those in times past who predicted an 'end to the world', even announcing a specific date ... The 'end' did not come. THEY WERE GUILTY OF FALSE PROPHESYING. (*Awake!*, 8 October 1968, p. 23.)

Quote ... Misquote

Here is one of the clearest pieces of evidence, proving beyond doubt that the WBTS is not the true prophet of God. Again and again, by judicial editing, they *deliberately* misquote reliable authorities, making it appear that the writers agree with the Society when in reality the opposite is true. We cite just a few examples here to illustrate the point but other examples will be found throughout the book. Present them to a Witness in this way: 'You know the Watchtower said that the *Encyclopaedia Britannica* agreed with them about...Have you read the exact quote? Why do you think the WBTS have mislead you over this?'

The quotes as printed in Society publications are in normal type. What the Watchtower failed to print is added in bold type.

EB, Vol. 10, 1976, p. 126. Quoted in WT, 1 August 1984, p. 21

Neither the word Trinity, nor the explicit doctrine as such, appears in the New Testament, nor did Jesus and his followers intend to contradict the Shema in the Old Testament: 'Hear, O Israel: The Lord our God is one Lord' (Deut 6:4). **The earliest Christians, however, had to cope with the implications of the coming of Jesus Christ and of the presence and power of God among them, i.e., The Holy Spirit, whose coming was connected with the celebration of Pentecost. The Father, Son, and Holy Spirit were associated in such New Testament passages as the Great Commission: 'Go therefore and make disciples of all nations, baptizing them in the name of The Father and of the Son and of the**

Holy Spirit' (Matt 28:19); and in the apostolic benediction: 'The grace of the Lord Jesus Christ and the love of God and the fellowship of the Holy Spirit be with you all' (II Cor 13:14). Thus, the New Testament established the basis for the doctrine of the Trinity. The doctrine developed gradually over several centuries and through many controversies.

EB, Vol. 4, 1976, p. 485. Quoted in WT, 1 August 1984, p.23

The basis for the doctrine of the Trinity. The Christian doctrine of the Trinity has its ultimate foundation in the special religious experience of the Christians in the first communities. This basis of experience is older than the doctrine of the Trinity. It consisted of the fact that God came to meet Christians in a threefold figure: (1) as Creator, Lord of the history of salvation, Father, and Judge, who revealed himself in the Old Testament; (2) as the Lord who, in the figure of Jesus Christ, lived among men and was present in their midst as the 'Resurrected One'; and (3) as the Holy Spirit, whom they experienced as the power of the new life, the miraculous potency of the Kingdom of God. The question as to how to reconcile the encounter with God in this threefold figure with faith in the oneness of God, which was the Jews' and Christians' characteristic mark of distinction over against paganism, agitated the piety of ancient Christendom in the deepest way. It also provided the strongest impetus for a speculative theology—an impetus that inspired Western metaphysics [philosophy] throughout the centuries.

NCE, Vol. XIII, 1967, pp. 449–450. Quoted in 'Reasoning', p. 377

There is no dichotomy [division] of body and soul in the O[ld] T[estament]. The Israelite saw things concretely, in their totality, and thus he considered men as persons and not as composites. The term *nepes* [*ne'phesh*], though translated by our word soul, never means soul as distinct from the body or the individual person... At death the *nepes* goes to Sheol, a place of insensitive, shadowy existence. Many psalms pray for the rescue of one's *nepes* from death, where the rescue means to be saved from dying, not to be raised from the dead... The term [*psy-khe*] is the N[ew] T[estament] word corresponding with *nepes*. It can mean the principle of life, life itself, or the living being. Through Hellenistic influence, unlike *nepes*, it was opposed to body and considered immortal. The *psyche* in Matthew 10:28...means a life that exists separately from the body.

'The Bible Translator', Vol. 15, 1964, p. 151. Quoted in a personal letter from the Society, ref: EC:SE, 26 September 1985 (copies available)

Finally, we felt it might be of some assistance to list a few comments by various scholars concerning the *New World Translation* particularly, highlighting the competence of its translators:...Professor Bruce M. Metzger: 'On the whole one gains a tolerably good impression of the scholarly equipment of the translators (their names are not divulged)...**Some of the translations which are simply indefensible include the following. The introduction of the word "Jehovah" into the New Testament...the translation of John 1:1...to insert four times the word "other" (totally without warrant from the Greek) before the word "things" in Col. 1:16f.'**

W. Barclay, 'Many Witnesses One Lord', 1973, pp. 23–24. Quoted in 'Reasoning', p. 417

If John had said *ho theos en ho logos*, using a definite article in front of both nouns, then he would definitely have identified the *logos* with God, but because he has no definite article in front of *theos* it becomes a description, and more of an adjective than a noun. The translation then becomes, to put it rather clumsily, 'The Word was in the same class as God, belonged to the same order of being as God.' **The only modern translator who fairly and squarely faced this problem is Kenneth Wuest, who has: 'The Word was as to his essence essential deity.' But it is here that the NEB has brilliantly solved the problem with the absolute accurate rendering: 'What God was the Word was.'** John is not here identifying the Word with God. To put it very simply, he does not say that Jesus was God. **What he does say is that no human description of Jesus can be adequate, and that Jesus, however you are going to define it, must be described in terms of God.**

NCE, Vol. 13, 1976, p. 575. Quoted in 'Reasoning', p. 407

Although the NT concepts of the Spirit of God are largely a continuation of those of the OT, in the NT, there is a gradual revelation that the Spirit of God is a person. The majority of N[ew]

T[estament] texts reveal God's spirit as something not someone; this is especially seen in the parallelism between the spirit and the power of God.

John L. McKenzie, 'Dictionary of the Bible', 1965, p. 317. Quoted in WT, 1 July 1986, p. 31

In the words of Jesus and in much of the rest of the NT the God of Israel (G[ree]k *ho theos*) is the Father of Jesus Christ. It is for this reason that the title *ho theos*, [the God, or God], which now designates the Father as a personal reality, is not applied in the N[ew] T[estament] to Jesus Himself; Jesus is the Son of God (of *ho theos*). **This is a matter of usage and not of rule, and the noun is applied to Jesus a few times.** J[oh]n 1:1 should rigorously be translated 'the word was with the God [=the Father], and the word was a divine being.' **Thomas invokes Jesus with the titles which belong to the Father, 'My Lord and my God' (J[oh]n 20:28). 'The glory of our great God and Saviour' which is to appear can be the glory of no other than Jesus (Tt 2:13).**

SECTION 3

History of Jehovah's Witnesses

Charles Taze Russell

1852 Born 16th February in Allegheny City, Pennsylvania, of Presbyterian parents. Joined Congregational Church. Had elementary education which would not help in the study of Greek and Hebrew (see Note 1).

1869 At seventeen discarded the Bible and studied Buddhism, Confucius and other Oriental religions.

1870 Joined the Second Adventists. With six others started home Bible study.

1873 At twenty-one published first booklet, *The Object and Manner of the Lord's Return*. Concluded that the Lord's return would be invisible (see Note 2).

1876 Met N. H. Barbour and they published *Three Worlds and the Harvest of the World* in which they taught the saints would be 'caught away bodily' in 1878 (see Note 3). When this didn't happen, Russell made the first major 'U-turn' of the Society, explaining that the resurrection of the dead began in 1878 and that *all* Christians dying after then would go straight to be with the Lord.

1879 6,000 copies of the first issue of *Zion's Watch Tower and Herald of Christ's Presence* were printed in July. Married Maria F. Ackley.

1881   Watchtower Bible and Tract Society formed. Incorporated in 1884.

1886   Volume 1 of *Millenial Dawn* published (today known as *Studies in the Scriptures*). Russell would write five other volumes and considered them *more important than the Bible* (see Note 4).

1897   Maria left him and the divorce confirmed in 1908. The judge concluded that the way Russell treated his wife 'would necessarily render the life of any sensitive Christian woman a burden and make her conditions intolerable'.

1911   15 June edition of the *Watch Tower* advertised, at sixty times the price of regular wheat, 'Miracle Wheat' that 'should produce ten to fifteen times as much proportionately to the amount sown'. Department of Agriculture compared it with a regular variety and found the latter was twice as fruitful! Claimed other 'miracle' plants such as the 'Millenial Bean' and the 'Wonderful Cotton Seed' and also cures for cancer and appendicitis.

1916   Died 31st October on a train at Pampa, Texas.

Joseph Franklin Rutherford

1869   Born 8th November in Morgan County, Missouri. Father was a Baptist but Joseph never liked their 'hell-fire preaching'.

1894   Bought three volumes of Russell's *Millenial Dawn*.

1906   Rutherford baptized.

1917   After bitter in-fighting elected second president of the Society on 6th January. On 17th July opposition erupted to Rutherford, when the seventh and final volume of *Millenial Dawn* was released. Opponents claimed that the book merely contained some quotations from Russell's pen, together with repudiations of his teachings and substitutions of newly invented errors. The Society's *1975 Yearbook* says 4,000 left, which would be approximately 20 per cent of the then membership! The split was explained as the 'fiery trial' of 1 Peter 4:12–13. Apparently this was the first, but since often repeated ploy of finding Scriptures to fit events after they happened, their aim being to 'prove' that the Society is 'God's organization' foretold by Jehovah in His Word.

1918   With seven others convicted of espionage and sent to Atlanta Penitentiary.

1919   With the war over and public opinion easing the offenders were released. The Society's 'historians' explain the imprisonment as the trampling down of those who look after the 'holy city' (Rev 11:2–11) and their spiritual killing. Their release is escape from Babylonish captivity. They fail to add that many 'Babylonish' clergymen were also in jail for the same reasons.

1920   *Millions Now Living Will Never Die* published. It foretold the return to this earth of Abraham, Isaac and Jacob during 1925.

1930   'Beth-Sarim', a house in San Diego, purchased for the resurrected Old Testament saints to live in.

1941   *Children* published with the advice to wait till after Armageddon to marry. A copy was given to every child at the summer convention, and they were told to use it in the 'remaining *months* before Armageddon'.

1942   Died 8th January of cancer. No in-fighting for leadership this time because individualism had been stamped out. Best highlighted by the changing of the 'faithful and discreet slave' from the one man, Russell, to the 'organization' (see Appendix 3).

In his life Rutherford had made many changes to the 'doctrine' of the Society:

'Other sheep' have earthly paradise (1923)
Importance of the name of Jehovah (1925)
Resurrection in 1918 not 1878 (1927)
Life is in the blood (1927)
Sombre dress at meetings (1927)
Christmas not to be celebrated (1928)
Not to use the cross as a symbol (1928)
The name Jehovah's Witnesses (1931)
'Other sheep' to be baptized (1934)
'Other sheep' same as 'great multitude' (1935)
Division between those who take the bread and the wine and those who don't (1935)
Must not salute the flag (1935)
Jesus died on a 'stake' not a cross (1936)
Correct understanding of neutrality (1939)

Nathan Homer Knorr

1905   Born 23rd April in Bethlehem, Pennsylvania. Belonged to Dutch Reformed Church.

1923   Baptized and soon after joined the headquarters staff.

1942   Elected third president on 13th January. Had a self-contained flat with valet and personal kitchen. Others had one room, communal bathroom and toilet and mass-produced meals. Less conspicuous than predecessors, it's said, 'Russell was fire, Rutherford was acid and ice, and Knorr rock and grey.' Described as a 'plodding man' but his forte was organization and he took the Society from a membership of approximately 108,000 to over 2,000,000.

1947   Undertook a world tour on which he arranged for all countries to be more closely tied to Brooklyn.

1950   Arranged for F. W. Franz to translate the New World Translation. Officially the translator's names have never been released (see Note 5).

1975   Another failed prophecy! Arranged the 'cover up', blaming Witnesses for making 'too much' of a date that the Governing Body only 'intimated was a possibility'. Many left, some estimate as many as 250,000 in the USA alone.

1976   Reluctantly agreed a change in the structure of the Governing Body, and six extra committees were formed. These took much of the traditional authority away from the office of president. Today any change needs a two-thirds majority of all the Governing Body.

1977   Died 6th May of a cancerous tumour.

Frederick W. Franz

1893   Born in Covington, Kentucky. Cut short his stay at university to become a full-time preacher. Took two years Greek at university and self-taught in Hebrew but still regarded as the best Bible translator the Society had! (see Note 6).

1950   In the August convention at Yankee Stadium, New York, he changed the 'princes' that Rutherford claimed would return to rule the earth in 1925 from the Old Testament saints to the congregational overseers. He then dramatically said that they were 'now amongst us'! This caused many Witnesses to feel cheated.

1977   Aged eighty-three elected fourth president.

1980   Shake-up at headquarters. Many disfellowshipped including Franz's own nephew, Raymond, a one-time member of the Governing Body.

Note 1

In a libel case Russell was questioned about his scholastic standing and admitted that he had left school at fourteen after only seven years tuition. He was then questioned as follows:

Q. 'Do you know Greek?'
A. 'Oh, yes.'
Q. (The attorney, Mr. Staunton, handed Russell a copy of Westcott and Hort's Greek New Testament.) 'Please could you read the letters of the alphabet at the top of page 447.'
A. 'I cannot.'
Q. Are you familiar with the Greek language?'
A. 'No.'

He also admitted he didn't know Hebrew and that he had never taken a course of philosophy or systematic theology. (Recorded from the trial transcript in *Some Facts and More Facts about the Self-styled Pastor Charles T. Russell*, by J. J. Ross.)

Note 2

The title page of the publication and the WT show that Russell wrote this pamphlet in 1877.

> Well, then, in the spring of 1877, or over two years before starting this magazine, the said Russell published a pamphlet entitled 'The Object and Manner of the Lord's Return.' (WT, 1 July 1949.)

But the Society's 'official' history changes the date of publication to 1873!

> Earnestly endeavouring to counteract such erroneous teachings, in 1873 twenty-one-year-old C. T. Russell wrote and published at his own expense a booklet entitled 'The Object and Manner of the Lord's Return'. Some 50,000 copies were published and it enjoyed a wide distribution. About January of 1876, Russell received a copy of the religious periodical *The Herald of the Morning*. (*1975 Yearbook of Jehovah's Witnesses*, p. 36).

The following quote shows us why they made the change.

> Looking back to 1871, we see that many of our company were what are known as Second Adventists, and the light they held briefly stated, was that there would be a second advent of Jesus... This, they claimed would occur in 1873... Well, 1873 came, the end of 6,000 years, and yet no *burning* of the world. (ZWTR, February 1881, p. 188.)

In 1874 Russell was looking for the 'visible' return of Christ. The 'visible' was only changed to the 'invisible' when the event did not happen. By changing the publication date to 1873 the Society make Russell appear to be a 'prophet' of Christ's invisible return (albeit forty years earlier than they now believe) whereas in reality he was a false prophet covering up another error.

Note 3

> Hence, if he is to COME TO *harvest* the EARTH, to gather his saints; and is also to come '*with* all his saints'; there must be two parts or stages of his coming... The harvest is a definite period of time... And yet the LIVING SAINTS ARE NOT TAKEN UNTIL NEAR THE END OF THE HARVEST... the harvest... began on the tenth day of the seventh month in 1874. And...measures three and a half years. (N. H. Barbour and C. T. Russell, *Three Worlds or Plan of Redemption*, 1877, pp. 28–30.)

Note 4

> Furthermore, not only do we find that people cannot see the divine plan in studying the Bible by itself, but we see, also, that if anyone lays the SCRIPTURE STUDIES aside, even after he has used them, after he has become familiar with them, after he has read them for ten years—if he then lays them aside and ignores them and goes to the Bible alone, though he has understood his Bible for ten years, our experience shows that within two years he goes into darkness. On the other hand, if he had merely read the SCRIPTURE STUDIES with their references, and had not read a page of the Bible, as such, he would be in the light at the end of two

years, because he would have the light of the Scriptures. (WTR, 15 September 1910, p. 4685; emphasis in original.)

Note 5

The translators are commonly believed to be Fred Franz, Nathan Knorr, Albert Schroeder and George Gangas.

Note 6

In a Scottish trial of 1954, Frederick Franz under oath answered as follows:

Q. 'Have you also made yourself familiar with Hebrew?'
A. 'Yes.'
Q. 'So that you have a substantial linguistic apparatus at your command?'
A. 'Yes, for use in my biblical work.'
Q. 'You, yourself, read and speak Hebrew, do you?'
A. 'I do not speak Hebrew.'
Q. 'You do not?'
A. 'No.'
Q. 'Can you, yourself, translate that into Hebrew?'
A. 'Which?'
Q. 'The fourth verse of the second chapter of Genesis?'
A. 'You mean here?'
Q. 'Yes?'
A. 'No. I wouldn't attempt to do that.'
(Purser's Proof pp. 6–7,102.)

Structure and Meetings of the Society

The above diagram, reproduced from the WT, 1 January 1977, p.16, shows that the modern-day WBTS believe that the Governing Body are only answerable to Jehovah God and indeed that they are the only mouthpiece for Jehovah on this earth today. The structure of the Society underneath the Governing Body, with its assisting committees, is a pyramid structure. The following information is taken from the Society's 1983 publication, *Organized To Accomplish Our Ministry*.

Zone overseer

Periodic appointment to help with branch problems and to visit missionaries.

34

Branch office

One in each country. Has branch committee of two or three mature men. One is co-ordinator. They handle all congregational matters in their territory.

District overseer

Serves a number of 'circuits' that make a 'district'. Gives 'upbuilding' talks, leads in group witnessing and encourages circuit overseer.

Circuit overseer

Regularly visits all congregations in his circuit. Checks records, speaks to individuals as well as elders together. Deals with any congregational problems and leads in field service.

City overseer

Appointed where there is more than one congregation in a city. Has no jurisdiction outside his own congregation, simply helps administratively.

Congregation overseers

There are three to five depending on the size of the congregation. One is the permanent presiding overseer. Where possible these men are responsible for the main areas of leadership in the congregation even if they need to take charge of more than one. They are kept informed by the secretary of the congregation.

Much of the routine work of the congregation is covered by the congregational service committee made up of the presiding overseer, secretary and service overseer.

Functions covered by the elders are the Watchtower study co-ordinator who prepares this weekly study; the book study co-ordinator who prepares this study and takes a lead in the field ministry; the theocratic ministry school overseer who trains Witnesses for field ministry; and the service overseer who co-ordinates field ministry.

Weekly Meetings

The Watchtower study is a one-hour meeting and the public meeting lasts forty-five minutes (these two are often combined into one two-hour meeting). The service meeting lasts for forty-five minutes and the congregational book study, held in small groups, lasts one hour. Then the theocratic school ministry takes forty-five minutes. Twice a week, often on Wednesday afternoon and Saturday morning, there is door-to-door 'ministry', every day for those who are in pioneer work.

Once or twice a year Witnesses attend weekend circuit assemblies and once a year three-or four-day district conventions.

Worldwide Membership

The 1987 worldwide figures of the WBTS are as follows, British figures in brackets:

Peak publishers:	3,395,612	(109,624)
New Witnesses baptized:	230,843	(5,948)
Hours on the doors:	739,019,286	(21,571,972)
Memorial meal attendance:	8,965,221	(209,172)
Memorial meal partakers:	8,808	

(Taken from WT, 1 January 1988)

The Organization

So much emphasis is placed upon 'God's organization' that the new Witness will not dare to question or entertain doubts about its validity. Indeed, although they may never admit it, the organization becomes as important as Jehovah and certainly more important than Jesus. For instance, Jesus is the only name given under heaven whereby men can be saved (Acts 4:12) and He said 'Come to Me.' But the Society say:

> ...the witness yet includes the invitation to COME TO Jehovah's ORGANIZATION FOR SALVATION... (WT, 15 November 1981, p. 21.)

You can see from their own literature that they practically worship the organization:

> If one renders obedient service to someone or SOME ORGANIZATION, whether willingly or under compulsion, looking up to such as possessing a position of SUPERIOR RULERSHIP AND GREAT AUTHORITY, then that one can SCRIPTURALLY BE SAID TO BE A WORSHIPER. (WT, 1 September 1961, p. 525.)

Other quotes (a few are cited here) show how dependent the Witness has been made on the organization for spiritual understanding, growth and security. Again and again it is not one's relationship with God that is the predominant feature, but with the organization. This is why the threat of disfellow-shipping fills many with fear and holds them in the Society; they would rather be unhappy in 'God's organization' than happy outside without any eternal hope.

> Consider, too, the fact that Jehovah's ORGANIZATION ALONE, IN ALL THE EARTH, IS DIRECTED BY GOD'S HOLY SPIRIT...ONLY THIS ORGANIZATION functions for Jehovah's purpose and to his praise. TO IT ALONE God's Sacred Word, the Bible, is not a sealed book...THE ONLY ORGANIZATION ON EARTH that understands the 'DEEP THINGS OF GOD'...THIS ORGANIZATION ALONE is supplied with 'gifts in men', such as evangelizers, shepherds and teachers... There is NO OTHER ORGANIZATION that is DOING THE DIVINE WILL or that is educating people for life everlasting...THE ONLY ORGANIZATION ON EARTH THAT IS SERVING JEHOVAH GOD UNDER HIS MESSIANIC KING...enthusiastically direct others to GOD'S ORGANIZATION. (WT, 1 July 1973, pp. 402,404,406.)

> We must take seriously what his Word says and what HIS ORGANIZATION REVEALS TO US...Would not a failure to respond to direction from God THROUGH HIS ORGANIZATION really indicate a REJECTION OF DIVINE RULERSHIP? (WT, 15 February 1976, p. 124)

> Thus the Bible is AN ORGANIZATIONAL BOOK and belongs to the Christian congregation as an ORGANIZATION, NOT TO INDIVIDUALS, regardless of how sincerely they may believe that they can interpret the Bible. For this reason the Bible CANNOT be properly understood WITHOUT JEHOVAH'S VISIBLE ORGANIZATION IN MIND. (WT, 1 October 1967, p. 587)

Any person who wants to survive into God's righteous new order urgently needs to come into a right relationship with Jehovah and His EARTHLY ORGANIZATION *NOW*. (WT, 15 November 1981, pp. 16–17.)

One Organization

To believe these statements a Witness must accept two things: firstly that Jehovah only has one visible organization, and secondly that the WBTS is that organization. To 'prove' the first point the Society make the case that there was only *one* organization in the early church and therefore there is only *one* organization today.

Reasoning, p. 280, shows on what basis a Witness is a member of Jehovah's earthly organization: 'Members of an organization are united by administrative arrangements and by standards or requirements.' The inward life of Christ has nothing to do with it—only outward standards and administrative decisions. The article goes on to seek to prove the two points mentioned above by showing Scriptures to answer the following questions:

Are God's heavenly creatures, the angels, organized?

How did God convey instructions to his servants on earth in times past?

Do Jehovah's works of physical creation indicate that he is a God of organization?

Does the Bible show that true Christians would be an organized people?

Are those who are faithful servants of God simply individuals who are scattered in the various churches of Christendom?

All these questions are answered in such a way to show that God is a God of order and that He wants there to be *one* people on the earth. But that does not prove there is *one* organization today with its headquarters in Brooklyn, New York, USA.

Reasoning, pp. 283–84, then lists seven identifying marks of Jehovah's visible organization. Summarized these are:

1. Exalt Jehovah as the true God.
2. Recognize Jesus's vital role in Jehovah's purpose.
3. Adhere closely to God's Word.
4. Keep separate from the world.
5. Maintain a high level of moral cleanliness.
6. Preach the good news.
7. Cultivate fruits of the spirit.

They do not conclude the article by saying they are the one but they certainly infer it. However, we would argue that they fall down on some of those points whereas other churches do not. But in the end we need to check, with the Scriptures, their claim that there is only *one* organization—the WBTS.

An article entitled, 'Direct New Ones To God's Organization' found in WT, 1 November 1984, makes several statements that we will check.

The Basis for One Organization

According to this article, Paul and other Christians did not make their own decisions on doctrinal matters but received 'authoritative answers' from the elders in Jerusalem. But we read in another article:

> Was the apostle Paul part of the Christian governing body? It is reasonable to conclude that Paul was a part of the Christian governing body in the first century (WT, 1 December 1985, p. 31.)

The article tells us that Paul went to Jerusalem to 'explain' the good news he was preaching. If he was part of the body, surely they would know! However, did Paul go to Jerusalem to check if he was 'running in vain'?

Why Did Paul Go to Jerusalem?

A careful look at all the Scriptures recording this episode will show clearly what happened.

Galatians 2:1–2 tells us that Paul went to those of reputation in Jerusalem because of the revelation given to him by the Lord.

He did not want the sharing of that revelation to be nullified by others preaching 'another gospel'.

Acts 15:1–2 mentions that Paul and Barnabas went to *complain* to the elders in Jerusalem that some of the members of their congregation were causing problems to new-born Christians in Galatia by preaching 'another gospel' of adherence to the law of Moses (see Gal 1:6; 2:4,11–14).

Galatians 2:6 shows the men of reputation in Jerusalem contributed nothing to Paul which is a very strange way of giving an authoritative answer!

Acts 15:22 reveals that Paul and Barnabas did not take the letter from the elders in Jerusalem but two men were appointed from that congregation to read it.

Galatians 2:10 indicates that the elders simply made a request to Paul and Barnabas that they should remember the poor, something they wanted to do anyway.

Galatians 2:11–14 records that later Paul had to strongly oppose Peter, one of the elders from Jerusalem, because he was not living the Christian life in a full and open way.

Summary

First, Paul and Barnabas did not go to Jerusalem to receive an authoritative answer for themselves but to complain that some in that congregation were preaching wrong doctrine.

Second, Paul did not go to 'check out' the gospel he was preaching but rather he wanted to make sure that all the work he had done was not brought to nothing (i.e. made vain) by someone preaching 'another gospel'.

Third, Paul and Barnabas were not instructed by the elders. Silas and Judas were sent from Jerusalem to read the letter which made clear the elders' agreement with Paul's complaint and showed an effort to right the situation. Paul and Barnabas taught the Word of the Lord (Acts 15:35) not the letter from Jerusalem.

Finally, Paul later instructed Peter an elder in Jerusalem, not vice versa.

It is evident that the WBTS's interpretation of these events is wrong. There was not one organization in the New Testament church and so there is no ground for one organization today. If a Witness still does not want to accept the truth of Scripture share this thought. The 'Governing Body' of this so-called one organization was allowing false doctrine to be preached until someone came in from the outside to correct them! Is it the same today?

Faithful and Discreet Slave

Although Scriptures clearly show there is no basis for one organization let us still look at the argument that the Witnesses use to 'prove' they are that one organization. It all hinges on the parable in Matthew 24 in which Jesus said He would put a 'faithful and discreet slave' over His household to give out food in due time. The WBTS say we, more accurately, the remnant of the 144,000 (approximately 8,800) left on this earth are that slave. Of course anyone who opposes or shows errors in the doctrine of the Witnesses is the 'evil slave' from the parable. The following, I believe, sums this up.

> Jesus was also referring to the living members of this 'body' on earth when he spoke of a 'faithful and discreet slave', authorized to 'feed' the 'domestics' (Matt 24:45–47). Individual Christians worldwide would have to recognize the authority of this 'slave' if they were to be 'fed' by it. This would result in an international association of Christians... Is there a similar 'whole association of brothers' today? Indeed there is. 'The faithful and discreet slave' still exists and still has responsibility for the 'feeding' of the 'domestics' (Matt 24:45–47). As in Paul's day, a governing body represents this 'slave' and directs the worldwide work of preaching the 'good news'. (WT, 1 November 1984, pp. 16–17.)

Appendix 3 shows the lies the WBTS have told about the 'faithful and discreet slave' as they did not want the 'authority' to die with first president, C. T. Russell. But we also need to look at the Scripture passage to see if the Witnesses' doctrine is sound biblically.

Most will not be surprised to find that an honest and sound

exegesis of this passage shows that it cannot be used to prove that the Governing Body of the WBTS represent the rest of the remnant as the 'faithful and discreet slave' today. The following points show this clearly.

First, the passage is set in Matthew 24, a chapter that the Witnesses use to show that Jesus returned in 1914. Second, the Lord Jesus sets this slave over His house and if he is the faithful one he will be doing a good job when his master returns. The conclusion to the Witness from these points must be that the Lord rewarded the faithful slave when He returned in 1914! Therefore the slave does not exist today.

Third, throughout the chapter Jesus has been talking about individuals, e.g. 24:13, the *one* who endures to the end; 24:40, *one* will be taken. But the Witnesses do not believe that this represents just one person or even one particular group of men. They say to all they preach to, if you endure to the end you will be saved. In other words, Jesus was personalizing this serious matter to bring it home but was actually speaking to anyone who would listen to Him and read the words in years to come. The evil slave, according to the Witnesses, is anyone who leaves the WBTS or who actively preaches against it.

The conclusion from this teaching is that although Jesus used the singular 'slave' He did not refer to only one of them but to any number that He gave authority to be His shepherds and teachers. This point is borne out by other New Testament Scriptures that show many were appointed as elders, teachers etc to 'feed the flock' (see 1 Peter 5:1–4; 1 Timothy 3:1–6 etc).

There is therefore no scriptural justification for the teaching that there was only *one* organization in the early church or that the 'faithful and discreet slave' is the Governing Body of the WBTS today.

Spiritual Jews

This subject needs to be dealt with briefly because it is another way that the WBTS 'prove', from Scripture, that they alone are God's people. They simply alter all the references to Jews in the Bible to read 'spiritual Jews'. WT, 15 September 1984, pp.

10–20, showed it like this. Romans 11:26, 'All Israel will be saved,' means that the full number of Jehovah's Witnesses have been brought in. At Pentecost a number of Jews, and at Cornelius' house a number of Gentiles, became part of the 'olive tree' (Rom 9:17ff.). The olive tree's '144,000 branches' were finally completed in 1935 'under the supervision of the Watch Tower Bible and Tract Society'.

We have dealt with the unscriptural nature of the 144,000 and so here we concentrate on Romans 9–11 and answer the question, 'Is it possible for the Watchtower to say that this refers to themselves as spiritual Jews?' Witnesses normally are very strong on 'keeping to the context', but this WT is noticeable for the way it does not deal with the context of Romans 9–11 but refers to other Scriptures which have no bearing on the subject. If you ever get on to the subject of 'spiritual Jews' make the following points, asking the Witnesses questions and getting them to follow in their Bibles.

Romans 9:1–5: in these verses Paul clearly shows he is talking about his kinsmen, i.e. real Jews.

Romans 9:6 shows that Gentiles can become part of spiritual Israel, i.e. enter into God's kingdom but Paul does not give them the title 'spiritual Jews'. The rest of the chapter is taken up with the matter of election which is not vital for us in this study except to underline the point that the choosing is God's sovereign decision and we cannot influence Him by doing or being a certain thing.

Romans 10: Paul again introduces his kinsmen and says how he longs for their salvation. He moves on to show that Jews had heard the gospel but were a disobedient people.

Romans 11:1–10 is where Paul continues to talk about his fellow Jews and shows that not all have been rejected but there is a remnant (v. 5) who have received Christ.

Romans 11:11–36 is the heart of the matter. The Jewish nation stumbled to allow salvation to come to the Gentiles (v. 11). There will be a fulfilment for the Jews, (v. 12), life from the dead (v. 15). The root from which the Jews come is holy and therefore the branches must be too (v. 16). Because of unbelief some of the natural branches (Jews) have been broken away from the tree and other branches (Gentiles) have been grafted in (v. 17). Gentiles should not become arrogant about this because they only stand by faith, and if God did not spare natural branches when they fell into unbelief we who are grafted branches need to take heed (v. 18–22). Indeed those cut off will be grafted in if they repent of their unbelief (v. 23–24). A partial hardening has happened to all natural Israel (Jews by birth) until the fullness of the Gentiles has come in and then all of natural Israel, those born Jews, who are destined for salvation, will come to know the Lord. There is no way that we can break into the logical argument of Paul and suddenly say it is spiritual Israel. The context forbids this.

The WT article (15 September 1984, pp. 10–20) points out that Russell and Rutherford, in his early days, saw the Jewish people as a sign of what God was doing in setting up His earthly kingdom, but then new light dawned. Ask the Witnesses to check the Scriptures and see which light was the correct light.

One sidelight from the passage in Romans 11 that we should mention is the phrase 'fullness of the Gentiles' (11:25). The WT article, p. 12, quotes Luke 21:24 as proof that this happened in 1914. Again please point out that the context of Luke shows that the Jerusalem mentioned is the literal one and that certainly was still being trampled underfoot in 1914. If Witnesses say it is the spiritual Jerusalem, ask them when the spiritual city had captives led away from it and when it was trampled underfoot.

Finally, if the Gentile Times ended in 1914 and all Israel was saved by 1935, where is this tremendous fulfilment of 'life from the dead' that the Bible promised would happen at that time?

The Witness at Your Door

You will have gathered from this chapter that the Witness calling at your door is not an individual but an 'organization'. Because of this they are sometimes difficult to draw into 'personal' conversation. However, please be loving and patient and seek to show them that the concept of 'organization' they have is not supported by Scripture, nor indeed is the concept that Jehovah's Witnesses are the special people of God, 'spiritual Israel' today. You will then be making a way to share the need we each have, as individuals, to enter into a personal relationship with Jesus Christ.

SECTION 4

Witnessing to a Jehovah's Witness About Jesus

First, here are a few simple suggestions that can be used to turn around whatever the Witness says to you sharing your personal testimony of Jesus and/or God's way of salvation. Whatever the Witness is expected to say is printed in *italics*. This may not be the exact wording but you should recognize the general drift.

'*I want today to talk to you about the future that Jehovah has in store for...*'

'Yes, I do believe that there is a wonderful future for people who do things God's way. However, the point is unless we conform to God's way there will be no salvation for us at all. Let me tell you what I believe God's way of salvation is...'

'*I want today to talk to you about world conditions, aren't things terrible...*'

'Yes, Satan is causing many problems for mankind, but Jesus tells us that we need not be overcome by them because He gives peace and victory. Let me explain...'

'*I want today to talk about the doctrines the churches teach such as an immortal soul, or hell etc...*'

'Well, to be truthful, I don't understand your reasoning or logic, but one thing is sure whether or not we have an immortal soul (or whatever the Witness was talking about) is not as important as whether or not we are going to have a future at all. You do believe in a future don't you? (Await reply.) Right, but there is only one way to please God and that is fitting in with His way of salvation. Let me explain...'

46

'I want today to talk about the Trinity. Does your church teach it? It's a pagan doctrine you know. How can Jesus be the same as Jehovah...'

'I actually believe the Bible teaches something different to that, though I would need time to research more thoroughly. But I don't think that's the main problem. Did you know that God accepts us on what we think of Jesus. Do you agree?'

Possible reply, 'Our view of Jesus is important but not as important as what we think of Jehovah.'

'Okay, but we show what we think of Jehovah the Father by obeying His instructions. Note what Jehovah says about what we should think of Jesus...' (see Scriptures below).

'Today I'm talking about the battle of Armageddon and the destruction of the wicked...'

'It is good to know that God is a just God. But it causes me to think seriously about my own position before God, am I pleasing Him or not? You see, whatever we do or say, if we've got it wrong then there is no good future for us at all. We must be absolutely positive that we are doing things God's way, and I know that I am because...'

Remember the Witness does not have a personal relationship with Jesus and is without the indwelling Holy Spirit but a Christian does and has! Therefore don't flannel but tell it as it is. After you've turned the conversation around to Jesus continue by giving your testimony of how you were saved or present the gospel simply. Here are some Scriptures to help you share in a relevent way with a Jehovah's Witness.

Jehovah's way of salvation

John 6:40 – *Look* to the Son
Matthew 17:5 – *Listen* to the Son
John 14:21 – *Obey* the Son
Acts 4:12 – *Only name*
John 14:6 – *Through* the Son

The reason we go through the Son

John 10:28 – He *gives life*
John 5:22 – He is *our Judge*

Matthew 11:28 – He gives *rest*
John 14:27 – He gives *peace*
Colossians 2:15 – He won the *victory* on the cross
John 5:23 – Therefore we give Him *the same* honour as the
Father

Jesus wants to live 'in' us

The Watchtower have translated 'in us' as 'in union with us', but
there is no justification for this (see literal Greek in Section 8).
John 17:26 – I *in* them
John 14:23 – Father and Son make home *in* us
John 1:12 – Receiving *Him* makes us children of God
Romans 8:1 – We are not condemned *in* Him
1 John 5:12 – Have Christ we have *life*
Romans 10:9 – Jesus, Lord *in* our lives

Being 'born again'

Matthew 6:33 – Seek first the kingdom of God
John 3:3, 5 – Can't see kingdom unless born again
2 Corinthians 5:17 – New creatures in Christ
Colossians 2:6, 7 – Receive Christ and walk in Him
Romans 6:3ff – Old self dead in Christ

What we must recognize

Romans 3:23 – All are sinners
Romans 3:10ff – Acknowledge our condition
1 Peter 2:24 – Christ took away our sin in His Body
Romans 4:25 – Christ died in our place
Luke 13:3 – We must repent or perish
Acts 26:20 – Our life must fit our repentance

Finally, three Scriptures that sum up the gospel of Jesus
Christ well are 1 Corinthians 15:3, 1 Corinthians 2:2 and Luke
24:46ff.

Most of the second group of suggestions in this Section,
again without any five-year guarantee, have been 'tried' with
some 'success'. They are for those who are willing and able to
speak in more depth with the Jehovah's Witnesses. Most times
the Witnesses will not admit they are preaching wrong doctrine

so do not be discouraged and continue to sow doubt in their hearts.

It is often important to start on a clear foundation and establish that our statements are the teaching of the WBTS otherwise they might have a loophole to exploit later. Where necessary we quote chapter and verse, but these need only be used if a Witness will not commit him/herself. Quote the article and ask, 'The Governing Body say it is true and so you believe it, don't you?'

If it's convenient, and you feel able, ask them in. If you have a problem over 2 John 10, don't go against your conscience, but surely if we are seeking to win the Witnesses for Christ does it matter where we speak to them? The tenure of the New Testament is to love all in order to win some and we need to put this verse in that overall context. The immediate context of 2 John is showing the importance of not allowing the perpetration of false doctrines in our homes or churches with spiritually weak members who are liable to stumble, not the geography of where we are talking to them. If, therefore, you are weak yourself or there are weak ones around—don't debate. But if the house is free and you want to win them, make them as comfortable as possible. (If your concern is also what the neighbours think, take around 'warning tracts' after you've finished and explain why you were talking to the Witnesses).

Let the Witnesses finish their opening speech because this relaxes them. Praying all the time for wisdom for you and light for them. When the appropriate time comes for a response start one of the outlines. They expect argument and rejection and often don't know what to do with love. In most cases this brings down their defences and their hearts are wide open to receive what you have to say. Remember it's your home so do not be intimidated. They have had their opportunity so now ask them firmly but politely to listen to you.

It is important that you are happy with what you use and feel at home with the Scriptures. The answers the Witnesses give are not always important, because many will twist and waffle, but still listen politely. Do not be side-tracked but lovingly steer the point you are making home to their hearts.

Worship

Reasoning, pp. 214–15.

I believe the Society teach that you should only worship Jehovah God and not Jesus Christ. Is this right? Please could you then explain Revelation 5:8,13–14. Isn't the Lamb, Jesus, receiving *the same* honour, glory and worship as Jehovah? Should we not do what heaven is doing? Please could you also explain why, when every *creature* worships and gives honour to Jesus, you teach that Jesus is a *created being*. If He is, there's idol worship in heaven, with creature worshipping creature.

Is He an Angel?

Reasoning, p. 218.

As you believe Jesus is an archangel, simply meaning an angel but the chief one, could you explain Hebrews 1:6–8 where there is a clear distinction made between Jesus and angels. When Jesus comes back to this inhabited earth (v. 6)—if you want to be side-tracked ask them when that will happen!—*All* angels will worship Him. In verse 7 God speaks to angels but in verse 8 He speaks different words to Jesus.

My Witnesses

Reasoning, p. 203.

You call yourselves Jehovah's Witnesses from Isaiah 43:10. I wonder why when Jesus said just before He left this earth, '...you shall be My witnesses...' (Acts 1:8). Reading on in Acts we find good reason to speak in and about the name of Jesus; people were baptized in *His name*, healed in *His name* and above all saved in *His name*. Acts 4:10–12 also makes it quite clear that there is salvation in *no other name* (compare Acts 2:21 in NWT—'Jehovah'). No wonder we must make much of the name of Jesus—He is our only hope of salvation.

Enthronement of Christ

Reasoning, pp. 96–97.

'You believe that Christ did not take His seat on His heavenly throne until 1914 so could you please explain Ephesians 1:20–22. When was Christ enthroned? This Scripture shows that Christ was certainly enthroned by the time the Letter was written in AD 60. Where does the Bible change the date of the enthronement to 1914?'

John 1:1

'I believe here your Bible shows you clearly that Jesus is God… oh, "a god". But what kind of God? True or false? So Jesus is a true god. That's very interesting in the light of Isaiah 43:10 which tells us there were no other gods formed before or after Jehovah, and also John 17:3 where we see there is only *one true* God. If Jesus is a true god the Bible shows that there are either two true Gods, which is impossible, or that Jesus is part of the Godhead. Hebrews 7:1–3 also shows us Jesus is eternal and only God is eternal! Mr Witness you may not understand with your head but who will you believe—the Bible or the WBTS? They can't both be right!'

Mighty or Almighty?

In Revelation 1:8 the Alpha and Omega is the Almighty God. In Revelation 22:10–16 Alpha and Omega is the one who is coming which verse 16 says is Jesus. (The Witness might say that the speaker changes in verse 13 if so…) The Alpha and Omega is also the first and the last. Revelation 1:17–18 shows that the first and last is Jesus, the Alpha and Omega, the Almighty God.

The Witness has been taught to say that even though they are both called Alpha and Omega that does not prove they are the same person or of equal rank. However, ask how many Alpha's and Omega's can there be? That is more to the point.

Jehovah and Jesus

Reasoning, pp. 197–98.

'You teach that God's name, is never applied to Jesus but have you read these Scriptures?

'Zechariah 11:12–13 (NWT) and Matthew 26:14–15—Who is valued at thirty pieces of silver?

'Jeremiah 17:10 (NWT) and Revelation 2:23 (2:18 for speaker)—Who searches the heart?

'Deuteronomy 10:17 (NWT) and Revelation 17:14—Who is Lord of lords and King of kings?

'Malachi 3:1 (NWT)—Jehovah sends the true Lord, Jesus. Hebrew for "true Lord" is *ha-Adon* which the Society say can *only* be Jehovah! (See Reachout Trust's Factsheet 1 for a detailed presentation.)

'Acts 2:21 (NWT) and Acts 4:10–12—Whose name saves us?

'Isaiah 43:10 (NWT) and Acts 1:8—Who are we witnesses of? (You can add to this Acts 9:20, 27–28. If anyone preached in the name Jehovah it would be Paul with his strict Jewish background, but he preached in the name of Jesus)'

These verses are not saying that the Father *is* Jesus but that the *name* of God is used of Jesus, showing two persons of the Godhead.

Glory of God

'Could we please read Isaiah 42:8. Is this Jehovah God saying that He will not give His glory to another? In this light please could we read John 17:5. How can Jesus Christ receive glory that never went to anyone else except God?'

Grandfather Jehovah

No you are not seeing things! This is what I call a conversation stopper, to be used in emergencies when all else fails! The WBTS have made some crazy statements but this surely is the winner:

The second Adam [Jesus Christ], however, has become a life-giving spirit. In this capacity he can fulfil Isaiah's prophecy and become the 'Eternal Father'... In such a way the heavenly Father of Jesus Christ will become the heavenly Grandfather of the restored human family. (*Worldwide Security Under The 'Prince of Peace'*, 1986, p. 169.)

There is so much you can do with this quote. When the present heavenly Father retires as a Grandfather and Jesus becomes the heavenly Father, surely I will be able to worship Him? That has so many implications!

Romans 8

'Please could we read Romans 8:1–5. How many types of people do you see here? *(Get them to establish there are two types—flesh and Spirit.)*

'Can we now read verse 9. What is the description of one who is, "of the Spirit". *(Get them to say it is to have "God's Spirit dwelling in you". If they mention Christ's Spirit too, you have the opportunity to show that they are the same!)*

'We've therefore established that to be of the Spirit means to have God's Spirit dwelling in us. Can we look further then at verse 14. What can we call those who are led by the Spirit of God? *(Sons of God.)*

'So we see these verses teach that someone who is of the Spirit becomes aware of what the Spirit tells them to do and thus they are led by the Spirit. The Scriptures teach that such a person is born of God. Do you agree?

'Surely these verses also teach us the opposite, i.e. if we are not led by the Spirit of God we are not of the Spirit and therefore we must be of what? *(The flesh).*

'That's right. We can only be one or the other, nowhere in between. To be of the flesh is a hopeless situation, in the light of verse 8. Don't you think so?

'In the light of this revealed truth from God's Word I would like to tell you what the Lord Jesus has done for me in my life...'

SECTION 5

The Name of Jehovah

There are many facets to the subject of the tetragrammaton (abbreviated to tetragram) meaning simply the four Hebrew letters that make up the name commonly pronounced 'Jehovah'.

It is widely accepted that 'Jehovah' is a mispronunciation of the tetragram (see Appendix 1). However, this is not the most significant aspect. There are three claims made by the WBTS regarding the use of 'Jehovah' in the New Testament and the early church which are of prime importance.

The three articles, published by the Society, we shall mainly refer to are ABU, pp. 882–94; NWT, with references, 1984, pp. 1561–66; and KIT, pp. 10–15.

The claims these articles make that we will investigate are:

1. The tetragram is found in the early Greek translation of the Old Testament, known as the Septuagint (abbreviated to LXX).
2. Jesus and His followers in the early church would pronounce the tetragram every time they came across it.
3. The tetragram was originally to be found in the Greek manuscripts of the New Testament but sometime during the second or third centuries it was removed by copyists who didn't appreciate, or developed an aversion for, the divine name.

If these claims are true then the Society have a case for using the name of Jehovah. But if they are false the fuss made over it will be seen to be of man.

54

Claim 1: the tetragram is found instead of a Greek word in the LXX

This is truth, but not the whole truth, and in any case here the Society contradicts itself. They base their case almost entirely on the discovery of a part copy of the LXX called 'P. Fouad Inv. No. 266' and pictured in a number of their publications. This is dated first or second century BC and contains parts of Deuteronomy 18:5–32:19. Their conclusion is that because this one copy of the LXX contains the tetragram then all copies must have, especially the ones that Jesus read. But in an earlier WBTS publication we read:

> 'Jehovah' does not occur in the *Septuagint* version, that name being represented by the Greek words for 'the Lord'. (*Equipped For Every Good Work* 1946, p. 53)

What makes this remarkable is that the Deuteronomy fragments were first published in 1944 and *Equipped for Every Good Work* didn't come out until 1946. A case where the 'new light' was a little late!

On a more scholarly note, most, if not all versions of the LXX are of Jewish origin and therefore the scribes, translating or copying, would be simply keeping to their traditions by using the tetragram. We should also note that the Society have carefully avoided mention of another portion of the LXX called 'P. Ryl. GK. 458' dated middle second century BC. C. H. Roberts points out in *Two Biblical Papyri*, p. 44, 'it is probable that kyrios was written in full.' In other words, this version probably did not contain the tetragram.

However, although the Society do not mention the above copy they do, in NWT, refer to nine other copies (see below— Number 1 is the P. Fouad Inv. No. 266 already mentioned) of the LXX in order to bolster their case, yet only one (Number 5) is dated before Christ, and that does not strictly contain the tetragram. This fact is vital when they are seeking to prove that Jesus would have read and pronounced the tetragram in the synagogue. Only BC manuscripts could prove this. Any written by Jewish scribes after Christ would simply show the desire to keep old traditions. We will look at this evidence to see what the Society's case is.

Number 2—LXX[VTS10a]

Dated end of first century. The review in *Supplements to Vetus Testamentum* Vol. X, 1963, pp. 170–78, declares it to be a 'recession of the ancient LXX', i.e. it was a revision. It also says that its wording was literal to the Hebrew—thus showing the reason for the revision is to harp back to the old Jewish traditions.

It is helpful here to note F. F. Bruce's explanation as to why there were many Jewish revisions of the LXX harping back to old traditions:

> There were two main reasons why the Jews lost interest in the Septuagint. One was that from the first century AD onwards the Christians adopted it as their version of the Old Testament... Another reason for the Jew's loss of interest in the Septuagint lies in the fact that about AD 100 a revised standard text was established for the Hebrew Bible by Jewish scholars... any version in another language which was to be fit for Jewish use must conform to it. (*The Books and the Parchments*, 1953 pp. 145–46.)

Number 3—LXX[IEJ 12]

Dated first century AD. Recorded in *The Israel Exploration Journal* Vol. 12, 1962, p. 201–07, by B. Lifshitz of the Hebrew University, Jerusalem. This is part of his account:

> Some ten years ago Père D. Barthélemy published a paper in which he made mention of, among other things, fragments of a parchment scroll containing the Greek Translation of the Minor Prophets... Père Barthélemy concluded that the version of this scroll is neither a new translation nor an independent one, but rather a recension of the Septuagint; and that its variations from the Septuagint are the result of an attempt to render Greek in a manner FAITHFUL TO THE HEBREW ORIGINAL. (p. 201.)

The NWT only mentions four verses in Zechariah where the tetragram is found. But B. Lifshitz, on p. 204 of the same article, shows an extract from Nahum 1:9 and comments:

> This small fragment is too meagre to allow for an attempt at reconstructing the version of the scroll; however, IT IS CLEAR THAT 'THEOS' APPEARS instead of kyrios of the Septuagint.

The same is written about Zechariah 4:8a and clearly shows the inconsistency of this version in using the tetragram. In both the above places the NWT has 'Jehovah', but this particular version does not have the tetragram and therefore must disqualify itself from being reliable evidence on behalf of the Society.

Number 4—LXX^{VTS} [10b]

The Society have tried to make this a separate case. However, you will notice its catalogue number is very close to Number 2 and indeed the fragments were reviewed in the same article. All that was said about Number 2 applies here.

Number 5—4Q LXX Lev^b

Found in the Quaram caves and definitely of Jewish origin. Dated first century BC. However, its review in *Supplements to Vetus Testamentum* Vol. IV, 1957, pp. 148–58, puts a different light on this find than the one the WBTS would want us to believe. Two points need to be made. Firstly, this fragment does *not* have the tetragram but a Greek substitute (IAW). The article comments:

> Its only special feature is that in the midst of the Greek text, familiar from the LXX codices, the divine name here appears NOT AS KYRIOS but as IAW.

What is apparent from this is that the majority of LXX codices contained *kyrios*, not the tetragram. And indeed that this version does *not* contain the tetragram.

The second matter to note is that although Quaram was a

bastion of Jewish tradition they did not use the tetragram. The *New International Dictionary of New Testament Theology* informs us:

> Members of the Quaram sect, in Heb [rew] biblical MSS [manuscripts], were writing *adonay*, Lord, instead of the tetragrammaton. (Vol. 2, p. 512.)

Number 6— LXX *P.Oxy.VII.1007*

Dated third century AD and described by A. S. Hunt in *The Oxyrhynchus Papyri*, 1910, Part VII. Here again the Society decide not to present all the evidence to its readers. Why is this representation of the tetragram there? A. S. Hunt explains:

> . . . a most remarkable abbreviation of the so-called Tetragrammaton, WHICH IN THE SEPTUAGINT IS REGULARLY REPRESENTED BY *kyrios*. This abbreviation consists of a double Yod, the initial of the sacred name, written in the shape of a Z with a horizontal stroke through the middle . . . A DECIDED TENDENCY TO OMIT THE WORD *kyrios* was, however, observable in the early Oxyrhynchus papyrus (656), where in one passage a blank space was originally left in which the missing word was supplied by a second hand. (pp. 1–2.)

From this information we understand three things about this version:

1. This is a remarkable, not a normal and often used, abbreviation. Therefore it would not be commonly found in the LXX.
2. It was a 'decided tendency' of the Jewish scribe to use this tetragram rather than *kyrios*.
3. A similar and older version 656, containing the end of Genesis 2 and beginning of 3, left a blank space four times. Later, *theos* or *kyrios* were added by another scribe in three of these places.

Numbers 7 and 8—Aq^{Burkitt} and Aq^{Taylor}

These are different versions of the same manuscript, translated by Aquila (about AD 100), dated around the fifth or sixth century. But who was Aquila? The WBTS themselves say:

> Aquila was a Jewish proselyte of Pontus in Asia, AN APOSTATE FROM CHRISTIANITY. (*Equipped For Every Good Work*, p. 52.)

We read from other sources:

> What is certain is that he was a pupil of the new rabbinical school...(his version) was an extraordinary production...No jot or tittle of the Heb[rew] might be neglected; uniformity in the tr[anslation] of each Heb[rew] word must be preserved...a bold attempt to displace the LXX. (*International Standard Bible Encyclopaedia*, 1978, Vol. 4, p. 2725.)

> Moreover, he followed the ANTI-CHRISTIAN bias of his master by using, in some passages interpreted Messianically by the Church, another word in place of *Christos* ('anointed') and in Isaiah 7:14 *neanis* ('young woman') instead of *parthenos* ('virgin'). (Sir F. Kenyon, *Our Bible and the Ancient Manuscripts*, 1958, p. 103.)

Surely in the light of this evidence these manuscripts cannot be brought in to prove the way *Christians* translated the Scriptures. F. Crawford Burkitt who published these fragments (Number 7), however, does not draw the same conclusions as the WBTS. For instance on p. 18 of his publication, *Fragments of the Book of Kings According to the Translation of Aquila*, he explains that one of the main tasks of scholars is to separate the pure from the mixture. He adds that this find is 'of very great importance for the textual study of the LXX' because it is a classic example of mixture!

He goes on to make it even clearer:

> To the scribe of our MS [manuscript] the Tetragrammaton must have been a mere symbol, blindly copied from the model...The Tetragrammaton in our MS [manuscript] was UNDOUBTEDLY INTENDED TO BE *pronounced kyrios*...Contractions are extremely infrequent in our MS [manuscript] and when they occur they are

always at the end of lines. The scribe, in fact, used contractions only to avoid dividing words. Now at the end of 4 Kings 23 24 [2 Kings 23:24 in our Bibles]... there was no room to write the Tetragrammaton in full, so instead... we find... ku. The Greek Synagogue, therefore, READ THE NAME *kyrios*. (pp. 15–16.)

The Society are deceptive in bringing this version in as evidence because it contains *kyrios* and also shows just how the name was pronounced.

Number 9—Sym[P.Vindob. G. 39777]

This version by Symmachus was a revision of the Aquila text around AD 200, to meet the needs of a Jewish sect who were dissatisfied with the LXX.

Number 10—Ambrosian 0 39 sup.

This is simply a compilation of various other versions and therefore adds no new evidence to the case.

The Chester Beatty Papyri

Before we summarize this section we need to underline another of the classic deceptions of the WBTS. Not only have they twisted the evidence they've presented but they've omitted evidence that disproves their point.

Several manuscripts found in Egypt containing parts of the Old Testament in Greek, as well as parts of the New Testament, called 'The Chester Beatty Papyri', were published under that name by F. G. Kenyon in 1937. Details are listed below and all contain abbreviations of *theos* and *kyrios*, not the tetragram.

Mss number	Scriptures covered	Dated
961	Genesis	early fourth century
962	Genesis	late third century
963	Numbers & Deuteronomy	early second century
965	Isaiah	early third century
966	Jeremiah	second/third century
967	Ezekiel and Esther	second/third century
968	Daniel	second/third century

p^45	Gospel and Acts	early third century
p^46	Pauline Epistles	early third century
p^47	Revelation	late third century

We conclude from the evidence presented that some uncommon LXX versions contain the tetragram but we cannot conclude from this that all or even most do. In fact we read:

> The LXX is characterized by the Hellenizing of Israelite-Jewish monotheism and by the reduction of the designations of God... The name Yahweh or Yah, which is mostly translated by *kyrios*, is replaced by *theos* only about 330 times. (*Dictionary of New Testament Theology*, 1971, Vol. 2, p. 70.)

Most of the early versions of the LXX are of Jewish origin and the scribes were determined to keep old traditions. These have nothing to do with the work of the Christians in the New Testament.

Claim 2: Jesus and His followers pronounced the divine name, and therefore we should today

As already shown, only two BC copies of the LXX have been brought forward for evidence. Therefore it is a wild assumption to say that the manuscript Jesus read in the synagogue contained the tetragram. However, just for a minute let us accept that this was the case. Would the Scribes and the Pharisees allow Him to pronounce the name without a violent outburst? Luke 4:22 tells us they all began to give favourable witness. I don't believe that this calm, appreciative reaction followed the first time the tetragram had been pronounced in a synagogue for hundreds of years! The reaction only comes later when the Jewish leaders realize He is talking about God choosing Gentiles before Jews.

Apart from the evidence we have already printed concerning how the name was pronounced, another factor to take into account is what do we have recorded in Luke's Gospel? Is it the verbatium words of Jesus? This is very doubtful. What we appear to have is Luke's recording of the words of Jesus, written from different texts. The quotations in Luke sometimes agree with the LXX but at other times with the Masoretic Text. Whatever the case, you cannot say that because of these words in Luke, Jesus must have read the tetragram. There is no evidence of that here.

Also, if the purpose of Jesus' ministry was to make known the name of God by pronouncing it, He failed. The NWT takes pains to show that Jesus used the divine name. However, apart from a dozen or so quotes from the Old Testament (we will look at the validity of these later) they can only find evidence to put 'Jehovah' in the mouth of Jesus twice! Jesus did not make the divine name known by pronouncing it.

We close this section with the comments of two biblical scholars about 'Jehovah' in connection with Jesus. It is worth noting that the first, Steve Byington, has translated a modern version of the Bible that the WBTS promote.

> If we need to argue the point of translating 'the Lord' where the Greek says 'the Lord', my argument would be that when Jesus and the apostles and their friends spoke an Old Testament text aloud, they said 'the Lord' for 'Jehovah' even in so careful a quotation as Mark 12:29 (the newly found manuscript of Isaiah may be cited as fresh evidence that the custom of saying 'the Lord' began before the time of Christ...), and we cannot presume that the apostles wrote otherwise than they spoke. (S. T. Byington, *The Christian Century*, 9 May 1951, p. 589.)

Referring initially to the tetragram in the Aquila Fragments, H. H. Rowley wrote in the *Expository Times* soon after Vol. 2 of the NWT Old Testament was released in 1955:

> Actually this offers no evidence that it was pronounced by the reader, any more than it was pronounced by the Jew who read from the Hebrew, where also it was written... if our Lord had rejected the unwillingness to pronounce the Name... it might have been expected that His disciples would have noticed and followed Him in this. Such evidence as we have indicates that when He quoted Psalm 110 He used words which mean 'The Lord said unto my Lord,' and not 'Yahweh said unto my Lord.' Similarly, there is no evidence that in Romans 9:29, 15:9, or

2 Corinthians 6:17 Paul ever wrote anything other than *Kyrios* to represent the [tetragram].

Claim 3: the tetragram appears in the original New Testament manuscripts

This is the WBTS's equivalent of the theory of evolution. There is no evidence but it must be. In fact all the evidence points in the other direction. There is *not one* New Testament manuscript known today in which the tetragram appears and there is no evidence of a conspiracy to get rid of the tetragram.

The Watchtower place their 'burden of proof' on a work by George Howard, published in the *Journal of Biblical Literature*, 1977. The KIT pp. 1137–38, quotes from his work:

> In the following pages we will set forth A THEORY that the divine name . . . was originally written in the N[ew] T[estament] quotations of and allusions to the O[ld] T[estament].

As we have emphasized, this is a theory, and Professor Howard maintains to this day that it should be treated as a theory until a New Testament manuscript is found with the tetragram. Howard starts his article, 'In order to support *this theory*', and ends:

> Concluding observations . . . We have refrained from drawing too many conclusions due to the revolutionary nature of THIS THEORY. Rather than state conclusions now in a positive manner it seems better only to raise some questions that suggest a need for further examination a) IF the tetragram was used in the NT, how extensively was it used . . .

Professor Howard clearly then saw the need for caution and further investigation. He still says that until a manuscript of the New Testament is found with the tetragram his theory remains a theory. But the WBTS are not content with that so they conclude the KIT article with a quantum leap:

> We concur with the above, with one exception: We do not
> consider this view a 'theory', but, rather, a presentation of the
> FACTS (???) of history as to the transmission of Bible manuscripts.

Please note our '???'! What facts? Actually the Society are
up to their normal tricks in missing out much of Howard's
article. One of the relevant parts is:

> We can imagine that the NT text incorporated the tetragram into
> its OT quotations and that the words KURIOS and THEOS were used
> when secondary references to God were made in the comments
> that were based upon the quotations.

Also the article dealt,

> primarily with the divine name AS IT WAS WRITTEN . . . NOT WITH
> WHAT WORD OR WORDS THE READER PRONOUNCED.

So even if the WBTS wish to consider this theory a fact, all
they can claim from it is that the divine name would be in the
New Testament Scriptures *only* where it quoted Old Testament
Scripture. They have, however, gone far beyond that, even to
claiming the pronouncing of the name which Howard says he
doesn't deal with.

KIT, p. 1137, actually claims to have another piece of
evidence to prove that the tetragram appeared in the Christian
Greek Scriptures:

> Matthew's Gospel account was first written in Hebrew rather than
> in Greek, as is indicated by Jerome, of the fourth and fifth
> centuries CE.

The KIT account continues with Jerome's description of
Matthew's Gospel in Hebrew. What they do not tell, or maybe
do not know, is that in his work 'Evangelium Secundum',
Jerome rejects this text as being the Gospel of Matthew and
identifies it with the apocryphal work of the Gospel to the
Hebrews. Many early scholars thought that this or similar
manuscripts were the original of the Gospel of Matthew but

modern scholars reject this completely:

> It is generally not difficult to discover when a Gr[eek] book of this period is a tr[anslation] from the Heb[rew] or the Aram[aic]. That our Mat[thew] was written originally in Gr[reek] appears, among other things, from the way in which it makes use of the O[ld] T[estament], sometimes following the LXX, sometimes going back to the Heb[rew]. (*International Standard Bible Encyclopaedia*, 1978, Vol. 3, p. 2010.)

These facts show that there is no proof for the claims of the Society.

A Greater Problem

However, there is a greater problem. If the divine name has been removed from the Scriptures, why did God allow it? And if He allowed it, has He ordained the WBTS to reverse the position? First, what do the WBTS say themselves about the New Testament Scriptures?

> But with these various families, and the many variations of texts within each family, the Scriptures have come down to us ESSENTIALLY THE SAME AS THE ORIGINAL WRITINGS. The many variations are mainly minor and immaterial. They are to be expected in the light of so much recopying. By careful study and comparison of manuscripts the ERRORS OF ANY CONSEQUENCE HAVE BEEN IRONED OUT and we enjoy today an authentic Bible text. (*Equipped For Every Good Work*, p. 63; more or less reprinted in ABU, p. 1107.)

> Appreciation of the reliability of the Bible is greatly enhanced when it is realized that, by comparison, there are only very few extant manuscripts of the works of classical secular writers and none of these are original, autograph manuscripts. Though they are only copies made centuries after the death of the authors, present-day scholars accept such late copies as sufficient evidence of the authenticity of the text...Manuscripts and versions of the Greek Christian Scriptures bear UNASSAILABLE TESTIMONY TO THE MARVELLOUS PRESERVATION AND ACCURATE TRANSMISSION OF THAT PORTION OF GOD'S WORD. (ABU, p. 1110.)

We conclude from this that they accept all these manuscripts as proof of the accuracy of God's Word today. But here, too, is a regrettably common twisting of the facts by the Society, depending on which hat they are wearing.

> However the papyrus manuscripts brought to the light of day during the nineteenth and twentieth centuries fill in what was once a blind spot in the chain of preserved Scripture copies. THEY BRIDGE OVER THE GAP OF THE SECOND AND THIRD CENTURIES. (*Equipped For Every Good Work*, p. 58.)

> Sometime during the second or third centuries CE, THE TETRAGRAMMATON (YHWH, OR JHVH) WAS ELIMINATED. (KIT, p. 10.)

You can't have it both ways. If you have the copies to prove the authenticity of Scripture then you know that the name was not removed.

So, with the 'non-existent evidence' that the name was removed from the New Testament, we must take a close look at the scholarship of the Society which 'puts it back in'. But just before we do let's summarize our findings so far.

1. A few versions of the LXX have the tetragram in one form or another.
2. Not one Greek manuscript of the New Testament has ever been found containing the tetragram.
3. Jewish translators of the Scriptures harp back to the traditions of their forefathers and add the tetragram to their works.

Scholarship

Anyone who's read the KIT or NWT will recognize 'J' references. These are the translations cited by the WBTS as giving them authority to 'replace' the name of 'Jehovah' in the Greek Scriptures. But do these translations really give such authority?

J2, which was written 'AGAINST Christianity' was revised as 'J3'
and later as 'J4'. J7 was revised as 'J8' and later, in part, as 'J10'.
The London Jewish Society published J11, J13 and J16, while
translators who helped prepare these publications also prepared
J14 and J15. This demonstrates a degree of commonality between
J11, J13, J14, J15 and J16. The extent of the Society's 'support' is
reduced even further when it is recognized that only 9 of the 19
Hebrew translations relate to the whole of the Greek Scriptures;
included in these 9 are J7 and J8 which are related, and also J11,
J13, J14 and J16, which are also related. (Doug Mason, *Witnessing
the Name*, 1981, p. 31.)

This shows the weakness of the 'J' evidence, and it becomes
further diluted when you discover that the oldest translation is
1385, the next 1537 and from there on up to 1981! Most are by
Jewish authors who have a reason for putting the name back in.

The authority of these 'J' references is accepted above that
of some of the oldest New Testament manuscripts. We'll look at
this in more detail presently, but first what do the WBTS say
about these manuscripts?

Biblical papyri of GREAT IMPORTANCE were among papyrus codices
found in Egypt about 1930 . . . three contain portions of fifteen
books of the Christian Greek Scriptures . . . The international
designation for Biblical papyri is a capital 'P' followed by a small
number . . . Quite noteworthy is P[46]. (ABU, pp. 1108–9.)

This article describes various finds of biblical manuscripts
and ends with the earlier comment that we can be sure we have
an accurate Bible because of these finds. They also quote Sir F.
Kenyon:

The interval then between the dates of original composition and
the earliest extant evidence becomes so small as to be in fact
negligible, and the last foundation for any doubt that the
Scriptures have come down to us substantially as they were
written has now been removed. Both the *authenticity* and the
general *integrity* of the books of the New Testament may be
regarded as finally established. (*The Bible and Archeology*
pp. 288–89.)

Here we discover the heart of the Society's deception. They will praise these manuscripts, of 'great importance', as being accurate and proof conclusive that the Bible is reliable, but will reject them for insignificant works of biased men.

The WBTS's 'replacing' of the name of 'Jehovah' in the New Testament 237 times is accomplished by:

1.   The fourth-century Vatican manuscript (B), widely held to be the oldest and best partial manuscript of the New Testament, being rejected 221 times in favour of questionable translations at least 10 centuries and in some cases even 15 centuries later.

2.   The fourth-century Codex Sinaiticus א containing all the New Testament, being rejected all 237 times in favour of the newer translations. Twenty-eight times a nineteenth- or twentieth-century translation is preferred.

3.   The fifth-century Codex Alexandrinus (A), a nearly complete New Testament, being rejected 213 times, over 20 times in favour of nineteenth- or twentieth-century translations.

4.   The fifth-century Codex Ephraemi resciptus (C) which contains almost half of the New Testament being rejected 16 times.

5.   The fifth- and sixth-century Bezae Codices (D) containing the Gospels, Acts and a fragment of 3 John being rejected 14 times.

6. P^{45}, containing portions of the Gospels and Acts, being rejected 3 times, once in favour of a 1981 translation!

7. P^{46} dating from the third century, containing nine of Paul's Letters and the Book of Hebrews, is called 'quite noteworthy' by the WBTS but still rejected 14 times in favour of translations up to sixteen centuries later.

That gives a general picture of the scholarship of the Society but there are one or two notable points that we should make. In 1 Corinthians 7:17 *all* of the above manuscripts are rejected in favour of no 'Js'. The WBTS cannot allow the Lord to be equated with *God* so they replace 'Jehovah' with *no evidence*.

There are times in the New Testament where it would be inappropriate, as far as the WBTS are concerned, to put 'Jehovah'. Here, all of a sudden, they accept the original manuscripts over their 'J' translations. This obviously has nothing to do with scholarship but the desire of the Society to put over their biased views.

Romans 10:9

J[12-14, 16-18, 22] all contain the Hebrew phrase *ha'adhon* which the NWT, p. 1568, tells us is limited '*exclusively to Jehovah God*'. But we find the translators prefer the manuscripts Χ A B because they have Lord. Well it wouldn't do to put Jesus is Jehovah in the NWT would it!

1 Thessalonians 4:16–17

Three times here there is a change, so that Jesus' coming isn't seen as Jehovah's coming. In verse 16 and the first instance in verse 17 J[7, 8, (13, 14)] have Jehovah, and in the second instance of verse 17 J[7, 8, 13, 14, 24] have Jehovah. This evidence was widely accepted before but now they prefer Χ A B.

2 Timothy 1:18

This must have given the translators a headache because 'the Lord is to grant mercy from the Lord.' There is no problem if you accept the biblical revelation of the Trinity but to the WBTS one must be the God, Jehovah and the other little god Jesus. However, a secondary problem comes in because according to their explanation of John 1:1 where the definite article *ho* is found that must be the God Jehovah, and where it isn't found it's the little god Jesus. Yet if you do that here it would appear that Jehovah is subservient to Jesus and so *ho kyrios* becomes the little god Jesus and *kyriou* becomes *the God* Jehovah. This clear twisting of their own teaching is in addition to the fact that *ho kyrios* in J[7, 8, 13, 14, 16] is Jehovah and the *kyriou* in J[7, 8, 13, 14, 16-18, 22-24] is also Jehovah. If they had been really honest they would have had to translate this verse, 'May Jehovah grant him to find mercy from Jehovah in that day.'

1 Peter 3:15

Probably this is the classic deliberate mistranslation, firstly it is an Old Testament quotation and therefore should be translated

Jehovah. Secondly, J[7, 8, 11-14, 16, 17, 24] all say Jehovah and according to WBTS's 'rules of translation' should have been chosen instead of manuscripts X A B C. We would then read, 'But sanctify Jehovah as Lord in your hearts...'

A. M. Stibbs, in his commentary on 1 Peter, says:

> 14...Peter here follows some of the phrases and ideas of Isaiah 8:12–13: 'Neither fear ye their fear, nor be afraid. Sanctify the Lord of hosts himself; and let him be your fear'...it is a plea...to reverence Jehovah and to take refuge in Him...15. In the Greek the reading 'Christ' instead of *God* is to be preferred. Language referring to Jehovah in Isaiah 8:13 is explicitly applied to Jesus, thus claiming for Him, and particularly for Him as 'the Christ'... worship as God. (pp. 134–35.)

Revelation 16:5

J[7, 8, 13, 14, 16] say, 'You, Jehovah', but the WBTS prefer the 'You' of X A C. However, we should read, 'You, Jehovah, the One who is *and was*...'

Conclusion

This brief look at the biased way the Society restore the name shows that their scholarship cannot be trusted. Since we have shown that the claims of the WBTS are false now we need to make some conclusions based on Scripture.

We've seen that the Old Testament revelation included the tetragram but the New Testament does not; so what revelation do we receive of God in the New Testament? Over a hundred times in the Gospels alone we read 'Father'. This is the New Testament revelation. The remote 'Jehovah' of the Old Testament has become the close intimate Father of the New. The personal name of God has been changed because of the new relationship—not calling Him by His personal name, as indeed we don't our earthly fathers, but Abba Father, that glorious secure family relationship.

We see in John 17:6,26 Jesus claimed that He had made the name known. However, we have already shown that Jesus did not pronounce the tetragram so what was he talking about? ABU itself gives much of the answer:

> For an individual to know God's name signifies MORE THAN A MERE ACQUAINTANCE WITH THE WORD... It means actually knowing the person... This is illustrated in the case of Moses... (he) was privileged... to 'hear the name of Jehovah declared'. That declaration was NOT SIMPLY THE REPETITION OF THE NAME 'JEHOVAH'... When Jesus Christ was on earth, he 'made his Father's name manifest' to his disciples (John 17:6,26). Although having earlier known that name and being familiar with God's activities as recorded in the Hebrew Scriptures, these disciples came to know Jehovah in a far better and grander way... CHRIST JESUS PERFECTLY PRESENTED HIS FATHER, doing the works of his Father and speaking, not on his own originality, but the words of his Father. (p. 1202.)

In other words it wasn't so much what Jesus said but what He did that made the name known. Time and time again Jesus said He did the will of His Father, spoke the words of His Father, did what He saw His Father doing. Not Jehovah but Father. This is the New Testament record. There is no removal of the name—it was never there. If Jesus was who the WBTS say He was then He should have used 'Jehovah' hundreds of times but He never did—My Father. That is our relationship today.

The Watchtower itself says in *Reasoning*:

> ...how would it be possible to identify the true God...Only by using His personal name ...1 Corinthians 8:5-6 (p. 197.)

And 1 Corinthians 8:6 in the NWT says, '...there is actually to us one God THE FATHER...'

We can now bring the subject to a close. We've seen that there is no case for the name being removed and that the Scriptures, as we have them today, are correct. We can now answer one final question, 'When the New Testament talks of the name what does it mean?' The following Scriptures are just

some that give the answer:
Acts 1:8—witnesses to the name of Jesus
Acts 2:38—baptized in...Jesus
Acts 3:6—healed in...Jesus
Acts 4:12—salvation only in...Jesus
Acts 9:12—suffer for...Jesus
Acts 11:26—called Christ ones.

The Old Testament revelation was Jehovah; the New
Testament is Jesus. The Old Testament was outward obedience
to Jehovah in sacrifices; the New Testament is knowing Jesus in
the heart. The Old Testament saints were to be witnesses of
Jehovah; the New Testament ones are to be witnesses of Jesus.
We today are privileged to be in the New Testament and we
need to live in the glorious free family relationship given to us.
We close with one final quote from *Knowing the Scriptures*
by A. T. Pierson, 1910, which talks about the name of 'Jehovah':

> Were this great name always reproduced in the English and
> especially in the New Testament quotations from the Old, it
> would prove that our Lord Jesus Christ is absolutely equal and
> identical with the Father, for passages which, in the Old
> Testament contain the name, 'Jehovah', are so quoted and
> applied to Him in the New as to demonstrate Him to be JEHOVAH-
> JESUS, one with God of the Eternal Past, Himself God manifested
> in the flesh...Hebrews 1:10... 'Prepare ye the way of Jehovah'
> (Matthew 3:3 from Isaiah 40:3). 'Jehovah our Righteousness'
> (Jeremiah 23:6; Romans 3; 1 Corinthians 1:30). Most complete
> and conclusive is Revelation 1:8,11,17,18...Rabinowitz said,
> 'What questioning and controversies the Jews have kept up over
> Zechariah 12:10: 'They shall look upon Me whom they pierced.'
> They will not admit that it is Jehovah whom they pierced, hence
> the dispute about the word '*whom*'; but this word is simply the
> first and last letters of the Hebrew alphabet—Aleph, Tav. Filled
> with awe and astonishment, I open to Revelation 1:7–8 and read
> these words of Zechariah, as quoted by John...and then heard
> the glorified Lord saying 'I am the Alpha and Omega.' Jesus
> seemed to say: 'Do you doubt who it is *whom* you pierced? I am
> the Aleph, Tav—the Alpha and Omega—Jehovah the
> Almighty.' (pp. 93–95.)

Talking to Jehovah's Witnesses About...

This Section will cover a number of subjects and show how you can talk to a Witness, without fear, on 'touchy' matters. These are not meant for the first-time doorstep meetings but for the Witness who is willing and interested to hear what you have to say.

Reasoning is used by most Witnesses today to argue their case and therefore, wherever possible, we will follow its arguments and show its falseness and deception.

A. THE TRINITY

The article on the Trinity in *Reasoning* covers some twenty pages (405–26) and for reason of space we will not cover every part of it. First, though, we'll check some of the publications that Witnesses call on to support their assertion that the Trinity doesn't exist. As in previous Sections the part in bold letters is the part they've left out. Where necessary we've added explanatory notes in [ ].

EB Vol. X, 1976, p. 126

> Neither the word Trinity, nor the explicit doctrine as such, appears in the New Testament, nor did Jesus and his followers intend to contradict the Shema in the Old Testament: 'Hear, O Israel: The Lord our God is one Lord' (Deut 6:4). **The earliest**

Christians, however, had to cope with the implications of the coming of Jesus Christ and of the presence and power of God among them i.e., The Holy Spirit, whose coming we connected with the celebration of Pentecost. The Father, Son, and Holy Spirit were associated in such New Testament passages as the Great Commission: 'Go therefore and make disciples of all nations, baptizing them in the name of The Father and of the Son and of the Holy Spirit' (Matt 28:19); and in the apostolic benediction: 'The grace of the Lord Jesus Christ and the love of God and the fellowship of the Holy Spirit be with you all' (II Cor 13:14). Thus, the New Testament established the basis for the doctrine of the Trinity. The doctrine developed gradually over several centuries and through many controversies... By the end of the 4th century... the doctrine of the Trinity took substantially the form it has maintained ever since.

NCE, Vol. XIV, 1967, pp. 295–99

It is difficult, in the second half of the 20th century to offer a clear, objective, and straightforward account of the... Trinity... Among the Apostolic Fathers, Clement of Rome... in the final decade of the 1st century, bears witness to God the Father, to the Son, to the Spirit... From what has been seen thus far, the impression could arise that the Trinitarian dogma is in the last analysis a late 4th century invention. In a sense, this is true; but it implies an extremely strict interpretation on the key words Trinitarian and dogma. The formulation 'one God in three Persons' was not solidly established, certainly not fully assimilated into Christian life and its profession of faith, prior to the end of the 4th century. But it is precisely this formulation that has first claim to the title *the Trinitarian dogma*. Among the Apostolic Fathers, there had been nothing even remotely approaching such a mentality or perspective.

EA, Vol. XXVII, 1956, p. 294L

What the WBTS omit to tell their readers about this quote is that it comes from an eight page article on Unitarianism. Unitarians are a group who openly deny both the deity of Christ and that Christ died for our sins. The part of the article we've added from p. 301 shows this clearly.

Christianity derived from Judaism and Judaism was strictly Unitarian [believing that God is one person]. The road which led from Jerusalem to Nicea was scarcely a straight one. Fourth-century Trinitarianism did not reflect accurately early Christian teaching regarding the nature of God; it was, on the contrary, a deviation from this teaching... **The alleged fact that Jesus died for our sins, and thus guarded us against the effects of the wrath of God, is categorically denied. To believe that Jesus' death did have this result would be to cast an aspersion on God's character... Moreover, man should not, Unitarians believe, accept such an offer on the part of Jesus...**

Once again, the WBTS are guilty of quoting an anti-Christian group to try to 'prove' their erroneous doctrines.

John L. McKenzie, '*Dictionary of the Bible*', 1965, pp. 899–900

The trinity of persons within the unity of nature is defined in terms of 'person' and 'nature' which are G[ree]k philosophical terms; actually the terms do not appear in the Bible. The trinitarian definitions arose as the result of long controversies in which these terms and others such as 'essence' and 'substance' were erroneously applied to God by some theologians... **This distinction between God and flesh is the NT basis for the affirmation of the unity of nature; the very identification of the Father with 'the God' shows that the NT writers intended to distinguish the Son and the Spirit from the Father. The NT does not approach the metaphysical problem of subordination as it approaches no metaphysical problem. It offers no room for a statement of the relations of Father, Son and Spirit which would imply that one of them is more or less properly on the divine level of being than another... any statement of this distinction which reduces the divinity of any of the persons is a false statement.**

NCE, Vol. XIII, 1967, p. 575

Although the NT concepts of the Spirit of God are largely a continuation of those of the OT, in the NT there is a gradual revelation that the Spirit of God is a person. The majority of N[ew] T[estament] texts reveal God's spirit as something not someone; this is especially seen in the parallelism between the spirit and the power of God.

NCE, Vol. XIV, 1967, p. 296

> **The God of the Christian, like the God of the Israelites, was**
> **unequivocally one. Nevertheless if as Justin notes (1 Apol. 13),**
> **Christians worship Christ in the second place and the Spirit in the**
> **third place, there is still no inconsistency; for the Word and Spirit**
> **are not to be separated from the unique Godhead of the Father** . . .
> The Apologists [Greek Christian writers of the second century]
> spoke too haltingly of the Spirit; with a measure of anticipation,
> one might say too impersonally.

Karl Rahner, Vol. 1, 'Theological Investigations', 1961, pp. 138,
143

> *Theos* [God] is still never used of the Spirit . . . **there are six**
> **complete texts in which** *o theos* **is used to speak of the Second**
> **Person of the Trinity** . . . *O theos* [literally, the God] is never used
> in the New Testament to speak of the 'holy spirit'.

McClintock and Strong, Vol. X, *'Cyclopedia of Biblical,
Theological, and Ecclesiastical Literature'*, 1981, p. 552

> McClintock and Strong's *Cyclopedia of Biblical, Theological, and
> Ecclesiastical Literature,* though advocating the Trinity doctrine,
> acknowledges regarding Matthew 28:18–20: 'This text, however,
> taken by itself, would not prove decisively either the *personality*
> of the three subjects mentioned, or their *equality or divinity*,'
> (1981 reprint, Vol. X, p. 552). Regarding other texts that also
> mention the three together, this *Cyclopedia* admits that, taken by
> themselves, they are 'insufficient' to prove the Trinity. (Compare
> 1 Timothy 5:21, where God and Christ and the angels are
> mentioned together.)

**The Society only refer to this book without quoting in full
because these scholars actually say the opposite!**

> The first class of texts taken by itself, proves only that there are
> three subjects named and that there is a difference between them;
> that the Father in certain respects differs from the Son, etc; but it
> does not prove, by itself, that all three belong necessarily to the
> divine nature and possess equal divine honour. **In proof of this,**

**the second class of texts must be addressed . . . These texts prove (a)
that the Son and Holy Spirit, according to the doctrine of the New
Test[ament], are divine, or belong to the one divine nature; and (b)
that the three subjects are personal and equal. (p. 552.)**

Other quotes will be mentioned at the appropriate time but
this brief look shows that the scholars do not say the Trinity is of
pagan origin or that it is not found in the Bible—in fact just the
opposite. How can the WBTS, who call themselves God's
channel of truth, twist things so much?

The fact that the Trinity 'dogma' was not written down
until the fourth century is true. The reason, though, is not
because it was only invented then but because this truth,
believed and taught in the early church, came under severe
attack at that time. The truth hadn't been questioned so fiercely
before and had never needed to be defined 'on paper'. Now
Christians wanted everyone to know what they believed.

From the quotes above you will be able to show that
scholars do not agree with the WBTS's teaching but remember,
we can never understand the Trinity with our minds. The divine
relationship of the Godhead (incidentally, because the word
'Trinity' is like a red rag to a bull it is usually better to use
'Godhead') can only be grasped by the Holy Spirit witnessing to
our spirits. This is a great disadvantage to Jehovah'a Witnesses
and even after hours of sharing many will not change their views
because they are blinded by the enemy. Share in love and
patience and above all pray that the Lord will have mercy on
them and open their eyes.

When sharing it is often best to forget about the scholars
and ask, 'Are you willing to accept the biblical revelation of the
position of Christ and His relationship with God the Father?'
The answer must be 'Yes', and so which Scriptures should we
use first? You must use the ones that you are comfortable with
but the ones I have found most helpful are the presentations of
Alpha and Omega, Hebrews 1 dealing with Jesus' superiority to
angels, and Revelation 5 re worship. All of these are mentioned
in Section 4.

John 1

John 1, especially verses 1 and 2 is dealt with on pp. 416–17 of
Reasoning. In the next sub-section we'll look at the Greek
aspects of these verses. But try just to get the Witness to read
the Scripture and then ask them to tell you what they've read.
Be persistent with them till they give the answer on the page.

Verse 1: In the *beginning*—the Greek phrase is exactly the
same as the Greek translation (Septuagint) for Genesis 1:1.
There God was *in* the beginning—*not created*; here the word is
in the beginning—not created. *Was*—not will be. He existed
before any creation took place (v. 3) and as seen this doesn't
mean he had a beginning. Use Hebrews 7:3 here, where even
the NWT shows the Son of God had no 'beginning of days or
end of life', i.e. He is eternal.

Verse 3: *All* things created by Him. The Word of God
offers no exceptions as the emphasis in this verse shows: 'apart
from Him *Nothing came into being.*' Only if you bring human
interpretation to bear can you say that Christ was created.

Verse 14: *Only-begotten.* The Greek word *monogenes* is
contrasted with the word for born, *gennao* in verse 13. Christ is
the unique one, not born as we are but begotten. Begotten can
never mean created.

We don't use the words *begetting* or *begotten* much in modern
English, but everyone still knows what they mean. To beget is to
become the father of: to create is to make. And the difference is
just this. When you beget, you beget something of the same kind
as yourself. A man begets human babies, a beaver begets little
beavers, and a bird begets eggs which turn into little birds. But
when you make, you make something of a different kind from
yourself... What God begets is God; just as what man begets is
man. What God creates is not God; just as what man makes is not
man. That is why men are not Sons of God in the sense that Christ
is. (C. S. Lewis, *Beyond Personality*, 1944, p. 12.)

We can only rightly understand the term 'the only begotten' when
used of the Son, in the sense of unoriginated relationship. 'The
begetting is not an event of time, however remote, but a fact
irrespective of time. The Christ did not *become*, but necessarily

and eternally *is* the Son. He, a Person, possesses every attribute of pure Godhood. This necessitates eternity, absolute being; in this respect he is not "after" the Father.' (VINE, Vol. 3, p. 140.)

For further biblical teaching on this matter see Reachout Trust's *An Alternative View* (order form at end of book).

Reasoning, pp. 416–24, mentions several other verses under the revealing heading, 'Texts from which a person might draw more than one conclusion, depending on the Bible translation used'. We list these texts and add a few comments.

John 8:58

The WBTS cannot have Jesus say that He is 'I AM', so He becomes the 'I have been'. They try to justify this with a quote from A. T. Robertson, but even he says this is impossible:

> The Progressive Present. This is a poor name in lieu of a better one for the present of a past action STILL IN PROGRESS... In John 8:58 *eimi* is really absolute. (A. T. Robertson, *A Grammar of the Greek New Testament in the Light of Historical Research*, p. 879.)

Other scholars' views on John 8:58 are found in Appendix 4.

Acts 20:28

As there is great debate amongst scholars as to whether the phrase here is church of God or church of the Lord it doesn't seem helpful to pursue this issue. We don't need to, anyway, with so much other clear evidence.

Romans 9:5

The punctuation is changed in the NWT so that Christ is not equated with God. They quote from the *International Dictionary of New Testament Theology*. However, they end the quote before this part on the next page:

> ...the passage cannot be treated as a doxology to God the Father, since it does not follow the form of doxologies elsewhere in the LXX and the NT. The application of *theos* to Christ suits the context...

> comparable assertions of divinity may be found in
> 2 Thess[alonians] 1:2; Tit[us] 2:13; Phil[ippians] 2:6; Col[ossians]
> 2:9; and 2 Cor[inthians] 3:17 ... 'God blessed for evermore' stands
> in apposition to Christ.

Once again they are found to be tampering with the Word of God without evidence.

Philippians 2:5–6

Witnesses argue that Christ can not be equal to God and, as usual, have a scholar who appears to agree with them, but the quote continues:

> Are we not obliged then, to think of the [Greek] *harpagman*
> (=*harpagma*) as something still future ... Observe how aptly the
> view fits the context. In verse 10, which is the climax of the whole
> passage, we read that God gave Jesus Christ *as a gift* ... the name
> above every name, i.e. the name (including position, dignity and
> authority) of *kyrios*, Lord, the name which represents the OT
> Jehovah. But this is the highest place Christ has reached. He has
> always (in Paul's view) shared the Divine nature ... But it is only as
> the result of His Incarnation, Atonement, Resurrection and
> Exultation that He *appears to men* as on an equality with God, that
> He is *worshipped by them* in the way which Jehovah is worshipped.
> (*The Expositor's Greek Testament*, 1967, edited by W. Robertson
> Nicoll, Vol. III p. 437.)

We must thank the WBTS for giving us the quote to show that Jesus is God.

Colossians 2:9

The Witnesses' argument that the Greek here is not to be translated 'Godhead', but 'divine quality', is full of Watchtower logic but not scriptural content. I think the answer lies in what Vine says:

> THEIOTES ... divinity ... is to be distinguished from *theotes*, in
> Colossians 2:9, 'Godhead' ... [in this passage] Paul is declaring
> that in the Son there dwells all the fullness of absolute Godhead;
> they were no mere rays of Divine glory which gilded Him, lighting

up His Person for a season and with a splendour not His own; but He was, and is, absolute and perfect God. (VINE, Vol. 1, pp. 328-29.)

Titus 2:13

Again the verse is changed to stop it saying Jesus is God. Again the apparently convincing scholarly quote. Again the ending missed off.

> ... Whichever way taken, the passage is just as important testimony to the divinity of our Saviour: according to (1) [*Jesus Christ, the great God and our Saviour*], by asserting His possession of Deity and right to the appellation of the Highest: according to (2) [*the great God and of our Saviour Jesus Christ*], even more strikingly, asserting His equality in glory with the Father ... (H. Alford, *The Greek Testament*, 1877, p. 421.)

In other words, whichever way you translate it, Jesus is still equal with the Father, God!

Hebrews 1:8

Repeat of introduction to Titus 2:13

> ... In whatever way then *o theos* be taken, the quotation establishes the conclusion which the writer wishes to draw as to the essential difference of the Son and angels. Indeed it might appear to many that the direct application to the divine Name to the Son would obscure this thought. (B. F. Westcott, *The Epistle to the Hebrews*, 1889, p. 26.)

Westcott's position is made abundantly clear on p. 20 of the same book:

> Nor is it without the deepest significance that in the fundamental passages, Ps[alm] 2:7, 2 Sam[uel] 7:14 the speaker is 'the Lord' and not 'GOD': The unique title of Christ is thus connected with God as He is God of the Covenant (*Jehovah, the* Lord).

The deviousness of the arguments in the *Reasoning* book, are made very clear when the original quotes are checked!

Old Testament Posers for Jehovah's Witnesses

Malachi 3:1

This verse and footnote in NWT, 1971 large print edition, gives the Witness all sorts of problems

> 'Look! I am sending my messenger, and he must clear up a way before me. And suddenly there will certainly come to His temple the [true] Lord, whom you people are seeking, and the messenger of the covenant in whom you are delighting. Look! He will certainly come,' Jehovah of armies has said. (NWT.)

Clearly Jehovah is speaking about the true Lord whom He will send. The true Lord whom the people *are seeking* and the only one ever to come to the temple, is Jesus. The footnote says that the Hebrew for 'true lord' is *ha-Adon* and cites eight other occurrences of the word. The 1970 NWT (p. 1455) explains further that *ha-Adon* is only ever used of Jehovah God. The nine Scriptures, Exodus 23:17; 34:23; Isaiah 1:24; 3:1; 10:16; 10:33; 19:4; Micah 4:13 and Malachi 3:1 are listed and every one of them links the name Jehovah with true Lord, usually 'the true Lord, Jehovah'. Every one that is *except* Malachi 3:1! The reason is obvious—first, the verse would show that Jehovah was sending Jehovah, but more devastating it would show that Christ is the true Lord, Jehovah.

Zechariah 2:10–12

> 'Cry out . . . O daughter of Zion; for here I am coming, and I will reside in the midst of you,' is the utterance of Jehovah . . . And you will have to know that Jehovah of armies himself has sent me to you. And Jehovah will . . . yet choose Jerusalem. (NWT.)

It is clear that Jehovah is the one coming and residing in Jerusalem, not Zechariah as some Witnesses will try to say. But it is also clear that Jehovah of armies has sent Him. A clear case of two Jehovahs in the NWT. The only possible answer is that God the Father is sending God the Son.

New Testament Posers for Jehovah's Witnesses

Which name?

Ask the Witness to explain these two Scriptures:

> And everyone who calls on the NAME OF JEHOVAH will be SAVED. (Acts 2:21, NWT.)

> ... in the NAME OF JESUS CHRIST ... does this man stand here ... Furthermore, there is NO SALVATION in ANYONE ELSE, for there is NOT ANOTHER NAME under heaven that has been given among men by which we must GET SAVED. (Acts 4:10–12, NWT.)

To worship or not to worship?

Luke 4:8 makes it clear that only God must be worshipped. But the Scriptures show that Jesus received worship. Oh no, Mr Trinitarian, Jesus only ever received obeisance. Look, for instance, at Hebrews 1:6: 'let all God's angels do obeisance to him.'

Interestingly, the same Greek word is translated 'worship' when used of the Father, but 'obeisance' when used of the Son. If that isn't translating the Bible to suit yourself I don't know what is. However, the Watchtower's 'evolution' of Hebrews 1:6 is worth a mention!

> And let all God's angel's WORSHIP him. (Heb 1:6, NWT, 1970.)

Back in 1970 it was all right for Jesus to receive worship.

> And let all God's angels DO OBEISANCE to him. (Heb 1:6, NWT, large print, 1971.)

By 1971 Jehovah had changed His mind, or had He? The verse had a footnote, 'Or "worship him". Compare Hebrews 11:21.' Jehovah wasn't sure! By the way Hebrews 11:21, which we must compare, is all about Joseph *worshipping*. Once again we find that the truth is there for any seeker to find. Jesus can and did receive worship which means He is either a fraud or God. See Section 4 for further information on this subject.

An interesting sidelight to worship is that today a Jehovah's Witness must not worship Jesus, but in 1916 they were told that many would worship Charles T. Russell:

> Charles Taze Russell, thou hast, by the Lord, been crowned a king...and thy enemies shall come and WORSHIP at thy feet. (ZWTR, 1 December 1916, p. 6015.)

Did they really believe that Russell was more important than Jesus?

And don't forget...

There are many other verses in the New Testament that can be used. Here are just a few with brief comments:

Matthew 28:19—What is the *name* of the Father, Son and Holy Spirit? Jehovah?

2 Corinthians 13:14—Why the threefold blessing? Why not all from Jehovah? Why is Jesus first?

1 Corinthians 12:4–6—three persons bringing fullness to the church.

James 1:1—How can James have two separate masters? He is serving Jesus with the same diligence as Jehovah.

Problem Verses for Christians

There are some verses, about the person of Christ, that are nearly always raised by the Witnesses and we need to be able to answer them clearly.

John 14:28

Jesus said His Father was greater than Him, therefore how can Jesus be God? The argument sounds logical and because the Witnesses rely so much on logic they have problems. However, what does 'greater' mean? Better? Different than? The same word is used in John 14:12: 'greater works you will do.' Are we going to do better or different works than Jesus? No, greater here simply means in more magnitude; they will be no better and certainly not different. The self-imposed limitations of Jesus' earthly life caused His Father to be greater only at that time and in that place. Incidentally, only things in the same magnitude can be compared. Jesus claimed equality and oneness with the Father—John 5:18; 10:30—and therefore could be compared with Him.

1 Corinthians 15:28

There is always right subjection in the relationship between the Father and the Son (see John 5:30). Jesus willingly allows this and it doesn't imply that He is lesser than the Father. The word for subjection is a military term meaning to put in rank—a right order created to achieve a desired end which does not imply inequality. For instance, Luke 2:51 tells us that Jesus was in subjection to His parents. Did this make Him less than His parents? No, it was just the right order which Jesus willingly accepted. Ephesians 5:21 shows us this relationship in the body of Christ and verse 22 within marriage, but neither indicate that one has to be less than the other—simply that there is a right order.

The Holy Spirit

Having shared the biblical teaching on the relationship of Father and Son you can then move on to add one or two comments concerning the Holy Spirit. Two areas need to be covered: first, to show that the Holy Spirit is a person not a force, likened to electricity; and second, that this person is the third member of the Godhead.

His personality

In an indirect way the WBTS show that the Holy Spirit is a person. Point out the following quote:

Is the Devil a personification or a person? . . . these accounts relate to conversations between the Devil and God, and between the Devil and Jesus Christ. Both Jehovah God and Jesus Christ are persons. Can an unintelligent 'force' carry on a conversation with a person? Also, the Bible calls Satan a manslayer, a liar, a father (in spiritual sense) and a ruler... ONLY AN INTELLIGENT PERSON COULD FIT ALL THOSE DESCRIPTIONS. (*Awake!*, 8 December 1973, p. 27.)

This is a good 'theocratic' rule and can be applied in other cases. Let's apply the principles to the Holy Spirit. First Witnesses say the Devil has to be a person because he talks to other persons:

> SO THE SPIRIT SAID to Philip... (Acts 8:29, NWT.)

> THE HOLY SPIRIT SAID... (Acts 13:2, NWT.)

> Just as THE HOLY SPIRIT SAYS... (Heb 3:7, NWT.)

The Holy Spirit talks with other people, therefore he cannot be an unintelligent force!

The second principle is that the names Scripture gives to the Devil show he must be a person.

> But the HELPER, the HOLY SPIRIT, which the Father will send in my name, THAT ONE WILL TEACH you all things... (John 14:26, NWT.)

> However when that one arrives, the spirit of truth, HE WILL GUIDE YOU into all the truth; for he will not SPEAK on his own initiative, but whatever he HEARS, he will SPEAK... (John 16:13, NWT.)

The Holy Spirit is a helper, a teacher, a guide, a speaker and a hearer, all of which clearly shows He is an intelligent person.

One name especially, 'helper' gives us a clear insight into His person. The Greek word is *parakletos* and this is what Greek scholar W. E. Vine says about the word:

> ...lit., called to one's side, i.e., to one's aid, is primarily a verbal adjective, and suggests the capability or adaptability for giving aid. It was used in a court of justice to denote a legal assistant, counsel for the defence, an advocate; then, generally, of one who

pleads another's cause, an intercessor, advocate, as in 1 John 2:1, of the Lord Jesus. In the widest sense, it signifies a succourer, comforter. Christ was to His disciples, by implication of His word 'another (*allos*, another of the same sort, not *hetros* different) Comforter', when speaking of the Holy Spirit, John 14:16. In John 14:26; 15:26; 16:7 He calls Him 'the Comforter'. (VINE, Vol. 1, p. 208.)

With this one description Vine has encapsulated so much proof of the person of the Holy Spirit. First, the definition of *parakletos* shows such a one who pleads and aids must be an intelligent force. Second, he shows that both the Lord Jesus and the Holy Spirit are called the *parakletos*. Third, he underlines the use of the word *allos* for 'another' which clearly means of the same sort, not different. These last two points link the Holy Spirit and Jesus together as beings of the same sort i.e., intelligent persons.

Besides the Witnesses own definition there are other indications that the Holy Spirit is a person. However, before we look at them we should mention one come-back that you might receive from the Witnesses. They are taught in *Reasoning*, p.380, that just because something is personified it doesn't mean it's a person, and 'wisdom' is given as an illustration. If this comes up please remind them of the following quote which turns this argument on its head:

> God's Son had a fondness for mankind even during his prehuman existence. UNDER THE FIGURE OF WISDOM PERSONIFIED, HE IS IDENTIFIED as God's 'master worker'... (WT, 15 April, 1980, p. 26.)

You can not argue the matter in both directions! Wisdom personified is the person of Jesus! The Holy Spirit personified is the person of the Holy Sprit. There are, however, other clear indications in Scripture.

He has the characteristics of a person

There are four characteristics that are only ever found in intelligent persons and never found in things. The Holy Spirit is

shown to have these qualities: Intelligence—John 14:26—
ability to teach; a mind—Romans 8:27; a will—1 Corinthians
12:11; affections—Ephesians 4:30—an unintelligent force can
not feel grief!

Original Greek

In John 14:17 the NWT refers to the Holy Spirit as an 'it' and in
the strict grammatical sense this is right because the word for
spirit, *pneuma*, is neuter and therefore the pronouns that refer
to it are also in the neuter. But even the WBTS have to call the
Holy Spirit *he* in John 16:13 where we have the neuter *pneuma*
and the masculine *eikinos*. Vine sums this up:

> THE PERSONALITY OF THE HOLY SPIRIT IS EMPHASIZED at the expense
> of strict grammatical procedure in John 14:16; 15:26; 16:8,13,14,
> where the emphatic pronoun *ekeinos*, 'He', is used of Him in the
> masculine, whereas the noun *pneuma* is neuter...(VINE,
> Vol. 4, p. 64.)

(As a sidelight, Vine is quoted in *Make Sure of All Things*,
1965, p. 488, as proving that the Holy Spirit does not have a
personality. Needless to say the words above were replaced by
'...'!)

The above is abundant proof that the Holy Spirit is a
person. Having established that He is a person removes one
barrier to the problem of Him being the third person of the
Godhead. The question of whether He is God or not can be
answered as follows.

He has the characteristics of God

Just as there are certain characteristics only found in a person so
there are also certain characteristics only found in God. The
Scriptures show the Holy Spirit to have these characteristics:
omnipresence—Psalm 139:7–10—only God is present everywhere!; all knowing—Isaiah 40:13–14—no one taught Him!;
sovereign—1 Corinthians 12:11—only God can do just as He
chooses; eternal—Hebrews 9:14
Some Witnesses might respond that because it's Jehovah's

active force, it represents God in these verses. Remind the Witnesses though that He is not just an active force but a person in His own right and therefore these Scriptures must talk of God the Holy Spirit.

He does the work of God

This work includes creation—Job 33:4, Psalm 104:30 (these verses should be read with Isaiah 44:24 where Jehovah says, I alone, Myself created!); regeneration—John 3:5,6, Titus 3:5; sanctification—Romans 15:16, 1 Corinthians 6:11, 2 Thessalonians 2:13, 1 Peter 1:1–2; and resurrection—Romans 8:11.

There are a couple of other verses which are worth sharing too. Acts 5:3–4, even in the NWT, indicates clearly that the Holy Spirit is God. Acts 5:3—'...play false to the holy spirit...'; Acts 5:4—'...played false...to God...' We are more used to the translation 'lied to', and remember it is impossible to lie to an active force!

Finally, ask the Witnesses to read from their own Bibles 2 Corinthians 3:16–18;

> But when there is a turning to Jehovah, the veil is taken away. Now Jehovah is the Spirit; and where the spirit of Jehovah is, there is freedom. And all of us, while we with unveiled faces reflect like mirrors the glory of Jehovah, are transformed into the same image from glory to glory, exactly as done by Jehovah [the] Spirit. (NWT.)

Then ask, 'What does "Jehovah *is the* Spirit," mean?'

Truly the Scriptures show beyond any doubt that the Father is God, the Lord Jesus Christ is God and the Person of the Holy Spirit is God. We may not be able to understand this with our mind but there is no need to reject it. God in His completeness and greatness manifests Himself in three distinct ways.

B. JOHN 1:1

Probably this verse causes more problems than any other. To show that Jesus is not God the NWT translates it, '...and the

Word was a god...' Indeed they appear to provide ample evidence to prove that this is the correct translation. Here we will examine this evidence.

Between 1962 and 1983 the WBTS quoted Johannes Greber to support their rendering of John 1:1. They did this even though they knew in 1956 that his wife acted as a spirit medium to produce the translation. They no longer quote Greber but it is still interesting to ask the Witness why they think their translation agrees with a spiritist Bible and why 'God's organization' knowingly used that spiritist Bible as a reliable source for many years. (For more detailed information see Reachout Trust's booklet, *The Truth Revealed*.)

Apart from *Reasoning* we will also look at an article in KIT, p. 1139.

'Reasoning From the Scriptures' (pp. 416-7)

Besides attempting to find scholarly evidence, the Society's main defence for their translation is:

> John 1:18 says: 'No one has ever seen God.' Verse 14 clearly says that 'the Word became flesh and dwelt among us...we have beheld his glory'. Also, verses 1, 2 say that in the beginning he was '*with* God'. Can one be *with* someone and at the same time be that person? At John 17:3, Jesus addresses the Father as 'the only true God'; so, Jesus as 'a god' merely reflects his Father's divine qualities—Heb[rews] 1:3. (p. 416.)

Does this sound convincing? Let's take a closer look. Firstly we reproduce John 1:14-18 from the KIT. (See p. 91.)

Note (v. 18) there is no definite article connected with the first *theon* which is translated God, but the second *theos* is followed by the definite article 'the one' and yet it is translated 'god'. When you add to this the meaning of the term 'only-begotten' (see previous part of this Section) this verse says no man has ever seen God but now God the unique Son clothed in flesh reveals God in a way that can be seen by men.

Look again at John 1:14. See how the Witnesses have lessened the impact from 'we viewed' definite to 'had a view of'

14 Καὶ   ὁ   λόγος   σὰρξ   ἐγένετο   καὶ
And   the   Word   flesh   became   and

ἐσκήνωσεν   ἐν   ἡμῖν,   καὶ   ἐθεασάμεθα   τὴν   δόξαν
tented   in   us,   and   we viewed   the   glory

αὐτοῦ,   δόξαν   ὡς   μονογενοῦς   παρὰ
of him,   glory   as   of only-begotten (one)   beside

πατρός,   πλήρης   χάριτος   καὶ
of father,   full   of undeserved kindness   and

ἀληθείας·   **15** Ἰωάνης   μαρτυρεῖ   περὶ
truth;   John   is witnessing   about

αὐτοῦ   καὶ   κέκραγεν   λέγων —   οὗτος
him   and   he has cried out   saying —   this (one)

ἦν   ὁ   εἰπών —   Ὁ   ὀπίσω
was   the (one)   having said —   The (one)   behind

μου   ἐρχόμενος   ἔμπροσθέν   μου   γέγονεν,
me   coming   in front   of me   has come to be,

ὅτι   πρῶτός   μου   ἦν·   **16** ὅτι
because   first   of me   he was;   because

ἐκ   τοῦ   πληρώματος   αὐτοῦ   ἡμεῖς   πάντες
out of   the   fullness   of him   we   all

ἐλάβομεν,   καὶ   χάριν   ἀντὶ
received,   and   undeserved kindness   instead of

χάριτος·   **17** ὅτι   ὁ   νόμος
undeserved kindness;   because   the   law

διὰ   Μωυσέως   ἐδόθη,   ἡ
through   Moses   was given,   the

χάρις   καὶ   ἡ   ἀλήθεια   διὰ
undeserved kindness   and   the   truth   through

Ἰησοῦ   Χριστοῦ   ἐγένετο.   **18** θεὸν   οὐδεὶς
Jesus   Christ   came to be.   God   no one

ἑώρακεν   πώποτε·   μονογενὴς   θεὸς
has seen   at any time;   only-begotten   god

ὁ   ὢν   εἰς   τὸν   κόλπον   τοῦ   πατρὸς
the (one)   being   into the   bosom   of the   Father

ἐκεῖνος   ἐξηγήσατο.
that (one)   explained.

14 So the Word became flesh and resided among us, and we had a view of his glory, a glory such as belongs to an only-begotten son from a father; and he was full of undeserved kindness and truth. **15** (John bore witness about him, yes, he actually cried out—this was the one who said [it]—saying: "The one coming behind me has advanced in front of me, because he existed before me.") **16** For we all received from out of his fullness, even undeserved kindness upon undeserved kindness. **17** Because the Law was given through Moses, the undeserved kindness and the truth came to be through Jesus Christ. **18** No man has seen God at any time; the only-begotten god who is in the bosom [position] with the Father is the one that has explained him.

and 'his glory' to 'a glory such as'. What is this verse saying in reality? We saw the glory that is unique to God being begotten in the flesh.

Also, don't be fooled by the argument of being 'with' therefore 'how can he be?' The Father is God, and Jesus is God. Therefore Jesus the Word was with God, but that doesn't make Him any less part of the Godhead.

Finally, take a look at Hebrews 1:3:

ΠΡΟΣ   ΕΒΡΑΙΟΥΣ
TOWARD HEBREWS

1 Πολυμερῶς καὶ πολυτρόπως πάλαι ὁ
In many parts and in many manners of old the

θεὸς λαλήσας τοῖς πατράσιν ἐν τοῖς
God having spoken to the fathers in the

προφήταις 2 ἐπ' ἐσχάτου τῶν ἡμερῶν τούτων
prophets upon last [part] of the days these

ἐλάλησεν ἡμῖν ἐν υἱῷ, ὃν ἔθηκεν κληρονόμον
he spoke to us in Son, whom he put heir

πάντων, δι' οὗ καὶ ἐποίησεν τοὺς
of all (things), through whom also he made the

αἰῶνας· 3 ὃς ὢν ἀπαύγασμα τῆς
ages; who being beaming forth from of the

δόξης καὶ χαρακτὴρ τῆς ὑποστάσεως αὐτοῦ,
glory and impress of the sub-standing of him,

φέρων τε τὰ πάντα τῷ ῥήματι τῆς
bearing and the all (things) to the saying of the

δυνάμεως αὐτοῦ, καθαρισμὸν τῶν ἁμαρτιῶν
power of him, cleansing of the sins

ποιησάμενος ἐκάθισεν ἐν δεξιᾷ τῆς
having made he sat down in right [hand] of the

μεγαλωσύνης ἐν ὑψηλοῖς, 4 τοσούτῳ
greatness in lofty [places], to so much

κρείττων γενόμενος τῶν ἀγγέλων
better having become of the angels

ὅσῳ διαφορώτερον παρ' αὐτοὺς
to how much more differing beside them

κεκληρονόμηκεν ὄνομα.
he has inherited name.

5 Τίνι γὰρ εἶπέν ποτε τῶν
To which one for he said sometime of the

ἀγγέλων Υἱός μου εἶ σύ, ἐγὼ σήμερον
angels Son of me are you, I today

γεγέννηκά σε, καὶ πάλιν Ἐγὼ ἔσομαι
I have generated you, and again I shall be

αὐτῷ εἰς πατέρα, καὶ αὐτὸς ἔσται μοι
to him into Father, and he will be to me

εἰς υἱόν; 6 ὅταν δὲ πάλιν εἰσαγάγῃ
into Son? Whenever but again he should lead in

τὸν πρωτότοκον εἰς τὴν
the Firstborn (one) into the

οἰκουμένην, λέγει Καὶ
being inhabited [earth], he is saying And

1 God, who long ago spoke on many occasions and in many ways to our forefathers by means of the prophets, 2 has at the end of these days spoken to us by means of a Son, whom he appointed heir of all things, and through whom he made the systems of things. 3 He is the reflection of [his] glory and the exact representation of his very being, and he sustains all things by the word of his power; and after he had made a purification for our sins he sat down on the right hand of the Majesty in lofty places. 4 So he has become better than the angels, to the extent that he has inherited a name more excellent than theirs.

5 For example, to which one of the angels did he ever say: "You are my son; I, today, I have become your father"? And again: "I myself shall become his father, and he himself will become my son"? 6 But when he again brings his Firstborn into the inhabited earth, he says: "And

Notice the NWT has 'reflection of'. The argument goes that you are not the same as your reflection! But the Greek word here *apaugasma*, is literally translated 'beaming forth from'. The light beams forth from a torch and that's not a reflection, the joy beams forth from a face and that's not a reflection, it's what is in the person coming out. The AV uses 'effulgence', more modern translations 'radiance'—and that is exactly what the word means: not looking at a reflection in the mirror but a shining out from that which is within. This is clearly underlined by the next phrase, 'the exact representation of his very being'. Jesus is not a pale reflection but from His very being shines forth that which He is, God.

Next in *Reasoning* the Society quote two publications— *Many Witnesses, One Lord* by W. Barclay and *Dictionary of the Bible* by J. J. McKenzie—which they claim give scholarly support for their translation of John 1:1. However, the deception of this is discovered when the missing parts of the quotes are inserted (see pp. 24–5 for the full quotes).

Finally, they quote other translations of the Bible. The American Translation and Moffat's translation that say Jesus 'was divine' cannot be proof because being divine means He has the qualities of God and therefore must be God because God alone has the qualities of God! (See also the comments on p. 95 by Bruce Metzger.) Ludwig Thimme's German translation is also quoted as saying, 'God of a sort the Word was.' Please not a capital G. There is no evidence here for 'a god'.

For more information *Reasoning* refers readers to the 1984 reference edition of the NWT. This article is the same as the one we'll look at in KIT.

The Kingdom Interlinear Translation of the Greek Scriptures (1985, pp. 1139–40)

The article lists eight versions of the Bible that the WBTS claim support their 'a god' translation. As one of them is the NWT itself we are left with seven to investigate.

1. The New Testament, in An Improved Version, Upon the Basis of Archbishop Newcome's New Translation: with a corrected text

The name of Archbishop Newcome is supposed to lend weight, but read carefully, an 'improved' version. However, that is a matter of opinion. As the photostats in Appendix 2 show, Newcome's text, originally published in Dublin in 1796, reads, '...the Word was God.' The version that the WBTS quote was published in London in 1808 and was the work of the Unitarians. Notice especially how many of the footnotes indicate Newcome's original text but not at John 1:1. The Watchtower are not quoting Archbishop Newcome but the Unitarians who we would expect to agree with them as they also deny the deity of Christ.

2. The Monotessaron; or, The Gospel History, According to the Four Evangelists (J. S. Thompson, 1829)

It is true that Thompson translated this verse, '...and the Logos was a god...' However, what is of interest is what he meant by it. This is shown by pages 32 and 33 of his pamphlet, 'A Second Vindication of the Deity, and Atonement of Jesus', 1816:

> The words '*theos en o logos*' which are translated, the word was God, are equally strong...if the want of the article before '*theos*' NULLIFY THE DEITY OF THE SON IT ALSO DISPROVES THE DEITY OF THE FATHER in the 12th and 18th verses of this chapter. Moreover Dr Middleton has shown that the pure construction Greek Language requires that '*theos*' be put without the article...But lest any should conclude that this rule tends to prove Jesus the Supreme God, i.e. Father, I observe, that though Dr. M[iddleton]'s rule be general, it is by no means universal...Perhaps some may ask, are you not here disproving what you designed to prove? I answer no, both the text and criticism combine to ASSERT CHRIST'S DEITY; but at the same time, to deny Polytheism.

In the light of the above, his translation may be unwise, but what He means is evident and it certainly is not what the

Jehovah's Witness wants it to mean. There can be no doubt what Thompson believes as he wrote in the same pamphlet:

> I do most solemnly declare, that I firmly believe the following Articles... 1. There is one Almighty... God... 2. The persons denominated Father, Son and Holy Ghost, Matt 28:19, ARE REALLY AND ESSENTIALLY GOD... 3. The Lord Jesus Christ, the eternal Logos, exists before all worlds, begotten of the Father, NOT MADE, VERY GOD OF VERY GOD. (p. 9.)

Maybe when the WBTS can assent to this they can quote Thompson properly!

3. The Emphatic Diaglott (Benjamin Wilson)

The WBTS are honest enough to say that 'and a god was the Word' is the interlinear reading, not the final translation. Much has been written about Wilson being a Christadelphian and be that as it may we seem to miss the fact that he translated the verse, '... and the Logos was God' (see photostat in Appendix 2). The Society have been devious here. The interlinear is a word for word translation and as a word for word translation 'a god' is a possibility because there is no indefinite article ('a', 'an' etc) in Greek. Therefore *theos* could be God, god, a God or a god. However, Wilson does not leave it as a literal translation but goes on to translate it with its proper full meaning as shown from the context of the passage, 'Logos was God'.

4. The Bible; An American Translation (J. M. P. Smith and E. J. Goodspeed)

This translation does not say 'a god' but, 'and the Word was divine'. I will leave comment on this to Bruce M. Metzger of Princeton Theological Seminary:

> As regards J[oh]n 1:1, Colwell's research casts the most serious doubts on the correctness of such translations as 'and the Logos was divine' (Moffatt Strachan), 'and the Word was divine' (Goodspeed), and (worst of all) 'and the Word was a god'... (*Expository Times*, Vol. 6 , 1952, p. 125.)

5. *Das Evangelium nach Johannes (Siegfrid Schulz)*

Although the Society say that Schulz said, 'and a god (or, of a divine kind) was the Word', the photostat in Appendix 2 shows he actually said 'and a God (or, God by nature) was the Word'. Either their German translators are not up to standard or this is deception. Schulz also said on pp. 18–19 of his commentary:

> God-ness characterizes the essence both of the 'Word' and of God himself. The word 'God' in the statement of v. 1c is not the subject—hence Luther's translation: 'God was the Word'—but the sentence predicate. The 'Word' is not 'the God' (thus v. 1b), i.e. God the Father. Nevertheless, the Logos is God by nature, of Godly being, identical in essence with God, so that the appropriate translation is: 'and of Godly nature was the Word.' (Translated from the German.)

6. *Das Evangelium nach Johannes (Johannes Schneider)*

This is a true translation: 'and godlike sort was the Logos.' Schneider, who was a Baptist, is now dead and we are unable to find out why he made this translation.

7. *Das Evangelium nach Johannes (Jurgen Becker)*

The photostat in Appendix 2 shows that Becker actually wrote, 'and a God was the Word.' Also, we have in our possession a letter dated 24 July 1984 (see translation below) from Jurgen Becker who is Professor of New Testament at Kiel University.

> The first part of the verse makes the following statements: First of all it is stated that the Logos (the Word) is not part of creation but belongs on the side of God. 'In the beginning' reminds us of Genesis 1:1. This is intentional and is usual in the context of statements relating to the role of wisdom as a mediator in creation . . . As a rule the creation of wisdom or of the Logos is said to be before all time . . . The test does not look back beyond the time of creation. Verse 1 does not speculate about pre-creation things but comments that the world which we know (v. 3) owes its being to the mediatory role of the Logos in creation who was

already with God before the world came into being (v. 1). With regard to your discussion with the Jehovah's Witness I can therefore confirm that the JEHOVAH WITNESS INCORRECTLY CITE ME AS THEIR SOURCE. In my view John 1:1 does not speak of the creation of the Logos but rather THE LOGOS WAS ALREADY IN EXISTENCE AT THE TIME OF CREATION.

What is clear is that all this apparent evidence amounts to very little. Out of the seven only two actually use 'a god', and one of these is a perversion of Newcome's translation. One German translation is very little evidence compared with at least twenty English translations, apart from foreign editions, that can be quoted as saying 'God'.

In an effort to sound convincing the Society then seek to make much of the fact that the first *theos* has the definite article and the second does not, thereby confirming that the first is 'the God' and the second 'a god'. They quote one authority in support that we need to investigate.

'Journal of Biblical Literature', Vol. 92, pp. 75–87, P. B. Harner

Whereas some of the article is quoted correctly the Society omit much of the flow of Harner's argument as to the best way to translate this clause. The concluding thoughts seem to sum up Harner's views:

> Perhaps this clause could be translated, 'the Word had the same nature as God.'

This, of course, is not what the Witnesses would want it to say.

Having checked the evidence, and seen that most of it does not support the Witnesses claims, we will add three further quotes from Greek scholars. The third one is of real interest to the Society as it is by B. F. Westcott whose Greek translation they use.

> It needs to be recognized that the Fourth Evangelist need not have chosen the word-order, and that his choice of it, though creating some ambiguity, may in itself be an indication of his

meaning; and Westcott's note (in loc.), although it may require the addition of some reference to idiom, does still, perhaps, represent the writer's theological intention: 'it is NECESSARILY WITHOUT THE ARTICLE *(theos* not *o theos)* inasmuch as it describes the nature of the Word and does not identify His person. It would be pure Sabellianism to say "the Word was *o theos*". No idea of inferiority of nature is suggested by the form of expression, which simply affirms the true deity of the Word...' (C. F. D. Moule, *An Idiom Book of New Testament Greek*, 1953, p. 116.)

...the theological significance of the rule [Colwell's] can be illustrated at once from the famous first words of the Fourth Gospel. It is well known that, although the English language is incapable, without a sacrifice of idiom, of marking any distinction in the two occurrences of 'God' in the sentence 'the Word was with God and the Word was God', the Greek in fact uses the article the first time but not the second and also transposes the word order: literally 'the Word was with the God, and God was the Word'. Commentators aver that the omission of the article in the second place is theologically significant; but if Colwell's canon is true, it may well be that the primary reason for its absence is to be found in the dictates of idiom, not of doctrine. This is not, of course, to deny that the Evangelist would have omitted the definite article in any case on theological grounds; BUT IT DOES MEAN THAT ITS OMISSION HERE IS NOT ITSELF A SOUND FOUNDATION FOR A THEOLOGICAL STRUCTURE. (C. F. D. Moule, *The Language of the New Testament*, 1953, p. 14.)

The three clauses contain all that is possible for man to realise as to the essential nature of the Word in relation to time, and mode of being, and character: He was (1) *'in the beginning'*: He was (2) *'with God'*: He was (3) *'God'*... *the Word was God*. The predicate *(theos)* stands emphatically first, as in 4:24. It is necessarily without the article *(theos* not *o theos)* inasmuch as it describes the nature of the Word and does not identify His person. It would be pure Sabellianism to say 'the Word was *o theos*'. No idea of inferiority of nature is suggested by the form of expression, which simply affirms the true deity of the Word... in the third clause 'the Word' is declared to be 'God', and so included in the unity of the Godhead. Thus we are led to conceive that the divine nature is essentially in the Son, and at the same time the Son can be regarded, according to that which is His peculiar characteristic, in relation to God as God. (B F. Westcott, *The Gospel According to St John*, Vol. 1, 1908, pp. 4–6.)

These three quotes, chosen out of many, show that the weight of scholarship is firmly stacked against the translation of the WBTS.

C. MICHAEL THE ARCHANGEL

Section 4 showed how to answer the Witnesses' claim that Jesus is Michael the archangel. However, there is another, more detailed, aspect of the Witnesses' own doctrine which we can look at. (I am indebted to Duane Magnani who has given me permission to use his study, *Where is Michael?*. This book can be obtained through Reachout Trust.)

Watchtower Quotations

A. There is Scriptural evidence for concluding that Michael was the name of Jesus Christ before he left heaven AND AFTER HIS RETURN. (WT, 15 May 1969, p. 307.)

The WT are saying that the angelic life form or spirit being called Michael became a man, and when that man died he again became a spirit being, an angelic life form. Is this possible even according to Watchtower teachings?

B. As mankind's source of salvation Jehovah God provided the perfect man, whose life could ransom the human race, by transferring the LIFE FORCE of his chief ANGELIC SON in the heavens to the womb of a virgin. (WT, 1 March 1960, p. 133.)

C. There is a body and a life principle, the UNION OF WHICH makes the SOUL. His experiences... his environment, his travels... all go to make up his personality. It is not his body, but his soul that has these experiences. (WTR, 15 January 1913, p. 5166.)

D. ... there can be no *being* or existence without *life and body* both... Any being is properly called a *soul* or person. This is the Scriptural sense and usage of the word *soul*... This principle of life pervades and is an essential element of all *being*...in man, in angels...Death is the *dissolution*, or separation of the things which combined, constitute *being*—namely, life and body. (ZWTR, April 1881, p. 205.)

E. Life itself is IMPERSONAL, incorporeal, being MERELY THE LIFE PRINCIPLE. (ABU, p. 1061.)

F. Thus the spirit could not have personality but must be an *impersonal* force. The invisible spirit or life-force active both in man and the animals might be compared with electricity, also an invisible force...The electric current...never takes on the characteristics of the machines or appliances in which it functions or is active. (*Awake!*, 8 August 1972, p.27.)

G. That the heavenly Word of God divested himself of everything as a God-like spirit except his life-force and that he lowered himself to become no more than a perfect man. (*The Kingdom is at Hand*, 1944, p. 46.)

Conclusions

1. B tells that the only part of Michael that was transferred to Mary's womb was his 'life force'.

2. C informs us that the personality of Michael is called his soul which is life principle (force) + body.

3. D shows us that the same principle of life and death pervades men and angels, i.e. when the life and the body are separated the death of that person takes place.

4. D, E and F together make it clear that only body + life gives personality. The life force or invisible spirit by itself is impersonal and does not give or take on any personality or characteristics.

5. G emphatically states that the only part of Michael that was transferred to Jesus was his life force which is impersonal.

Therefore there is no personal connection between Jesus and Michael and Jesus did not take on any of the characteristics of Michael!

Do You Believe in Evolution?

The WBTS, quite rightly, reject the theory of evolution, but when it is compared with the 'life history' of Michael what's the difference?

They make true statements such as, 'life comes only from life' (*Awake!*, 22 August 1978, p.7) and 'life proceeds from life and not from inanimate matter' (*Awake!*, 8 April 1965, p. 8). But when Michael became Jesus he came from an inanimate life force (see previous quotes).

Again the Society ask, 'Does one kind of life evolve into another? The answer found was NO! (*Awake!* 22 April 1967, p.10). But of Michael becoming Jesus they say, 'That change was only a transfer of existence...from spiritual nature to human nature' (ZWTR, February 1888, p. 1005).

Further, the Society conclude that scientists should not be trusted because, 'Theories that were held yesterday may be abandoned tomorrow' (*Awake!*, 8 November 1982, p. 7). Yet the Watchtower's theories regarding Michael have also changed. At one time they said he was NOT the Son of God and another that he was the Antichrist (see ZWTR, November 1879, p. 48 and December 1879, p. 55).

Take time to study these passages and ask the next Witness you talk to why, when they do not believe in the theory of evolution, do they believe in the theory of Michael/Jesus. Write out the Watchtower references to show that there is no personal connection between Jesus and Michael and ask them to come back in a couple of weeks with a clear outline that disproves the facts you show them. After that do be sure to share with them about the real Jesus, the Son of God with all power and authority.

D. SOUL, DEATH AND HELL

We begin this section with a look at what the WBTS teach about the soul.

In the Bible 'soul' is translated from the Hebrew *nephesh* and the

Greek *psykhe*. Bible usage shows the soul to be a person or an animal or the life that a person or an animal enjoys. (*Reasoning*, p. 375.)

...the Scriptures show that both *psykhe* and *nephesh*, as used with reference to earthly creatures, refer to that which is material, tangible, visible and mortal. (ABU, p. 1532.)

Thus, the Scriptures clearly show that *nephesh* and *psykhe* are used to designate the animal creation...Man was distinct from the animal creation, but that distinction was not because he was a *nephesh* ('soul') and they were not...So, too, the 'spirit' (Heb[rew] *ruahh;* Gr[eek] *pneuma*) or life force of man is not distinct from the life force in animals. (ABU, p. 1533.)

This is the belief of the Jehovah's Witnesses. They conclude that there is no immortality of the soul, no consciousness after death and certainly no eternal punishment in hell. However, whereas the WBTS categorically state that immortality of the soul, hell etc are not scriptural teachings, Christians believe they are, and therefore we need a simple way to communicate these truths to the Witnesses. First, let's get acquainted with the Greek and Hebrew words.

The Hebrew word *nephesh* literally means 'a breathing' creature but is used widely. *Psykhe* is the Greek word denoting the breath, the breath of life, then the soul in all its meanings. The literal meaning of the Hebrew word *ruach* is 'wind' and by resemblance breath. Primarily the Greek word *pneuma* denotes the wind, but also breath and then especially the spirit which like the wind is invisible, immaterial and powerful.

All four words, in their literal sense, have to do with breath and breathing, but how are the words used in their scriptural context? To discover this we'll follow some of the arguments in *Reasoning*. The article on the soul begins on p. 375 with the question:

What does the Bible say that helps us to understand what the soul is?

The Scriptures quoted here are Genesis 2:7, 1 Corinthians

15:45, 1 Peter 3:20, Genesis 9:5 and Joshua 11:11. The WBTS, in saying that the word can mean the person or the life of the person, take no account of the other different meanings that every biblical Greek and Hebrew scholar is aware of. They conclude from Joshua 11:11 that the soul cannot be the part of man that survives death because it's struck by the sword. However, the word *nephesh* is used here as the person and so no evidence about the inward man can be gleaned. Unfortunately the average Witness will not see this. But with the Society's definition of soul we must ask, 'Can we translate *nephesh* "a person or an animal or the life that a person or an animal enjoys" each of the 754 times that the word is used?' Ask the Witness, with their own definition before them, to explain the following Scriptures.

Leviticus 17:11
If my soul is no different to that of an animal why make blood atonement for the soul?

2 Samuel 11:11
Is Uriah repeating himself? Surely he is showing that the soul is more than just life.

Isaiah 42:1
God who is a spirit has a soul which obviously transcends animal or human life.

Psalm 42:1–2
This is not the natural life of a man. As the psalmist says in verse 7 deep calls to deep.

Before we leave the Old Testament we must comment on Genesis 2:7 because the Society's misunderstanding, whether deliberate or in ignorance, starts here. First we quote a Christian theologian:

> Man was thus made up of only two independent elements, the corporeal and the spiritual: but when God placed the spirit within the casing of the earth, the combination of these produced a third part, and man became a living soul. Direct communication between spirit and flesh is impossible: their intercourse can be carried on only by means of a medium, and the instant production of one was the result of their contact in Adam. He became a living

soul in the sense that spirit and body were completely merged in this third part. (E. H. Bancroft, *Christian Theology*, 1980, pp. 187–88.)

The Jehovah's Witnesses may not agree with that but help them by asking these two questions about Genesis 2:7. First, was Adam completely formed before he was called a *nephesh*? Second, was the *nephesh* Adam's life or was God's breath put in him to make him a *nephesh*?

What is clear is that Adam was complete as a person but was not called a *nephesh*—soul. Then 'life' was placed in him by means of God's breath. That life was not *nephesh* but made him a *nephesh*. In other words in this verse neither 'a person' nor 'the life of a person' defines *nephesh*.

The New Testament also has problems of definition for the Jehovah's Witnesses.

Mark 8:35

It's nonsense if we say whoever loses himself or the life within him...shall save it. The only way you can lose your life is to die and that in itself does not save you. Jesus was obviously saying that we are to lose our soul, our immortal part, to Him.

Matthew 10:28

The Watchtower's argument on this verse is basically that men can kill the body but not the person for all time and because God can destroy the soul it is not immortal or indestructible. This is not logical and is a smoke-screen but remember the average Witness will believe it. The things to point out are that no one on earth can destroy the soul, therefore it is immortal. The fact that the immortal eternal God can destroy it does not mean that it is not indestructible or immortal—God can do anything! Also, the fact that God can destroy the soul, in the after life ('destroy' and 'Ghenna' will be dealt later) proves that there is immortal life going beyond death.

John 10:17–18

The WBTS say once Jesus laid down His soul it was gone,

therefore He could not take it up again. But Jesus clearly says He has authority over His soul before and after death.

Revelation 6:9; 20:4

A dead person cannot be a soul!

3 John 2

A clear distinction is made between the good health of the life and the welfare of the soul.

Conclusion

The Scriptures reveal that the WBTS's definition of soul is not God's definition. The Bible often uses it just to describe the person, but in its fuller sense it describes that part which was formed to enable flesh and spirit to communicate. It is the deep invisible and immortal part of the man which at death leaves the body and returns to God. It does not cease to exist because God alone has power over the destiny of the soul and He has given it immortality.

The next question answered is:

> Where does the Bible say that animals are souls? (*Reasoning*, p. 376.)

When we understand the different uses of *nephesh* we see there is nothing wrong with both man and animals being called by that term. The following quote should help to give clarity:

> ...an animal is call[ed] a *nephesh* as long as it is living. A dead animal is never called a *nephesh* because its body would be devoid of the life principle. In this sense, once the life principle was breathed into the body of Adam, he became a *nephesh*, i.e., a living creature (Gen 2:7). When the life principle departs from the bodies of animals or men they die. Thus, the Old Testament used *nephesh* to refer to the principle of physical life approximately 150 times...Third, *nephesh* is used to describe the part of man which transcends the life principle, separates him from animals and likens him to God...God swears by His *nephesh*...The *nephesh*,

or soul, of God is His transcendent self...In no way can God's *nephesh* be reduced to the principle of physical life...When *nephesh* is used of God, it obviously transcends the mere life principle of animals...In the same way, *nephesh* is used to describe the part of man which transcends the life principle. (Dr R. A. Morey, *Death and the Afterlife*, 1984, p. 46.)

Reasoning then asks:

Do other scholars who are not Jehovah's Witnesses acknowledge that this is what the Bible says the soul is? (*Reasoning*, 1985, p. 377.)

We list here the scholars quoted as 'proof' that they agree with the Society. As usual what the Society have missed out is supplied in bold type.

NCE, Vol XIII, 1967, pp. 449–50

There is no dichotomy [division] of body and soul in the O[ld] T[estament]. The Israelite saw things concretely, in their totality, and thus he considered men as persons and not as composites. The term *'nepes'* [*ne'phesh*], though translated by our word soul, never means soul as distinct from the body or the individual person... **At death the** *'nepes'* **goes to Sheol, a place of insensitive, shadowy existence. Many psalms pray for the rescue of one's** *'nepes'* **from death, where the rescue means to be saved from dying, not to be raised from the dead...** The term [*'psy-khe'*] is the N[ew] T[estament] word corresponding with *'nepes'*. It can mean the principle of life, life itself, or the living being. **Through Hellenistic influence, unlike 'nepes', it was opposed to body and considered immortal. The psyche in Matthew 10:28...means a life that exits separately from the body.**

EB, Macropaedia, Vol. 15, 1976, p. 152

The Hebrew term for 'soul' (*'nefesh'*, that which breathes) was used by Moses..., signifying an 'animated being' and applicable equally to nonhuman beings. **The Hebrews used the term to apply to the entire personality but reserved the concept** *'ruah'* **('spirit') to denote a principle of life, 'mind,' and occasionally 'heart'.** *'Nefesh'* **was often used as if it were the seat of appetite, emotion, and passion and, conjoined with 'heart', was held to encompass**

intellect, will, and feeling. New Testament usage of *'psyche'* ('soul') was comparable to *'nefesh'*.

'The Jewish Encyclopedia' Vol. VI, 1910, p. 564

The belief that the soul continues its existence after the dissolution of the body is a matter of philosophical or theological speculation rather than of simple faith, and is accordingly nowhere expressly taught in Holy Scripture...**It is the Psalmist's implicit faith in God's omnipotence and omnipresence that leads him to the hope of immortality.**

The *Reasoning* article continues:

Is the soul the same as the spirit? (*Reasoning*, p. 378.)

In a brief outline such as this it is not possible to answer this question in depth. However, we can say that although the Scripture shows that the soul and the spirit are separate (see 1 Thessalonians 5:23 and Hebrews 4:12), it also shows that they are linked. We do, though, need to comment on the following verse found under this heading:

Eccl[esiastes] 12:7: 'Then the dust returns to the earth just as it happened to be and the spirit [or, life-force; Hebrew, *ruach*] itself returns to the true God who gave it.' (Notice that the Hebrew word for spirit is *ruach;* but the word translated soul is *nephesh*. The text does not mean that at death the spirit travels all the way to the personal presence of God; rather, any prospect for the person to live again rests with God. In similar usage, we may say that, if required payments are not made by the buyer of a piece of property, the property 'returns' to its owner.)

This is another of the Witnesses' 'even though it says this what it actually means is...' explanations. But try to get them to think about the verse for themselves. The illustration is there to make us believe the Scripture says other than it does; if they use it ask to look at the Scripture itself. The dust is said to 'return' to the earth, i.e. the body goes back to the place from where it was created. Therefore the point being made about the spirit is that it too 'returns' (same Hebrew word) to where it came from—to God.

Under this heading, and in the section on 'Spirit', the WBTS base their teaching, almost entirely, on Ecclesiates 3:19-22. Their argument is that man has nothing, as a result of birth, that gives him supremacy over the animals. Therefore just as when an animal dies, it is dead, so a human dies without any eternal spirit or soul. A person has to rely entirely on God's memory to reactivate the life pattern at some future point. (This is the WBTS's definition of resurrection.)

However, using these verses from Ecclesiastes to 'prove' this shows an ignorance for the revelation of the whole of God's Word—Old *and* New Testaments, and especially of the Book of Ecclesiastes. Ecclesiastes is in the 'Wisdom' section of the Old Testament and as such shows us how to live, not what to believe. There are two speakers in the Book, the humanist in chapters 1—11, apart for two brief passages, and the theist (speaking for God) in chapter 12. What is recorded in chapter 3 is from the humanist and therefore it is man's opinion and not God's. Maybe it shows a good deal about the WBTS that they base so much on humanist thinking.

That Ecclesiastes expresses man's viewpoint is clearly seen when it is compared with Proverbs, another 'Wisdom' book, which obviously puts God's viewpoint. In Ecclesiastes 1:18 wisdom brings vexation but in Proverbs 3:13 wisdom brings happiness and Proverbs 8:11 says there is no other delight equal to wisdom. Compare Ecclesiastes 1:18 which says knowledge brings pain with Proverbs 2:10 where knowledge is said to be pleasant to the soul. When we see how the Bible is written the heart of the argument using this Book falls away.

Another question *Reasoning* poses is:

What is the origin of Christendom's belief in an immaterial, immortal soul? (*Reasoning*, p. 379.)

Again the misleading editing and moreover much ignored evidence leads the Witnesses to believe that immortality of the soul is nothing but a product of Greek mythology and was not taught or believed in the early church. However, we again supply the words missed out from their 'scholarly' proof.

NCE, Vol. XIII, 1967, pp. 452, 454

(Two pages of contrary evidence are omitted from the quote, we've only included a fraction of it.)

> The Christian concept of a spiritual soul created by God and infused into the body at conception to make man a living whole is the fruit of a long development in Christian philosophy. Only with Origen [died c. 254 CE] in the East and St. Augustine [died 430 CE] in the West was the soul established as a spiritual substance and a philosophical concept formed of its nature... **The early Fathers were not directly concerned with the nature of the human soul, although they could not avoid treating this question at least implicitly when discussing the soul's immortality... The apologist Athenagoras (c. 177)... (taught that) a clear emphasis on the Chrisitian view of man as a unit, a living whole, even if the immortal soul is the more important element...** His [Augustines's] doctrine... owed much (including some shortcomings) to Neoplatonism, **yet was much more strikingly Christian in approach and content... (he taught that) the soul is a completely immaterial substance... God is the creator and maker of every soul and that the soul is not an emanation from the divine substance but a creature made to God's image.**

M. Jastrow, Jr, 'The Religion of Babylonia and Assyria' Boston, 1898, p. 556

> The problem of immortality, we have seen, engaged the serious attention of the Babylonian theologians. **While the solutions they had to offer could hardly have been satisfactory either to themselves or to the masses, it must not be supposed that the denial of immortality to man involved the total extinction of conscious vitality.** Neither the people nor the leaders of religious thought ever faced the possibility of the total annihilation of what once was called into existence. Death was a passage to another kind of life **and the denial of immortality merely emphasized the impossibility of escaping the change in existence brought about by death.**

The fact that Plato is quoted here doesn't mean a thing (see the second quote below). That the Greek's believed in the immortality of the soul is irrelevant. The relevant questions are, does the Bible show it to be true, and did the early church believe it? We've already shown Scripture teaches it but what about the early church? The following quotes are, I believe, convincing proof that they did.

> For reflect upon the end of each of the preceding kings, how they died the death common to all, which if it issued in insensibility it would be a godsend to all the wicked. But since sensation remains to all who have ever lived, and eternal punishment is laid up...see that ye neglect not to be convinced and to hold as your belief that these things are true...even after death souls are in a state of sensation. (Ante-Nicene Christian Library, Vol. 2, *First Apology Of Justin Martyr* [approx. AD 150], p. 22.)

Interestingly, the WBTS have given their 'blessing' to Justin Martyr, calling him, 'an early Christian writer' and quoting him as a reliable authority (see WT, 15 January 1974, pp. 47–48).

> For Moses is more ancient than [Plato and] all the Greek writers. And whatever both philosophers and poets have said concerning the immortality of the soul, or punishments after death...they have received suggestions from the prophets and have enabled them to understand and interpret these things. (Ante-Nicene Christian Library, Vol. 2, *First Apology Of Justin Martyr*, p. 45.)

> O Father of Thy beloved and blessed Son, Jesus Christ, through whom we have come to know Thee, the God of angels and powers and all creation, and of the whole family of the righteous who live in Thy presence, I bless Thee for counting me worthy of this day and hour, that in the number of the martyrs I may partake of Christ's cup, to the resurrection of eternal life of both soul and body in the imperishability that is the gift of the Holy Spirit. (Polycarp [approx. AD 160], at his martyrdom. Eusebius, *History Of The Church*, translated by G. A. Williamson, 1966, p. 173.)

> ...the purpose of Him who fashioned us, according to which he made man of an immortal soul and a body...it is quite clear that the resurrection is plainly proved. (Ante-Nicene Christian Library, Vol. 2, *Athenagoras on the Resurrection of the Dead* [approx. AD 177], pp. 439–40.)

> The Lord has taught...that souls not only continue to exist...but

that they preserve the same form... When God therefore bestows life and perpetual duration, it comes to pass that even souls which did not previously exist should henceforth endure [for ever], since God has both willed that they should exist, and should continue in existence. (Ante-Nicene Christian Library, Vol. 5, *Irenaeus Against Heresies* [approx AD 180], pp. 250,251,253.)

What the soul is in the body, that are Christians in the world. The soul is dispersed through all the members of the body, and Christians are scattered through all the cities of the world. The soul dwells in the body yet is not of the body; and Christians dwell in the world, yet are not of the world. The invisible soul is guarded by the visible body... The immortal soul, dwells in a mortal tabernacle. (Ante-Nicene Christian Library, Vol. 1, *The Epistle to Diognetus* [second century], pp. 308–9.)

Having looked at the soul and its immortality let us turn to the subject of death.

Definition of Death

The WBTS say death is,

The ceasing of all functions of life. After breathing, heartbeat, and brain activity stop, the life-force gradually ceases to function in body cells. Death is the opposite of life. (*Reasoning*, p. 98.)

Does this definition match up with the scriptural definition? Look at Luke 9:60 and ask, how can those whose life force has stopped functioning possibly bury those whose life force has stopped functioning? Read Ephesians 2:1 and consider how can we 'stop breathing in our trespasses and sins?'

Whereas *Reasoning* doesn't mention these matters under the heading of 'Death', ABU does, and it makes this revealing comment:

The death state is used to illustrate the SPIRITUALLY DEAD CONDITION... (Luke 9:60... Eph 2:1) ... a Christian's being freed or liberated from sin... is also likened to death... The one figuratively dying in such a way, of course, IS STILL ALIVE PHYSICALLY. (p. 432.)

The WBTS admit that Scripture uses death in a way which does not mean annihilation. However, if the actual meaning of death is non-existence then figuratively it has to mean the same, i.e. the Christian becomes non-existent to sin, which of course is not true. But if death means a continuation in a different state, then the example is perfect! For Jehovah's Witnesses to understand this you only need to turn them to 1 Kings 17:22 where the widow's son was raised from the dead. We read:

> Finally Jehovah listened to Elijah's voice, so that the soul of the child came back within him and he came to life. (NWT.)

The soul had lived on somewhere in a different state and returning to the body caused the boy to live again.

Origin of death

Death was never intended to be part of man's experience. It was not God's original plan. The first occurrence of death in the Bible is Genesis 2:17 where it is punishment of sin. Romans 5:12,17; 6:23 and James 1:14–15 all show that death is only as a result of, and punishment for, sin. Therefore we must ask ourselves, and our local Witnesses, 'What punishment is there in non-existence?' Punishment has to be felt and experienced, non-existence is not. Another interesting verse is Matthew 26:24. If the death of Judas meant non-existence, and certainly before he was born he knew nothing, why would it have been better if he had never been born? His 'after-death' had to be worse than his 'before-birth'!

Separated

The first occurrence of a word in Scripture shows its meaning and 'death' is first found in Genesis 2:17. This verse explains the punishment if man should take of the tree of good and evil. Even the NWT puts it clearly enough:

> ...in the DAY you eat from it you will positively die.

Whereas it's true the word 'day' can mean varying lengths

of time, in this situation it cannot logically mean, 'within the period of about 900 years after you have eaten you will die'. Adam's physical death took that long after he ate, but what happened *on the day* he ate? Genesis 3:24 shows Adam and Eve were put out of the garden, i.e. they were separated from God. Any honest reading of the Bible clearly shows that in the day Adam ate of the fruit he was separated from God—thus the Bible's clear definition of death is separation from God. Read Luke 9:60 and Ephesians 2:1 again with this definition and you'll see how much sense it makes. Also see that eternal separation from God is punishment which will be experienced.

But Ezekiel 18:4 says...

This verse is often used to 'prove' that the 'soul' dies and nothing lives on. However, read the verse with the Watchtower's definition of soul and death.

> ...The person or life of that person that is sinning—it itself will cease to live and become non-existent.

Having established what the verse means to a Jehovah's Witness, go through the rest of Ezekiel 18 and ask them to explain verses 9, 17, 19, 21, 22, 23 and especially 27. Here are the Watchtower definitions for two of these verses:

> Verse 17: ...he himself will not cease to live and become non-existent... He will positively keep on living which is the opposite of death.

> Verse 27: ...he is the one who will preserve his own person or the life of his person alive, he will remain in the state opposite to death.

Most Jehovah's Witnesses will not want to listen to such an argument, but keep lovingly plugging away until they promise to come back with an answer to the questions you've posed.

Dead or alive—communication!

This opens up another problem area for Witnesses. There are several Scriptures clearly showing that in either death or life we have direct communication with God.

Philippians 1:20–24: Christ would be *magnified* in Paul's death; death would be *gain* for him; leaving the earth would mean being with Christ. Does this sound like a man who believes in non-existent soul sleep for 1,900 years?

2 Corinthians 5:1–10: When the body is dissolved we are to have an everlasting 'house' in the heavens; we desire to put this on so that mortal may be swallowed up; while in the body we are absent from the Lord and when absent from the body we are home with the Lord! Death to Paul was an immediate release from the confines of his body and a being instantly with the Lord.

1 Thessalonians 5:10: Even the NWT is self-explanatory:

He died for us, that, whether we STAY AWAKE or ARE ASLEEP, we should LIVE TOGETHER with him.

Alive or dead we live with Him!

And finally…

If death is cessation of life and a period of sleep that we are unaware of, if we are simply waiting to be remembered by God and brought back to life. Then why in 1 Corinthians 15:26 is it called the last *enemy*? Ask a Jehovah's Witness for their comments on these verses:

1. Verse 55—What is the victory of death? To take away our breath? God is in control of that anyway! What is the sting of death? We feel nothing, we know nothing.

2. Verse 56—The sting of death is *sin*. What is the only way to overcome the sting of death? Dealing with *sin*. If I die with *sin* in me and the penalty of *sin* against me, will I ever have a resurrection to life? No!

3. Verse 57—The victory has been given in Jesus Christ. We need to know this *before* we go into death!

Hell

The Watchtower's teaching is explained on pp. 168–75 of *Reasoning* and is summarized as follows:

> The Hebrew (word) *sheohl* and its Greek equivalent *haides*, which refer, not to an individual burial place , but to the common grave of dead mankind; also the Greek (word) *geenna* which is used as a symbol of eternal destruction. (p. 169.)

On p.175 emphasis is given to the fact that the Babylonians and other heathen empires believed in hell. This is simply a smoke-screen. The only evidence that matters is whether the Bible teaches that there is a hell! They conclude by saying that the concept of hell comes from the Devil, *not* from God. This is a very strong statement and we believe a very dangerous one that shows up the roots of the WBTS.

With their belief the Jehovah's Witnesses can 'prove' that hell is not a literal place and that when a man is dead he is unconscious and unaware of what is happening, therefore there is no eternal soul. We've already dealt with the eternal soul and so now we will concentrate on the words translated hell, grave etc to see if the WBTS's definitions are correct. We'll do this in a way which, in theory, a Jehovah's Witness will agree with. We'll check the context of the surrounding verses and also check the usage of the word in the whole of Scripture.

Hebrew word 'sheol'

Can this refer to the common grave of mankind? If so there can be no eternal spirit and we would be just a memory in the mind of God waiting to be remembered and restored. However, this definition gives problems with the following Scriptures, amongst others. Check them in the NWT.

'Even Sheol underneath has become agitated...At you it has awakened those impotent in death...All of them speak up and say...' (Isa 14:9–10). How can they speak?

'...the distressing circumstances of Sheol themselves found me' (Ps 116:3). What are the distressing circumstances?

'...that you may deliver his very soul from Sheol itself' (Prov 23:14). It's possible not to go to Sheol!

'...Let them go down into Sheol alive...' (Ps 55:15). You can get there and still be alive!

'This is the way of those who have stupidity...they have been appointed to Sheol itself...God himself will redeem my soul from the hand of Sheol, for he will receive me' (Ps 49:13–15). The psalmist saw a distinct difference between himself and the stupid with relation to sheol.

Greek word 'hades'

'...and the gates of Hades shall not overpower it' (Matt 16:18). If hades were the place of the unconscious it would go without saying that it couldn't overpower the church.

'And in Hades he lifted up his eyes...cried out and said...' (Luke 16:23–24). The WBTS want to dismiss this as a parable but even so it must be a true story and therefore the rich man was alive in hades.

'And Hades gave up the dead...and they were judged...' (Rev 20:13). From hades there is no resurrection to this life but straight to judgement.

Greek word 'gehenna'

'It is finer (better) for you to enter into life maimed than with two hands to go off into Gehenna, into the fire that cannot be put out' (Mark 9:43, NWT). Being maimed in this life is a serious matter how would it be better to go into unconsciousness?

Notice also the 'everlasting' quality—a fire that cannot be put out. This is shown clearly in other Scriptures. Matthew 25:46 is an example of this that the Witnesses try to get around by giving a secondary meaning to the word 'punishment'. (See 'An Alternative View' for futher details on this matter.) However, this is a smoke-screen because the importance of this verse is that it contrasts the righteous going into eternal life i.e.

a life that will last for ever with the wicked going into eternal cutting-off (NWT). There is nothing eternal about being annihilated—this verse only makes sense if the contrast is between two sorts of eternal existence.

Greek word 'paradeisos'

The WBTS make much of Luke 23:43 in *Reasoning*, pp. 286–87, therefore we must also look at this here. They can't believe the eternal soul of the thief could continue in part of heaven or hades so they relegate it to 'resurrection' on earth at some time in the future. What is the evidence concerning the Greek word?

> PARADEISOS...In Luke 23:43, the promise of the Lord to the repentant robber was FULFILLED THE SAME DAY; Christ, at His death, having committed His spirit to the Father, went in spirit IMMEDIATELY INTO HEAVEN itself, THE DWELLING PLACE OF GOD. (VINE, Vol. 3, p. 158.)

Reasoning, also rightly says that J. B. Rotherham's Emphasized Bible agrees with their way of punctuating the verse, 'I say to you today,...' But it doesn't tell you that as a footnote it shows, 'I say to you, Today...' as a correct alternative.

A smoke-screen is being laid using the word 'paradise'. The WBTS are trying to make Scripture say there is no immediate life after death when, in actual fact, it is saying the very opposite.

Summary

Our conclusion therefore is that the Scriptures do not back up the definitions given to the three words by the WBTS, but rather they show that sheol and hades are the place of waiting after death for those who will yet receive judgement from the Lord in the last days. The part of man that is eternal is 'alive' there during this time. And gehenna is the final place of everlasting punishment to which the wicked are banished after a fair judgement from the Lord.

It is comfortable to have a gospel without hell—the choice is annihilation or life—but that isn't the choice that is manifested in the gospel of Jesus Christ.

The main problem Witnesses and others have with the biblical position is the logical one that, 'God is too good to cast people into hell'. The answer though is clear within the Scriptures. The Lord has willingly given His life for us that we do not need to go to hell. His desire is that we all will be saved and He longs for it to happen with all His heart. However, in the final analysis if we refuse to accept His forgiveness and love we condemn ourselves to hell. His judgements are right and just. May this spur us on to share the true gospel with the Witnesses at our door.

E. THE RESURRECTION

What a Witness understands by the word 'resurrection' is summed up on p. 333 of *Reasoning*:

> (It) literally means 'a standing up again' and it refers to a rising up from death... Resurrection involves a reactivating of the life pattern of the individual, which life pattern God has retained in his memory. According to God's will for the individual, the person is restored in either a human or a spirit body and yet retains his personal identity, having the same personality and memory as when he died.

The source of this definition is undisclosed. In the pages that follow not one Scripture is put forward to support their view that God remembers us and reactivates our life pattern. Next time you meet a Witness ask them where they get the definition from. Meanwhile we'll check the definition against the Scriptures.

Christ's Resurrection

What happened to Jesus in His resurrection will in measure happen to us. So, did God the Father remember the life pattern of Jesus and bring Him back with the same 'personal identity, having the same personality'? If He did, it appears from Luke 24:13ff, John 20:15 etc that something went wrong because people did not recognize Him. The WBTS explain this by saying Jesus materialized different bodies but this would, at the least, be deception. In any case there are clear reasons (e.g. it was dark) why the people did not recognize Him. (See *An Alternative View* for a more complete covering of this aspect.) However, there are other verses that have to be explained too, for instance John 10:17–18:

> I lay down My life that I may take it again. No one has taken it away from Me, but I lay it down on My own initiative. I have authority to lay it down, and I have authority to take it up again. This commandment I received from My Father.

It's definite—Jesus had authority to take up his own life again. If every part of Jesus died why did the Father give Him a commandment to take up His own life? The only answer to that is to twist Scripture. Added to this is John 2:19–21 where again Jesus said I will raise up My body. Did Jesus tell lies? Of course not! He was both showing His clear authority as God and that there is part of man that is eternal.

This is the resurrection of Jesus as shown in Scripture. But does that mean we have authority to take up our lives again? In one way the answer is yes, as we will shortly explain, but first we'll look at two other points that *Reasoning* raises.

Summarizing pp. 334–35 of *Reasoning* we read that Jesus only materialized bodies and therefore did not have His resurrection body. He was resurrected a spirit as 1 Peter 3:18 and 1 Corinthians 15:45 clearly show. This is despite the fact that He said in Luke 24:36–39, 'a spirit does not have flesh and bones as you see that I have.'

If Christ did not have His original, but now glorified body, then He was a liar and a hoaxer, and the faith of Thomas and other early Christians would have been based on a cruel confidence trick. We must therefore ask, do the phrases, 'made alive in the spirit' of 1 Peter 3:18 and, 'life-giving spirit' of 1 Corinthians 15:45 mean, as the WBTS claim, that Jesus was raised a spirit creature?

The resurrection life of Christ was obviously a 'spiritual life', no longer with the confines of the human body. But how does Scripture describe this life?

> So also is the resurrection of the dead. It is sown a perishable body, it is raised an imperishable body; it is sown in dishonour, it is raised in glory; it is sown in weakness, it is raised in power; it is sown a natural body, it is raised a spiritual body. If there is a natural body, there is also a spiritual body. So also it is written, 'The first man, Adam became a living soul.' The last Adam became a life-giving spirit. (1 Cor 15:42–45)

The context of 1 Corinthians 15 is clearly the body becoming imperishable and immortal.

Greek scholar W. E. Vine comments on the Greek word, *soma* which is translated 'body' in the above Scriptures:

> The Body is an essential part of the man and therefore the redeemed are not perfected till the resurrection, Heb 11:40; no man in his final state will be without his body, John 5:28–29; Rev 20:13. (VINE, Vol. 1, p. 136–37.)

Scripture uses 'body' in the sense that at the resurrection we'll have spiritual bodies. Just as we've had bodies suitable for this earth so we'll have bodies suitable for our new spiritual life. Jesus was not raised a spirit creature but with a new spiritual body that didn't have the limitations of His old earthly one. Scripture also describes Christians with 'bodies' now as 'in the spirit' (see Romans 8:8–9), therefore there is no problem with the use of a similar term in 1 Peter for Christ with a resurrection body.

Our Resurrection

Revelation 20:4 shows the 'firstfruits' in the resurrection—those who have gone through the tribulation without worshipping the beast. Verses 12 and 13 then make it clear that *all* others, good or bad, will receive a resurrection, not just those whom God remembers. The division is then made at the judgement between those who receive eternal life and those who receive eternal death.

Reasoning, pp. 338–39, through 'illogical' logic and twisting of words seeks to prove that the rest of the dead not coming to life until after the 1,000 years refers to more than their resurrection, thus allowing them to say they are resurrected during the 1,000 years but only come to life, i.e. attain human perfection, after the 1,000 years. However, the KIT shows that this isn't true as the word used here in Revelation 20:4 is the same as the one used in Romans 14:9 of Christ's resurrection which is complete and full already.

The WBTS also claim that no one who is resurrected is to be consigned to a second death. The explanation for this conclusion in *Reasoning*, p. 338, is a classic piece of Watchtower contortionism:

> *What is the meaning of John 5:28,29?* It says: 'All those in the memorial tombs will hear his voice and come out, those who did good things to a resurrection life, those who practiced vile things to a resurrection of judgement.' What Jesus said here must be understood in the light of the later revelation that he gave to John. (See Revelation 20:12–13 . . .) Both those who formerly did good things and those who formerly practiced bad things will be 'judged individually according to their deeds'. What deeds? If we were to take the view that people were going to be condemned on the basis of deeds in their past life, that would be inconsistent with Romans 6:7: 'He who has died has been acquitted from his sin.' IT WOULD ALSO BE UNREASONABLE to resurrect people simply for them to be destroyed. So, at John 5:28–29a, Jesus was pointing ahead to the resurrection; then, in the remainder of verse 29, he was expressing the outcome after they had been uplifted to human perfection and been put on judgement.

In other words, 'the Scripture says . . . but we don't believe it therefore we will say it says . . .' The Scriptures in John 5 and in Revelation 20 clearly show that the judgement comes after the resurrection and on the basis of what is already written within the books. So far as bringing in Romans 6 is concerned that is simply a peg on which to hang an illogical conclusion. It is obvious in the context of Romans 6 that Paul is not talking about physical death but spiritual death in Christ, and therefore there is no way that you can claim verse 7 means physical death. As a sidelight, it is amazing that the Witnesses teach here that people are not going to be judged on the basis of their past deeds, but at the same time they also teach that unless you are doing the 'works' you may not endure to the end and so lose your hope of a resurrection. These two teachings are contradictory.

Back in the mainstream we see that the similarity of our resurrection to Christ's is this: the resurrection to life depends on knowing Jesus in our hearts now, before we die, and it is because of Him that we have authority to 'take up our lives again'. Unless we have had our sins cleansed by the precious blood of Jesus and our names written in the Lamb's Book of Life there is no resurrection to life. Nowhere in the Bible do we find the doctrine of the second chance. Just as Jesus knew before He laid His life down that He would take it again so we too know before we die that we will be raised to eternal life.

Paul expounds this in 1 Corinthians 15. Verse 20 tells us that Christ's resurrection is the firstfruit, i.e. there are more to come of the same kind. Then in verse 42 following he shows that the body that is sown is raised again a different body. Instead of being a perishable, weak, natural body it will be an imperishable, powerful, spiritual body. These verses again show just how wrong the Witnesses definition of resurrection is. This fact is underscored when in verse 50 following he clearly shows that resurrection is not just an important coming back to where we left off, hoping for better things, but a powerful, mighty tool of God that swallows up the last enemy—death.

The evidence is there within the Scriptures. The best way to get these things across to a Jehovah's Witness is to quietly but firmly read the verses, ask them to confirm your findings and plant within their minds the fact that what the Bible teaches is different to what 'God's earthly organization' teaches—who will they choose? They may not respond positively to you straight away but you've planted a seed within them that can be watered, grow and finally bring forth fruit.

F. THE 144,000

A summary of the WBTS's teaching on the 144,000 is that Luke 12:32 shows only a 'little flock' inherit the kingdom. Revelation 7:1–8 and 14:1–5 show this 'little flock' to number 144,000 and Revelation 5:9–10 further shows they will rule as 'kings and priest'.

The 144,000 are in direct contrast with the 'great crowd' who do not have a heavenly future but an earthly one. John 10:16 shows this earthly group are called 'other sheep' or 'great crowd' (Rev 7:9–17). During the millennium, when the earth is a paradise, all those counted worthy of a resurrection (John 5:28–29) will have an opportunity to learn obedience and loyalty to the organizational structures that God establishes through the 144,000 and Jesus Christ reigning in heaven (Rev 20:11–15).

How scriptural is this? We'll check some of the WBTS's statements about the 144,000.

> Those who are called by God to share in such heavenly service are few in number. As Jesus said, they are a 'little flock'. Years after his return to heaven, Jesus made known the exact number in a vision to the apostle John, who wrote: 'I saw, and, look! the Lamb standing upon Mount Zion, and with him a hundred and forty-four thousand... who have been bought from the earth.' (*The Truth That Leads To Eternal Life*, 1968, p. 77; see also *Reasoning* p. 166.)

What is the scriptural link between the 'little flock' and the 144,000? According to the Society, the 'little flock' promise was made to the apostles, literal Israel, but the '144,000' are spiritual Israel. The two are not the same (see p. 42). Also note that the 'little flock' of verse 32 are few compared with the thousands of verse 1.

Indeed in John 10:16 Jews were told that there were 'other sheep' who would be brought into 'one flock with one shepherd'. Ephesians 2:11–16 explains that the 'other sheep' are Gentiles who would become 'one body' with Jews through Jesus. This means there is no place for two distinct groups anyway.

144,000 redeemed from Earth to be Kings and Priests with Christ in Heaven...Rev 14:1,4...Rev 5:9–10. (*Make Sure Of All Things*, 1965, p. 303.)

The Bible does not link the two Scriptures mentioned as being the same people. In fact the 144,000 are shown to be different to the people in Revelation 5: Revelation 7:4—'... from every tribe of the sons of Israel'; Revelation 5:9—'...from every tribe and tongue and people and nation'. Those in Revelation 5 are not the 144,000 but they are a kingdom of priests to God. Indeed Scripture shows they are the great crowd! Revelation 7:9—'...from every nation and all tribes and peoples and tongues.'

Revelation does not say of them [the great crowd] as it does of the 144,000, that they are 'bought from the earth'...The description of them as 'standing before the throne and before the Lamb' indicates not necessarily a location, but an approved condition... The expression...literally, 'in sight of the throne'. (*Reasoning*, p. 167.)

First, we must note that when we compare Revelation 5:9 with 7:9, as above, we find the great crowd *are* bought. Second, there is another phrase, other than 'before the throne', used of the great crowd. Revelation 7:15 shows them to be 'in His temple', the divine habitation. The Greek word is *naos*, about which Greek scholar W. E. Vine says;

...a shrine or sanctuary...into which only the priests could lawfully enter, e.g., Luke 1:9,21,22; Christ, as being of the tribe of Judah, and thus not being a priest while upon earth...did not enter the *naos* (VINE, Vol. 4, p. 115.)

The great crowd must be where the Lord is, not just in an approved condition. Indeed Revelation 19:1 in the NWT talks of the 'great crowd IN HEAVEN'.

The confusion that arises from twisting Scripture is seen from these two quotes:

And when God's purposes toward the earth are fulfilled, we shall no longer live just a few years and then die... Anyone who loses his life then will lose it only because HE WOULD NOT OBEY the instructions of the good King, Jesus Christ. (*From Paradise Lost To Paradise Regained*, 1958, p. 223.)

Many remaining members of the 'little flock' will also live through Armageddon. But sometime after Armageddon the last member of the little flock will finish his earthly service AND DIE. (*From Paradise Lost To Paradise Regained*, 1958, p. 216.)

If the only way to die is to disobey Jehovah then the 144,000 will never be able to be made up to its full number!

There is also the very practical problem of knowing when to begin and end the numbering.

But Jesus' resurrection to spirit life in the heavens opened up a new way of hope for his followers. After Jesus died and was resurrected men and women could be set aside to become the 'little flock' of 144,000 persons who make up the heavenly, spiritual nation of God. (*From Paradise Lost To Paradise Regained*, 1958, p. 231.)

However, each year, on the anniversary of Christ's death, the few remaining members of the 'little flock' yet on earth keep the Memorial of Christ's death. (*The Truth That Leads To Eternal Life*, 1968, p. 80.)

Since 1931 the Right Shepherd has been gathering his 'other sheep'. So the hundreds of thousands of persons now associating with the New World society are 'other sheep'. (*From Paradise Lost To Paradise Regained*, 1958, p. 195.)

People with the Scriptural hope of everlasting life in an earthly paradise have been benefitted. Since the momentous year of 1935 CE they have come out of all nations... (*Man's Salvation Out Of World Distress At Hand*, 1975, p. 302.)

How did the Society work out how many places of the 144,000 were still vacant when the required number started to be filled up in Russell's day? Indeed it appears a mistake was made because in a book published in 1958 we are told the number was complete in 1931 but in a book published in 1975 we are told 1935!

Conclusion

All the biblical evidence shows that the 144,000 cannot be who the WBTS say they are. In fact Scripture says just the opposite. A careful reading of Revelation 6:12 to 7:10 shows that all the 144,000 are on earth, being sealed just before the battle of Armageddon. Whereas the great crowd are shown to be in heaven as kings and priests.

We, then, have seen who the 144,000 are not, but the question remains who are they? The WBTS teach that Israel have been rejected for ever because they rejected Jesus. But Scripture tells of a time when God will again show favour to the Jews and many will be saved (see Romans 10–11; Zechariah 12:10–14; Revelation 1:7). Though God's day of wrath is devastating (Zeph 1:2– 3,14,18), survival is possible (Zeph 2:1–3). Some Jews will be saved 'through the fire' (Zech 13:8–9), and this could well correspond with the protective sealing of the Jews in Revelation 7. Surely, too, the group of 144,000 represents the remnant mentioned in Romans 10 and 11.

G. SALVATION

The WBTS's teaching on salvation is one of double standards. Ask a Witness if they believe in salvation by faith and they will honestly say, yes. However, asking the same Witness what would happen to them if they left the Society shows that in reality they believe their salvation is in the WBTS.

The WBTS define salvation as follows:

> Preservation or deliverance from danger or destruction. That deliverance may be from the hands of oppressors or persecutors. For all true Christians, Jehovah provides through his Son deliverance from the present wicked system of things as well as salvation from bondage to sin and death. For a great crowd of

faithful servants of Jehovah living during 'the last days', salvation will include preservation through the great tribulation. (*Reasoning*, p. 356.)

This sounds great, but the double standard appears when the above is compared with the following quotes:

Remember, though, that you MUST WORK HARD to receive these blessings. It will COST YOU time and effort... We therefore urge one and all to lay hold on God's promises and to trust him fully. By continued diligent study of the Bible and by application of its wise counsel you MAY attain to the grandest of blessings, including everlasting life in a paradise earth! (WT, 1 July 1984, p. 6.)

Salvation cannot be *earned* by attendance at meetings or in any other way. It is *free*, a gift from God. Yet, Jehovah God does REQUIRE EFFORTS on our part if we are TO RECEIVE his gift of everlasting life. (WT, 15 January 1986, p. 10.)

This must be salvation by C.O.D. The gift is free but we must pay before we receive it.

Actually it should not surprise us to find that the Witnesses' gospel of salvation is not the one of Scripture when we read:

But the Kingdom witnessing of Jehovah's Witnesses since 1914 has been something FAR DIFFERENT FROM what Christendom's missionaries have published both before and since 1914. (WT, 1 October 1980, p. 28.)

We'll show two examples of this 'far different' gospel. In a WT article on being 'born again' the WBTS claim that Jesus was 'born again' and those ruling with Him will be 'born again'. Then it changes the scene to speak of the great crowd:

What about these anointed footstep followers of Jesus Christ? When are they 'born again'? What steps must they take before Jehovah acts on their behalf, bringing them forth as spiritual sons?... There are SIX DISTINCT STEPS that these must take. But let it be noted that God requires these same things of all who would become true Christians and GAIN salvation... To begin with, such persons must *take in accurate knowledge* about Jehovah God, their Creator and Life-Giver, and about his Son, Jesus Christ, their Savior and Redeemer...A person must *exercise faith*...The very first WORK that is required as proof of a person's faith is that of *repentance*...A person must take the step of *conversion*...Then just as Jesus presented himself at the Jordan...the next step required...is to present themselves to God. Today, this includes making a *dedication* to Jehovah God, after which they must follow in the footsteps of his Son, Jesus...Further, as a sixth step they must symbolize this dedication and make an open confession of it by undergoing *baptism*...(WT, 1 February 1982, pp. 25–26.)

Only after taking all six steps will we *gain* salvation and as taking in knowledge and exercising faith are ongoing steps we can never know if we've attained to the standard.

The definition of justification is also rewritten. To the Christian it is the glorious fact that we who could never attain to God's righteous standard are declared righteous by the work of the Lord Jesus and can therefore live in God's presence. To Jehovah's Witnesses it's the possibility that if during the millennium they 'accomplish appropriate "deeds"' they'll attain to perfection (see WT, 1 December 1985, pp. 4–18).

Despite all the attempts of the WBTS to say otherwise, the definition of salvation in the Scriptures is clear and final:

> For by grace you HAVE BEEN saved through faith: and that NOT OF YOURSELVES, it is the gift of God; NOT AS A RESULT OF WORKS, that no one should boast. (Eph 2:8–9.)

Notice the past tense *have been* saved—nothing more need be added. It has *nothing* to do with works.

The WBTS pay lip service to this but a closer investigation of their publications shows they have rewritten these two verses of Scripture as follows:

> For by grace you MIGHT YET BE saved through faith: and that MUST HAVE SOMETHING TO DO WITH YOURSELVES, it is NOT ENTIRELY the gift of God; IT IS AS A RESULT OF WORKS, that WE should boast IN THE

SOCIETY. (Eph 2:8–9, Watchtower revised.)

Here are the quotations that show where this comes from.

> Jehovah God offers you something wonderful—everlasting life...you must have faith in Jehovah...However, MORE THAN FAITH IS NEEDED. There must also be works...(*You Can Live Forever In Paradise On Earth*, 1982, p. 250.)

> What does God REQUIRE of those who will reside forever upon his Paradise earth?...Jesus Christ identified a FIRST REQUIREMENT... *taking in knowledge*...Many have found the SECOND REQUIREMENT more difficult...*obey God's laws*...A THIRD REQUIREMENT is that we *be associated with God's channel*...The FOURTH REQUIREMENT...*loyally advocating his Kingdom rule to others*. (WT, 15 February 1983, pp. 12–13.)

> Though getting baptized is evidence that you are spiritually progressive, remember that baptism is just A BEGINNING STEP... dedication may be compared to APPLYING FOR EVERLASTING LIFE in God's new system...Afterward you MUST faithfully live up to your dedication IN ORDER TO RECEIVE GOD'S GIFT OF EVERLASTING LIFE. (WT, 15 August 1987, p. 16.)

Once you've said that you've said everything. We must first apply to receive everlasting life and then we must faithfully live up to the WBTS's standards in order to receive God's gift. But the moment I have to do anything in order to receive it, it's no longer a free gift. This is clearly nothing more than Watchtower double-talk.

The Mediator

Apart from the double-talk concerning salvation there is the serious matter of who brings salvation to the majority of Jehovah's Witnesses? Biblically of course the mediator of our salvation is Jesus Christ and He alone can give us eternal life (see John 10:28). However, what is the WBTS's position?

> What, then, is Christ's role in this program of salvation? Paul proceeds to say: 'There is one God, and one mediator between

God and men [NOT, *all* MEN], a man Christ Jesus'... The new covenant between 'our Saviour, God', and spiritual Israel continues as long as there are spiritual Israelites still in the flesh as 'men' here on earth. So the covenant is in force today... There are still more than 9,000 who profess to be spiritual Israelites in the new covenant... Evidently the new covenant is nearing the end of its operation for the purpose of producing 144,000 spiritual Israelites... Today, according to authentic records, there is a 'great crowd' of dedicated, baptized Christians who actively collaborate with the small remnant of spiritual Israelites... THEY ARE NOT... IN THE NEW COVENANT MEDIATED BY JESUS CHRIST, nor part of the 'chosen race, a royal priesthood, a holy nation'.... Yet they do benefit from the operation of the new covenant... To keep in relationship with 'our Saviour, God', the 'great crowd' needs to remain UNITED WITH THE REMNANT of spiritual Israelites. (WT, 15 November 1979, pp. 26–27.)

So in this strict Biblical sense Jesus is the 'mediator' ONLY for anointed Christians... The 'great crowd' of 'other sheep' that is forming today is NOT IN THAT NEW COVENANT. However, BY THEIR ASSOCIATING WITH THE 'LITTLE FLOCK' of those yet in that covenant they come under benefits that flow from that new covenant. (WT, 1 April 1979, p. 31.)

Your ATTITUDE towards the wheatlike anointed 'brothers' of Christ and the TREATMENT you accord THEM will be THE DETERMINING FACTOR as to whether you go into 'everlasting cutting-off' or receive 'everlasting life.' (WT, 1 August 1981, p. 26.)

This pastoral King tells us how a person may be considered fit to be separated to the side of divine favor in contrast to the goatlike people. It is by DOING GOOD TO THOSE YET REMAINING ON EARTH OF THE SPIRITUAL 'BROTHERS' of the reigning King... (WT, 1 January 1983, p. 13.)

Summarizing these quotes we find that the 'great crowd', i.e. the vast majority of Jehovah's Witnesses alive today, are not in the new covenant mediated by Jesus Christ, therefore Jesus Christ cannot be their mediator. However, as everyone needs a mediator, who is the mediator of the 'great crowd'? The 144,000! Therefore the 'great crowd' do not worry so much about their relationship with Jesus Christ but their relationship with the 144,000 represented by the remnant of approximately 8,800 still alive on the earth today. How can the WBTS be God's organization when the Son of God has been replaced by men and women of the Society!

H. THE KINGDOM

Reasoning sums up the WBTS's teaching about the kingdom as follows:

> The Kingdom of God is the expression of Jehovah's universal sovereignty toward his creatures, or the means used by him to express that sovereignty. The term is used particularly to designate the manifestation of God's sovereignty through the royal government headed by his Son, Jesus Christ. 'Kingdom' may refer to the rulership of the one anointed as King or to the earthly realm ruled by that heavenly government. (pp. 225–26.)

That by itself is fine, but as the article continues they show what they really mean. Commenting on Luke 17:21 they affirm that as Jesus was speaking to the Pharisees He could not possibly mean that, 'the Kingdom was in *their* hearts. But the Kingdom as represented by Christ was in their midst' (p. 226). They conclude that the kingdom will be a literal one, ruled over by Jesus and the 144,000. Next comes a list of all the benefits that this kingdom will enjoy. They conclude by showing that the kingdom began in 1914. Two other passages to note are:

> Is it simply a condition centered within the hearts of believers? In other words, when enough people are converted to Christianity, will God's kingdom be here? Some persons have reasoned that way... But if their conclusion is correct, the kingdom of God is getting even farther away... this should bring home to us, too, that the kingdom is a real kingdom, an actual government, even as its King is an actual person. (*Let Your Kingdom Come*, 1981, pp. 8–9.)

When does this mighty King, unwanted by the nations, start his reign over our earth? All the evidence points to the year 1914 CE. (*Let Your Kingdom Come*, 1981, p. 111.)

Summary

First, the kingdom is a literal place set up in heaven with Jesus Christ as its actual King. Second, the kingdom began in 1914. Third, the 'other sheep' left on earth after Armageddon will not actually be in the kingdom but they will benefit from it. Finally, 'princes' from the Old Testament, e.g. Abraham, David and Moses, will be brought back to earth and be among the earthly rulers (see *From Paradise Lost to Paradise Regained*, 1958, p. 218).

What Does the Bible Teach?

Hebrews 12:28 in the literal Greek shows that we receive the kingdom *now*!

Luke 17:21, Matthew 3:2 and 12:28 all show that the kingdom exists wherever the King is manifested and accepted in His rightful position.

Luke 12:32, we are told by the WBTS, is the heavenly kingdom being received by the 144,000. But the same Greek word, *basileia*, is used in Matthew 25:34 where we are told the earthly ones are receiving their 'kingdom'. It is amazing that the Greek makes no distinction between the heavenly kingdom and the earthly kingdom.

Revelation 21:24 shows that the kings of the earth will bring their glory into the 'capital city' of the heavenly kingdom. How can that be if the two kingdoms are completely separate? The Bible actually teaches a restoration to the life, albeit more complete, that there was before the Fall. (Compare Genesis 1 and 2 with Revelation 21 and 22). Then there was no great gulf between heaven and earth. God walked on the earth and spoke to Adam. The Bible does not teach a great gulf—it teaches a new heavens and a new earth but undivided, mingled together as it was in the beginning.

Luke 13:28 and Matthew 8:11 show Abraham, Isaac and

Jacob in the heavenly kingdom, but Matthew 8:12 shows the sons of the kingdom thrown out! Why were they thrown out but the Old Testament saints included? Because they were too bigoted to accept Jesus as God but the prophets of old were not. It is the same judgement and reward today.

The Greek word for 'kingdom' is always *basileia* which according to Greek scholar W. E. Vine,

> is primarily an abstract noun, DENOTING SOVEREIGNTY, royal power, dominion... then, by metonymy, a concrete noun, denoting the territory, or people over whom a king rules. (VINE, Vol 2, p. 294.)

A more literal rendering of the Greek is 'kingship', i.e. the kingdom is only in existence because the King is ruling. No King, no kingdom. The word has much more to do with the act of ruling than the literal territory of the kingdom.

The Scriptures teach that the kingdom mainly affects us in a spiritual way at the moment and the completeness of the literal kingdom will only take place when Christ returns to this earth. The WBTS have placed an over emphasis on this literal expression and practically ignore the spiritual effect on our lives today.

I. NEW HEAVENS AND A NEW EARTH

Reasoning, p. 113, asks the question, 'Will God himself destroy the earth by fire?' In answer to this two portions of Scripture are quoted: 2 Peter 3:7,10 and Revelation 21:1, from the King James version.

> The heavens and the earth, which are now, by the same word are kept in store, reserved unto fire against the day of judgement and perdition ['destruction', RS] of ungodly men... The day of the Lord will come as a thief in the night; in the which the heavens shall pass away with a great noise, and the elements shall melt with fervent heat, the earth also and the works that are therein shall be burned up ['burned (burnt) up', RS, JB; 'will vanish', TEV; 'will be made manifest', NAB; 'will be laid bare', NE; 'will

discovered', NW]. (Note: The Codex Sinaiticus and Vatican MS 1209, both of the 4th century CE, read 'be discovered'. Later manuscripts, the 5th century Codex Alexandrius and the 16th century Clementine recension of the Vulgate, read 'be burned up'.

And I saw a new heaven and a new earth: for the first heaven and the first earth were passed away; and there was no more sea.

The argument then goes that we must take these verses in context and discover that it is not a literal burning up but a symbolic one.

It is that symbolic 'earth', or *wicked human society*, that is 'discovered'; that is Jehovah will sear away as by fire all disguise, *exposing* the wickedness of ungodly human society and showing it to be worthy of complete destruction. That wicked society of humans is also 'the first earth', referred to at Revelation 21:1. (*Reasoning*, p. 115.)

This teaching is amplified in a WT article:

The survival of Noah and his family ... [is] picturing survival by some here on earth of the fast-approaching world destruction, the ... end of this wicked, polluted system of things ... it will be by the harmonizing of one's course of action with God's purpose ... A waterproof wooden ark was all right for surviving the end of the 'world of that time'. Such an ark would not do for the 'great tribulation' with which the present 'world' or human society will end. (WT, 1 November 1974, p. 665.)

Would it harmonize with God's original purpose concerning man and his earthly home for God to burn up this earth with literal fire? ... The watery deluge of Noah's day did not destroy the earth, but merely swept the 'world of ungodly people' off the surface of the earth and cleansed it, gave it a good bath. Likewise, the fire of Jehovah's day, the coming day of judgement, will not destroy the earth, neither all creature life in it, but will destroy off earth's surface the society of ungodly people and also their works that are out of harmony with God's purpose ... A profusion of Bible texts indicate that the 'fire' of the coming day of world judgement is symbolic. (WT, 1 November 1974, p. 666.)

How to survive into that 'new earth' under the 'new heavens' of Christ's kingdom is now the question...Noah built an ark as told by Jehovah God...Accordingly, Noah pictured Jesus Christ, and his wife pictured the 'Bride' of Christ, or, more particularly, the remnant of that collective 'Bride' that still finds itself on earth. The three sons of Noah and their wives picture those baptized worshipers of Jehovah God who now associate with the remnant of the 'Bride' class and who expect to become the earthly children of the Eternal Father, Jesus Christ, under his millennial kingdom...the 'time of the end' of this present 'world' began in...1914...Noah's ark would therefore picture that provision for survival that God makes through Christ...That divine provision is the spiritual paradise into which God has brought his faithful worshipers since the year 1919 CE, in which they live as his people restored to his favor and...to peaceful relationship with Jehovah God in 1919, as it were to their God-given spiritual homeland, the spiritual paradise was built up, MANY CONGREGATIONS OF JEHOVAH'S CHRISTIAN WITNESSES BEING ESTABLISHED AROUND THE EARTH. (WT, 1 November 1974, pp. 666–67.)

We can summarize this as follows:

1. The story of Noah is a prophetic picture. Noah = Jesus Christ. Noah's wife = the remnant of the Bride of Christ still on earth. The sons and their wives = the great crowd. The ark = spiritual paradise into which God has brought worshippers.
2. The fire that is coming is not all literal, although part of it may be. The earth will be cleansed and become a perfect place to live.
3. 'Heavens' and 'earth' are not literal, but represent 'systems of governments'.
4. The fulfilment of this 'prophecy' began in 1919.
5. The ark = spiritual paradise = Jehovah's Witness congregations.

What Does the Bible Teach?

In 2 Peter 3:13, already mentioned, the judgement of Noah's flood is compared with the judgement of fire in the last days.

The Bible never confuses us and always means what it says. Verses 3 and 4 show that these mockers were not prepared to believe that Christ promised to come again, because it seemed to them that everything had remained unchanged since the beginning. Peter shows that they were proved wrong and then compares the past judgement of the flood with the judgement of fire yet to come.

Verse 5—Literal heavens and earth existed in the past
Verse 7—Literal heavens and earth exist now
Verse 6—Literal water was used as a judgement
Verse 7—Literal fire will be used as a judgement
Verse 6—Everything in the world (*kosmos*) was destroyed
Verse 7—Ungodly men will be destroyed
Verse 10—Heavens and earth will be burned up

Everything was literal at the flood and the Bible clearly shows that everything will be literal in the last days. The Greek words used for heaven, *ouranos*, and earth, *ge*, are used in Scripture for the literal earth and the literal heavens. There is nothing here to suggest that the words should be spiritualized as a 'system'. Indeed there are three sets of heaven and earth mentioned and each set is literal.

Verse 5—The original ones created by the Lord
Verse 7—The present ones instituted after the flood
Verse 13—The new ones yet to come

The heavens will pass away, literally 'will loosen', 'be dissolved'. The elements, i.e. the substances of this material world, will be destroyed. And the earth, with all its works, will be burned up. As with the flood, all the inhabitants are to be destroyed unless they are in the 'ark' of the New Testament.

It has to be literal because the 'evil systems' will not be burned up by intense heat. They are spiritual, not physical. The Bible does not say this will happen any more than He destroyed the Devil and his demons in the flood. In the flood He destroyed mankind who had co-operated with the Devil, and the same will take place in the fire.

The Greek work for 'new' used in these verses is *kainos* which has the meaning of 'new in quality not time' and of 'a different nature from of old'. The very heavens and earth will undergo a change which could never be brought about by a thousand years of work by all the Jehovah's Witnesses. It is an essential change of character that only the miraculous working of God can produce. He created this world perfect in the first place. He must recreate it back into its original condition, no act of man can do that! Romans 8:20–21 shows clearly that the creation is in subjection to God and only He can release it, not the Jehovah's Witnesses.

To conclude we'll look at the 'pictures' that the WBTS deduce from Noah, his wife, his children and the ark.

Noah

Noah pictures Jesus Christ. As a preacher of righteousness he does picture our Lord Jesus. But if the inference is that Noah brought salvation that is wrong because 1 Peter 3:20 shows us that Noah was one of those delivered, not the deliverer.

Noah's wife

Noah's wife pictures the remnant of the 144,000 who are alive on earth at Armageddon. However, Revelation 7:3–4 shows that all the 144,000 are sealed together and there is no question of some going to heaven while some still remain of earth.

Noah's sons and wives

These picture the 'great crowd' of baptized Jehovah's Witnesses who associate with the Bride. Here the typology falls apart. All are in one ark going to the same destination, but Noah and his wife are going to heaven and the rest are going to earth! There is no 'two-tier' salvation shown by Noah's ark—the Witnesses have rewritten the Bible.

The ark

The 'ark' pictures 'the spiritual paradise into which God has brought his worshipers today'. But the ark only enabled Noah and his family to ride out God's judgement, it was a temporary dwelling place. 1 Peter 3:20 shows the ark as the means of salvation, not a place of long residence.

The worst part of this typology is that their 'ark' is being a baptized member of the WBTS and actively associating with the local congregation. This is blasphemy because they have placed themselves instead of Jesus Christ. 1 Peter 3:18–22 shows clearly that Jesus Christ is the Ark that will bring us safe through God's judgement into eternal life.

Conclusion

First, the only security for surviving the coming judgement is a 'born-again' relationship with Jesus Christ. Second, the WBTS have misconstrued the phrase 'new heavens and new earth' to fit in with their theology. Third, the typology of the Society is so confused that no honest Bible scholar can accept it as coming from Jehovah, the God of order.

J. THE 'PAROUSIA'

The Greek word *parousia* is used by the WBTS to show that Jesus returned invisibly in 1914.

> Before leaving the earth, Jesus Christ promised to return...there is a difference between *coming* and *presence*. Thus, while a person's coming (associated with his arrival or return) occurs at a given time, his presence may thereafter extend over a period of years. (*Reasoning*, pp. 340–41.)

> According to the 'sign' that Jesus foretold and also according to certain Bible time measurements, his invisible 'presence', or parousia, began in autumn of 1914 CE. (WT, 15 June 1979, p. 23.)

The WBTS therefore today can extend Christ's invisible *parousia* from 1914 to whatever date they choose. This is another of the WBTS's 'U-turns'.

But, 'If I go away, I will come again,' *cannot* refer to a spiritual coming *again*, because, spiritually, He never went away, as He said, 'Lo, I am with you alway, even to the end of the world,' [age]. Therefore, Jesus taught his *second* PERSONAL *coming*. (ZWTR, July 1879, p. 4; emphasis in the original.)

It is clear that originally Russell and his followers were looking for a physical return not a spiritual, invisible, return of Jesus. Even though the WBTS have changed their teaching the argument in their 1879 magazine is still true—Jesus could not return invisibly because He never went away invisibly!

The WBTS also have to explain away a number of other Scriptures. For example Acts 1:9–11 (*Reasoning*, p. 342), where we are told that Christ returns in the same manner He left, is twisted to mean that only the disciples saw Him go therefore the world in general will not see Him again. But in the same manner surely means that He went—feet on ground—up in the air— into the clouds and therefore will come—from the clouds— through the air—feet touch the ground.

Revelation 1:7 'every eye shall see Him' (*Reasoning*, pp. 342–43), is spiritualized and made to say every eye shall 'discern from events on the earth that he is invisibly present'. However, that is not happening—Jesus has been present for more that seventy years and very few are aware of it! What's wrong?

What then does the Greek word *parousia* mean?

a presence ... denotes both an arrival and a CONSEQUENT PRESENCE with. (VINE, Vol. 1, p. 208.)

The word is used twenty-four times in the New Testament: seventeen times of Christ, once of the lawless one, and six times of other people. All six used of other people speak of a bodily presence: 1 Corinthians 16:17, 2 Corinthians 7:6,7:7,10:10, Philippians 1:26,2:12.

Note the following references concerning Jesus Christ:
2 Peter 1:16—bodily presence of the Lord on the earth, up to AD 33!
1 Thessalonians 4:15,16—descended from heaven, not enthroned in heaven!
Matthew 24:27—light up the sky; everybody will know

Matthew 24:37,39—a sweeping away: all alive will know
Matthew 24:40—this did not happen in 1914
2 Thessalonians 2:8—the Devil will be slayed completely
James 5:7—no need of patience after *parousia*; full fruit obtained
It is obvious from these Scriptures that *parousia* cannot refer to the invisible return of our Lord Jesus in 1914.

There is also one other piece of evidence that the WBTS would like to hide. In their own publications you can see conclusively that the *parousia* did not take place in 1914. Below we quote 1 Thessalonians 4:15–17 (NWT large print edition) which speaks of the *parousia*.

> ...we the living who survive to the presence [*parousia*] of the Lord SHALL IN NO WAY PRECEDE those who have fallen asleep [in death]...we the living who are surviving will, together [footnote: AT THE SAME TIME] with them, be caught away...

The living and the dead will meet the Lord 'at the same time.' Which time? His *parousia*. The literal Greek of 1 Thessalonians 4:17 from the KIT shows the same thing:

> We the living the (ones) being left around AT THE SAME TIME together with them we will be snatched.

K. THE JUDGEMENT

The WBTS sum up the time of judgement as follows:

> These 144,000 joint heirs of Jesus Christ, instead of being judged, will sit with him on thrones of judgement... There was a previous judgement period for these 144,000 when they were on earth... For redeemed mankind in general to have a time of judgement here on earth there needs to be a resurrection... Jesus said... that the 'hour' would come... during the 1,000-year reign of Jesus Christ with his 144,000 glorified joint heirs... Of course, during their sleep of death there comes no change in their personality. (WT, 1 September 1978, pp. 21–22.)

What Does the Bible Teach?

Hebrews 9:27: We die once and then comes judgement. There is not one Scripture that teaches that anyone will be raised again during the 1,000 years and be given a second chance.

Revelation 20:1-15: These verses clearly show the events of the judgement.

Verse 1—This is the beginning of the 1,000 years

Verse 4—According to the WBTS those on the thrones are the 144,000

Verse 5—Therefore they are alone during the 1,000 years, because the rest of the dead do not come alive until after the 1,000 years are complete

Verse 7—End of 1,000 years

Verse 12—Now the dead are judged

Verse 13—They are judged individually according to their deeds—not because they belong to the WBTS

Verse 15—The basis of judgement is whether or not my name is found written in the Lamb's Book of Life, when I die. It cannot be written there after I have died. There is no second chance.

SECTION 7

Chronology

The Chronological Institute was founded in London in 1852 and its aims included, 'To promote...a more comprehensive acquaintance with chronological literature, and a more exact study of THIS SCIENCE, both historically and mathematically...'

The emphasis above that chronology is a science is confirmed by the definitions of chronology in the EA, *Oxford English Dictionary* and *Webster's International Dictionary*.

In contrast to these definitions the complex chronology of the WBTS is anything but scientific. Indeed the first thing we'll establish is that their chronology did not begin with Russell at all, as clearly admitted in an article about the parable of the ten virgins:

> ...much of this parable met its fulfilment in 1843 and 1844, when William Miller and others, Bible in hand, walked out by faith on its statements, expecting Jesus at that time...We merely notice here that the Bible chronology, first dug from Scripture by Bowen, of England...Brother Barbour first began to preach the message...If these movements were of God, and if Bros. Miller and Barbour were his instruments...the 'Bridegroom *came*' in 1874. (ZWTR, October and November 1881, pp. 288–89.)

Carl Olof Jonsson, in his book *The Gentile Times Reconsidered* (available from Reachout Trust), goes into detail of the development of Bible chronology. We will not be so detailed but must underline that Russell accepted dates that had been fixed before him. He simply 'juggled around' with starting and finishing points to arrive at a date in the future, not one that had already passed.

John Aquila Brown seems to be the first to use the figure of 2,520 years (see later in the Section) as the period basically from the time of Nebuchadnezzar to the Lord's return to earth, called the Gentile Times. For Brown this time ended in 1844. William Miller, mentioned in Russell's article, was an American but undoubtedly influenced by the British school of chronology. He accepted all the work completed before him but predicted the return of Christ during the Jewish year of 21 March 1843 and 21 March 1844. We know now that these dates were false.

Nelson H. Barbour (mentioned in Russell's article), an associate of Miller was severely disappointed at the fact of a failed prophecy for the Lord's return. However, he overcame the disappointment and checking the calculations of Miller against the work of the Revd Christopher Bowen (mentioned in Russell's article) he corrected them to arrive at 1874 as the date for Christ's return. Now Russell comes on to the scene. He accepted all the false calculations and false prophecies that had gone before and simply now claimed this is of God. But further changes would have to be made. When Christ did not return visibly in 1874 it was said He came invisibly but that He would end all things and set up His kingdom on earth in 1914. Later still the 1874 date was dropped altogether and Christ did not come invisibly till 1914. What is evident is that Russell took on failed prophecies and then twisted them to make further wrong prophetic statements.

All this would be bad enough but Russell then went on to use the pyramid, calling it God's second witness in stone, as proof of the dates calculated above:

> Then measuring *down* the 'Entrance Passage'... we find it to be 3,416 inches, symbolizing 3,416 years from the above date, BC 1542. This calculation shows AD 1874 as marking the beginning of the period of trouble... (SS, Vol. 3, 1901, p. 342.)

However, when the Society needed to change the dates

because 1914 did not bring the end that started in 1874, the
pyramid seems to have stretched!

> Then measuring *down* the 'Entrance Passage'...we find it to be
> *3,457* inches, symbolizing *3,457* years from the above date, BC
> 1542. This calculation shows AD *1915* as marking the beginning of
> the period of trouble... (SS, Vol. 3, 1923, p. 342.)

This is simply another indication that it is not God's dates
that are being proven. Rather facts are stretched and twisted to
fit in with dates that man has chosen. Actually after Russell died
the second president of the WBTS, J. F. Rutherford, decided
that the pyramid was not God's witness. But he still kept the
false chronology and went on adding many other dates of his
own.

In all the chronology of the WBTS there seems to be only
one common theme—1914. Even this has a different meaning
today than it did originally as we'll show later. First, however,
let's see what Jehovah's Witnesses have been taught.

> Two dates are fixed with considerable certainty...the beginning
> of the reign of Cyrus in 536 BC [see Note 1]...(this) is a very
> important aid; for the Bible chronology ends with the '70 years
> desolation of the land,'...the Bible alone, supplies such a
> chronology as the people of God can rely upon...Why not
> believe that God intended thus to provide a chronology as long as
> it was needed—down to the point where secular history *could* be
> depended upon as accurate [the Society would not agree with that
> today!]...We do so believe. (ZWTR, 15 May 1896, p. 1975.)

From their beginning the Society have seen the usefulness
of chronology to promote their message of impending doom.
Today the Society still use chronology to establish the vital date
of 1914, around which their 'prophetic' message is built.
However, they do not accept *all* chronology, only the parts that
confirm their teaching. This can be seen clearly in the article on
'Chronology' (ABU, pp. 324–48) where eleven pages are spent
dismissing as inaccurate Egyptian, Assyrian, Babylonian and
Persian historical records, astronomical calculations,

archaeological dating and contemporary historians. But then, the statement is made:

> ...we must use...a date in history that has SOUND BASIS for acceptance...as a pivotal point is the year 539 BCE, supported by VARIOUS HISTORICAL SOURCES. (ABU, p. 333.)

Chronic Chronology

Before we can check the accuracy of the WBTS's chronology we must understand the heart of their teaching on dates and numerical calculations. This is explained by the following quotes:

> An *absolute date* is a calendar date that is proved by secular history to be the actual date of an event recorded in the Bible...A prominent event recorded both in the Bible and in pagan secular history is the overthrow of...Babylon...October 11–12, 539 BCE. (*All Scripture Is Inspired Of God And Beneficial*, 1963, pp. 281–82.)

> Once this *absolute date* is fixed, calculations forward or backward from this date are made from accurate records in the Bible itself...the Bible record shows...by late in 538 BCE Cyrus acceded to the throne, and...at least before spring of 537 BCE, he issued his famous edict...This would give ample opportunity for the Jews...to come up to Jerusalem...about October 1, 537 BCE. (*All Scripture Is Inspired Of God And Beneficial*, 1963, pp. 281-82.)

> With the exit of the insubordinate Jews from the land of Judah, the foretold 70 years of desolation of the land without resident Israelite and domesticated beast started off. (WT, 1 March 1980, p. 16.)

> About two lunar months after the calamity upon King Zedekiah, his realm, the land of Judah, became totally desolated. There the 'seven times' of the nations, 'the times of the Gentiles', began their run of 2,520 years, to end in 1914 CE. (WT, 1 February 1980, p. 26.)

> There is no basis for doubt that Nebuchadnezzar's dream [Daniel 4] of the heaven-high tree was prophetic...(it) symbolized the

UNIVERSAL SOVEREIGNTY of...Jehovah God...True to that dream, Divine Sovereignty as exercised through the line of Davidic kings...toppled...in 607 BCE...For how long was this debased appearance of Jehovah's Universal Sovereignty to continue? For 'seven times', which were prophetically illustrated by the 'seven years' of Nebuchadnezzar's dethronement...A 'time'...used in connection with Bible prophecy averaged 360 days...The 'seven times' or seven years would therefore amount to 7 times 360 days, or 2,520 days. (*Our Incoming World Government—God's Kingdom*, 1977, pp. 83–84, 86–87; emphasis in the original.)

So each of these 2,520 days must be treated according to the Bible rule: 'A day for a year, a day for a year, is what I give you.' (Ezekiel 4:6; compare Numbers 14:34.) This would mean that the 'seven times' of domination on the earth by Gentile world powers...would extend for 2,520 years...607 BC...to...1914. (*Our Incoming World Government—God's Kingdom*, 1977, p. 88.)

Before we look in detail at each step we'll summarize the Society's calculations.

Step 1   An absolute date is chosen—the fall of Babylon 539 BC.

Step 2   Two years later, 537 BC, Cyrus decreed that the Jews could return to Jerusalem.

Step 3   537 would be the end of Jerusalem's seventy years of desolation, which therefore began, at its fall, in 607 BC.

Steps 4 and 5   Daniel's dream and the 'Bible rule' that a day equals a year, show that the Gentile Times, which began at Jerusalem's fall in 607 BC, would be 2,520 years long, ending in 1914.

Step 1: The Absolute Date

There are no 'BC' dates in the Bible. The moment we date any event in the terms of our modern-day calendar we have moved away from strict biblical chronology and have accepted evidence from scientific chronology. This fact is important because Witnesses will tell you they are using biblical chronology, but that can only place events in their right order with the correct interval of years in between. Their own publications show the reliance on historians.

An article in the WT, 15 August 1968, entitled 'The Book of Truthful, Historical Dates', shows their method of establishing the absolute date of 539, and backs this up with twenty-five reliable authorities. Out of these twenty-five reliable authorities the twenty-two that have been traced bring evidence to also prove that Jerusalem fell in 586/587 BC, not 607 as claimed by the WBTS. So, if these authorities are reliable over 539 BC, are they not reliable over 586 BC? Anyway, why choose 539 as the 'absolute date' when we could equally prove 586 as an absolute date and miss out the first two calculations? The answer is that the date of 539 can be moulded to fit their 'prophecies', but other dates cannot.

So we must either accept both 539 BC and 586 BC as reliable or reject both as unreliable. We cannot choose just one of them—they stand or fall together. We also need to understand the basis of fixing the date of 539 BC. This is explained in the WT article mentioned above:

> ...a stone document...(which) gives precise details...This, in turn, enables modern scholars, with their knowledge of astronomy, to translate these dates into terms of the Julian or Gregorian calendars. (p. 490.)

On this basis we can fix many absolute dates, especially, for instance, for the fall of Jerusalem in 586 BC. This date is based on a clay tablet with precise details that can be translated into terms of our modern-day calendar by the same accurate astronomical tables used for 539 BC. Again, we must ask why the WBTS only accept this one date when another far better can be fixed by exactly the same method?

Conclusion

The Society is not honest in its approach to chronology. The Governing Body of Jehovah's Witnesses must have realized it was skating on thin ice because a few years after the article in the WT was published this amazing about-turn was printed:

> ...the co-relation of astronomical data with human events in the past is subject to various factors and human interpretation, allowing for error. (ABU, p. 330.)

If this statement is true, 539 BC is not an absolute date and there is no WBTS chronology.

Step 2: From 539 To 537

Once 539 BC is accepted, Jehovah's Witnesses will proudly tell you that from then on only the Bible is used to establish their chronology. The first step is to get from 539 to 537. This is the two years between the fall of Babylon and the decree of Cyrus allowing the captives to return to Jerusalem. Where are these two years found mentioned in the Bible? The answer is nowhere! Do not let Witnesses get away with this. If they want to use the Bible for their chronology, stick on this point till they show you. It's not there as even the Society itself agrees!

> ...it is very PROBABLE that the decree was made by the winter of 538 or toward the spring of 537 BC (ABU, p. 333.)

This is why it cannot be proved from the Bible. Babylon fell to Darius the Mede in the seventh month (Tishri—equivalent to early October) 539 BC. The Bible does not tell us how long Darius the Mede reigned before Cyrus took over. So if the reigns of Darius the Mede and Cyrus the Great were concurrent the chronology would be the seventh to twelfth months of 539 were in the ascension year of Cyrus. All of 538 was the first year of Cyrus. The decree would be made in 539 or 538 and with the four-month journey (Ezra 7:9) from Babylon to Jerusalem the first people would arrive 538 or 537. Or, if

Darius' reign is separate from Cyrus' as Daniel 5:31 and 6:28 seem to indicate, and because he reigned at least one year (Dan 9:1), the chronology would be the seventh to twelfth months of 539 were in the ascension year of Darius. All of 538 was the first year of Darius and when Cyrus ascended to the throne. All of 537 was the first year of Cyrus. The decree would be made in 538 or 537 and the people would arrive 537 or 536.

Conclusion

Starting from 539 BC, and using the Bible alone, all we can say for certain is that the people returned to the land in 538, 537 or 536.

Step 3: Seventy Years of Desolation

The WBTS are adamant that the seventy years began with the fall of Jerusalem in 607 BC and ended with Cyrus' decree in 537 BC. We have already shown that these dates are suspect and it is not surprising that the 'simplistic attitude' the Society take over this matter of the seventy years is also suspect. Much could be written on this subject alone but the pivotal point is the question, was Jerusalem actually desolate for seventy years or did the seventy years begin when Nebuchadnezzar first came to Jerusalem? There is no simple answer, even though the WBTS would like to think there is. In fact, taking the starting-point of the seventy years as Nebuchadnezzar's first visit to Jerusalem (605/604 according to the most reliable records) satisfies both biblical and historical records (see Note 2 for a further look at this matter).

Conclusion

Even if we allow the Witnesses the seventy years desolation, it still only gives us an approximate date for the fall of Jerusalem—608, 607 or 606—and therefore does not alter the fact that their chronology is not exact.

Step 4: 'The Times of the Gentiles'

The dream of Nebuchadnezzar recorded in Daniel 4 is the basis of this calculation. The tree in the dream represents 'divine rulership... through the kingdom of Judah' and the seven periods that elapsed after it was cut down are the 'Gentile Times'. The kingdom being restored to Nebuchadnezzar after these seven periods represents the Lord Jesus taking His seat on the throne vacated by King Zedekiah. We will look at this interpretation.

Unlike other dreams recorded in Daniel, the fulfilment of this one is also recorded. It is not for the 'end times' as others are. In fact the word used for 'fulfilled' in verse 33 means 'to have an end of'.

The tree represents Nebuchadnezzar, the king of Babylon. It is difficult to equate that with the understanding of the Society that it actually represents divine rulership. 'What was really meant was... domination exercised by the kingdom of God' (*Babylon the Great has Fallen*, 1963, p. 177). It is a foolish man that seeks to correct God, but that seems to be what the WBTS has tried to do.

Luke 21:24 is the Scripture that mentions the 'Time of the Gentiles'. It explains that during this time Jerusalem will be trampled down, and that could not possibly end in 1914. The Jehovah's Witness will try to wriggle out of this by saying it is the heavenly Jerusalem that was trampled down till 1914. Don't be fooled with this illogical ploy. God did not lose His place in heaven in 607 BC—Zedekiah lost his throne on earth. The trampling started on earth and therefore must finish there. The mind boggles at the lengths to which the Society will go to twist Scripture to their own ends. Is it scriptural to say that the heavens were trampled down till 1914? See Ephesians 1:20–23 (past tense in AD 60!).

According to the dating of the WBTS, Daniel was taken to Babylon in 617 BC (see Note 3) and the fall of Jerusalem was ten years later in 607 BC. Also according to the WBTS, this dream is a prophecy concerning the fall of Jerusalem. However, these two statements cannot be reconciled. The dream indicated a future event, to take place at least one year later (Dan 4:29). If that event is the fall of Jerusalem then the dream must have been received at the latest in 608 BC. That is impossible because the dream in Daniel 4 must come after the dream in Daniel 2 (compare 2:48 with 4:9). The WBTS date Daniel 2 (albeit falsely) as 605 BC, two years after the fall of Jerusalem.

The word for 'time' here is only found eleven times in the Old Testament and all are in the Book of Daniel. It is against sound biblical exegesis to isolate this one instance and compare it with Scriptures in Revelation, no matter how logical the WBTS make it appear. Daniel speaks of seven 'times'. These were times when there was no king of Israel ruling. Instead God's people were dominated by a foreign power who did not recognize the God of the Jews. Revelation 12:6,14 shows another time of great testing for the people of God where three and a half 'times' equals 1,260 days. This translates into the fact that seven 'times' equals 2,520 days. Revelation is talking about another specific period of trouble for God's people that lasts seven years. This, of course, is not enough and therefore has to be linked with the next step.

Step 5: Dayears

The WBTS need to transfer days into years and call upon the year for each day theory, or as they say a 'Bible rule'. If it is a rule we must expect to find it often in the Scriptures. It actually appears only twice. The first time is in Numbers 14:34 which speaks of the guilt of the children of Israel; they spied out the Promised Land for forty days but still disobeyed God and would not enter. They would therefore bear the guilt for forty years— a *year* for every *day*. The second example is Ezekiel 4:6 which speaks again of the guilt of God's people. Ezekiel was a 'visual aid' for forty days—a *day* for every *year*.

Conclusion

There is no historical or biblical evidence to use a calculation of 2,520 years as the period of the Gentile Times. Both the Scriptures called on to turn days into years speak of the same matter—the guilt of God's people—therefore the rule is not general but specific. And in any case the verses do not say the same thing: Numbers 14:34 is a year for a day but Ezekiel 4:6 is a day for a year. Consequently the 'Times of the Gentiles' according to Ezekiel is seven days.

Summary

1.   The fall of Jerusalem in 607 BC is disproved by scientific chronology.
2.   The date of 586 BC for the fall of Jerusalem is established both by scientific and biblical chronology.
3.   Starting from an absolute date of 539 BC it is impossible, solely using the biblical record, to show that Jerusalem fell in 607 BC.
4.   The way the WBTS use Scripture is not sound interpretation but a taking of individual passages at random to prove a point that has been determined beforehand.
5.   The result of these conclusions is that 1914 is not proven as the significant date of Christ's invisible return.

Note 1

It is interesting to note that the WBTS have had three other 'absolute dates' before 539 BC (see quotes below) but because of minor changes in the way they calculated the Gentile Times they could always end at AD 1914. This in itself shows the deception of the Society in 'fixing' the date of Christ's enthronement.

> . . . the first year of the reign of Cyrus is a very clearly fixed date—both secular and religious histories with marked unanimity agreeing with Ptolemy's Canon, which places it BC 536. (SS, Vol. 2, 1889, p. 80.)

> According to the most accurate histories . . . Cyrus came to power, in 537 BC. (*The Kingdom is at Hand*, 1944, p. 183.)

> The first year of Cyrus . . . 538 BC. (WT, 1 November 1949, p. 326.)

Note 2

We see from the context of Jeremiah 25:11 what the Scriptures really say:

Verse 1   The prophecy was given in the first year of Nebuchadnezzar.

Verse 3   This was twenty-three years after Jeremiah had begun to bring the Lord's Word.

Verse 8   Because no one had listened in these twenty-three years Jehovah now said, 'I will'. There would be no further opportunity for repentance. Having made this statement it is highly unlikely that the Lord would wait a further eighteen years (Jerusalem fell in the eighteenth year of Nebuchadnezzar) to fulfil this promise, as the WBTS would have us believe.

Verse 11   The first part of this verse is a statement: the land must be devastated and must be an object of astonishment. But at this point there is a conjunction, 'and', and the subject of the sentence ceases to be the land and becomes servitude to the king of Babylon. Thus, the seventy years is only connected with servitude to the king of Babylon.

The context of Jeremiah 29 should also be noted, as I believe this is very conclusive evidence.

Verse 1   Letter sent to those in exile in Babylon.

Verse 3   This letter was sent while Zedekiah was still on the throne—*before Jerusalem finally fell*.

Verse 10   However, already Jeremiah is talking about the *seventy years*.

We should also note Daniel 9:2, where through reading Jeremiah, Daniel saw the seventy years captivity was up. Because Daniel only used Jeremiah, what did he read? First, Jeremiah 25:11 foretelling that nations must serve the king of Babylon seventy years. Then Jeremiah 25:12 and 29:10 which tell how, after seventy years, judgement would befall Babylon. Nowhere does Jeremiah link the seventy years with the destruction of the Temple therefore neither could Daniel!

Finally, we must also note that the seventy years of Daniel 9:2 is linked to devastations of Jerusalem. In the WBTS's teaching only one devastation comes within the seventy years, but according to Scripture Nebuchadnezzar came twice to devastate Jerusalem.

Note 3

> Early in 617 BC...Daniel...[was] taken...by Nebuchadnezzar. (ABU, p. 415.)
>
> Ezekiel...was...taken to Babylon by Nebuchadnezzar with Jehoiachin in 617 BC. (ABU, p. 552.)

The WBTS say that Ezekiel and Daniel were taken captive in the same year thus ruling out Nebuchadnezzar coming to Jerusalem in his first year. Whereas this makes it impossible for the seventy years to start then, it does cause other problems.

1.   Daniel 1:3–4 tells us that when Daniel was taken it was not a general exile. Just a few of the 'elite' were taken to the palace.
2.   Daniel does not mention king Jehoiachin but Ezekiel does. It would be strange not to report the king being taken to the palace.
3.   If Daniel was not taken to Babylon till 617, how could he interpret Nebuchadnezzar's dream in the second year of the king (Dan 2:1) which according to the Watchtower is 624/23? (Remember BC dates work backwards—617 is seven years *after* 624!)

What Did Russell Say About 1914?

There are many quotations in WBTS literature which show the present-day attitude to 1914.

> Consider, too, the fact that Jehovah's organization alone, in all the earth, is directed by God's holy spirit... To it alone God's Sacred Word, the Bible, is not a sealed book... How very much true Christians appreciate associating with the only organization on earth that understands the 'deep things of God'! Direction by God's spirit enables Jehovah's servants to HAVE DIVINE LIGHT... For instance, long ago they understood that 1914 CE would mark the end of the Gentile Times or 'appointed times of the nations'...*Zion's Watch Tower* of March 1880 had declared: '"The Times of the Gentiles" extend to 1914, and the heavenly kingdom will not have full sway till then.' (WT, 1 July 1973, p. 402.)

> From the outset, the *Watch Tower* showed that at Christ's second coming his *parousia* would be an invisible presence as a mighty spirit person... this journal's early issues (March and June 1880) pointed to 1914 CE as a climactic year. It was to mark the close of the 2,520-year-long Gentile Times, during which non-Jewish nations would rule the earth without interference by any kingdom of God. (WT, 1 July 1979, p. 5.)

> By the date of October 1 of 1914 World War I had been raging for more than two months... So, first of all, we will ask: Who were the ones that, many years beforehand, pointed out to the whole world that 'the Times of the Gentiles' would end in the latter half

of 1914? It was the International Bible Students ... Today they are known worldwide as Jehovah's Witnesses. Have world events vindicated them? Yes! ... have those opposers who far outnumber Jehovah's Witnesses won the hot dispute concerning the setting up of God's Kingdom by Christ in the heavens in 1914 CE? ... No! (WT, 1 January 1983, pp. 10–11.)

To summarize, the WBTS make the following claims concerning their past 'prophetic' statements:

1. With their 'Divine Light', they pointed to 1914 as a special year, more so than any other year they named.
2. The 'Gentile Times' would end on 1 October 1914.
3. Christ's kingdom would be a *heavenly* one.
4. Christ's kingdom would start in 1914.
5. Christ's coming would be an *invisible* one.

Since 1914 is such a corner-stone to Watchtower 'theology', and since they claim that for the 100+ years of their existence they have always spoken consistently about 1914 and the related events, we need to check the record. Below we record what C. T. Russell actually said in the early publications of the WBTS:

But, 'If I go away, I will come again,' *cannot* refer to a spiritual coming *again,* because, spiritually, He never went away, as He said, 'Lo, I am with you alway, even to the end of the world,' [age]. Therefore, Jesus taught His *second* PERSONAL *coming.* (ZWTR, July 1879, p. 4; emphasis in the original.)

'The Times of the Gentiles' extend to 1914, and the heavenly Kingdom will not have full sway till then, BUT as a 'Stone' the kingdom of God is set up '*in the days* of these (ten Gentile) kings,' and by consuming them it becomes a universal kingdom—a 'great mountain and FILLS THE WHOLE EARTH.' (ZWTR, March 1880, p. 82.)

The presence (of the Bridegroom) ... began in the fall of 1874. (ZWTR, April 1880, p. 87.)

True, it is expecting great things to claim, as we do, that within the coming twenty-six years all present governments will be overthrown and dissolved ... In view of this strong Bible evidence...we consider it an established truth that the FINAL END of the kingdoms of THIS WORLD, and the FULL ESTABLISHMENT of the Kingdom of God, will be accomplished by the end of 1914 AD. (SS, Vol. 2, 1889, pp. 98–99.)

It is not only possible but highly probable that not only Anarchists and the Seventh Day Adventists and ourselves, but others of God's children...will be hindered in the spread of the truth...it will not at all surprise us if this condition of things may come to pass by the year 1900—OR SOONER. (ZWTR, March 1890, p. 1198.)

The date of the CLOSE of that 'battle' is definitely marked in Scripture as October, 1914. It is already in progress, its beginning dating from October, 1874. (ZWTR, 15 January 1892, p.1355.)

...the final overthrow of present governments will be at the same time as the fall of ecclesiasticism, and will be followed by FROM FIVE TO SEVEN YEARS of socialism and anarchy, TO END WITH 1914 by the establishment of Christ's Millennial government. (ZWTR, 1 August 1892, p. 1434.)

The question comes from many quarters; 'Brother Russell, are you not possibly mistaken...that the great trouble will ALL BE OVER BY AD 1915, and that in its severity it will *probably* not reach us before AD 1906 to 1908?... We answer, No. (ZWTR, 1 and 15 September 1893, p. 1581.)

The CULMINATION OF THE TROUBLE in October, 1914 is clearly marked in the Scriptures; and we are bound therefore to expect a beginning of that *severe* trouble NOT LATER THAN 1910. (ZWTR, 15 September 1901, p. 2876.)

Universal Anarchy—just before OR AFTER October, 1914 AD. (ZWTR, 1 July 1904, p. 3389.)

The final spasm, which WE LOOK FOR IN 1915, will give birth to the new dispensation of peace and blessing, the Millennial reign of Messiah. (ZWTR, 1 January 1908, p. 4111.)

Finally, let us remember that we did not consecrate either to October 1914, nor to October 1915, nor to any other date, but 'unto death'. (WTR, 1 December 1912, p. 5142.)

Indeed, as respects the date 1914, which we have emphasized, and respecting which we have repeatedly expressed our faith, our conviction—even respecting this date we have never knowingly spoken IN INFALLIBLE TERMS. We have always admitted that it is a matter of faith and conviction, RATHER THAN ABSOLUTE KNOWLEDGE. (WTR, 1 June 1913, p. 5249.)

Only one thing did the Editor fear in respect to the influences mentioned and the able addresses of the speakers. He fears that the dear friends in several instances were over-stimulated by TOO POSITIVE ASSURANCE that the present year will witness the 'change' of the church, establishment of the kingdom etc. With all due respect for the opinions of the brethren, we believe that the present is a time for great soberness of mind, avoidance of speculation and waiting for whatever the Lord may be pleased to bring to pass. We greatly fear that some of the dear friends will experience sharp disappointments, if some of the confident statements made on the convention platform miscarry. At no time has the Editor ever spoken or written AS POSITIVELY as some of these dear brethren are speaking now. In the books, STUDIES IN THE SCRIPTURES, as well as in THE WATCH TOWER, we have set forth the chronology, NOT AS INFALLIBLE, but nevertheless declared our confidence in it... In recent numbers of THE WATCH TOWER we have plainly stated that fulfilments of the prophecies, although marked and manifest, ARE NOT AS FAR DEVELOPED FOR THE TIME AS WE HAD EXPECTED. (WTR, 15 July 1914, p. 5502.)

September 20 of this year, 1914 PROBABLY marked the end of the Gentile times. (WTR, 1 November 1914, p. 5566.)

Bible students all over the world have been expecting certain things to occur; and we have been HOPING that the Lord's time is near for the setting up of the kingdom... but if it should not come as soon as expected, we will still hold fast our confidence... God HAS PROMISED that he will give his true children the LIGHT at the time appointed... Even if the time of our change should not come within ten years, what more should we ask? (WTR, 15 December 1914, p. 5595.)

We see no reason for doubting, therefore, that the Times of the Gentiles ended in October, 1914; and that A FEW MORE YEARS will witness their utter collapse and the full establishment of God's kingdom in the hands of Messiah... OUR MISTAKE WAS... that some historians put the end of the Jewish Time of Trouble as April AD 73, which would correspond to April 1918. (WTR, 1 September 1916, pp. 5950–51.)

These statements are but the tip of the iceberg as far as the early chronology of the WBTS is concerned but from these we can draw the following comparisons to the modern-day claims of the WBTS.

1.   Russell emphasized a number of years, including 1915 and 1918, and so the WBTS cannot claim that they pointed exclusively to 1914. In fact, the record shows that the nearer 1914 came the more Russell doubted his original 'prophecies'.
2.   Russell first said that the 'Gentile Times' ended on 20 September 1914, and later saw 'no reason for doubting' October 1914.
3.   Russell always said that the kingdom would be an earthly one. What the Witnesses teach today about Christ's invisible reign has nothing to do with Russell's teaching of the end of the world's governmental systems.
4.   Neither by December 1914, nor by his death in 1916, had Russell received the 'light' that God had promised to his true children and not once did he claim that the kingdom was set up in 1914.
5.   The very first issue of ZWT clearly taught Christ's personal coming. This view has been slowly modified over the years.

Above all, Russell himself warned that these were only suggestions and not a prophetic warning concerning 1914. Even though he was still alive some two years into World War I, Russell never claimed any significance to it. Yet today the Society show that event, above all else, as 'proving' Russell's 'prophecies'.

How can a Society that blatantly twists the words of its own founder be the mouthpiece of Jehovah God? The record shows that in seeking to prove that they are God's prophet they have deceived and lied. Having examined the record, we must conclude that beyond any reasonable doubt, the WBTS is a false prophet and is not Jehovah's means of communication to man today.

Changes in Watchtower Chronology

The fixed and definite explanation of the WBTS's chronology in Section 7A is all the more amazing when you are aware of the changes that have taken place in the past years. Indeed, the WBTS themselves have sometimes even questioned whether chronology is reliable:

> Can we feel absolutely sure that the Chronology set forth in the DAWN-STUDIES is correct?...we have never claimed our calculations to be infallibly correct; we have never claimed that they were *knowledge*, nor based upon indisputable evidence, facts, knowledge; our claim has always been that they are based on *faith*. (ZWTR, 1 October 1907, p. 4067; emphasis in the original.)

However, at other times they've clearly stated that it's God's chronology and absolutely true:

> We have no doubt whatever in regard to the chronology relating to the dates 1874, 1914, 1918, and 1925. Some claim to have found new light...(but) the Lord has placed the stamp of his seal upon 1914 and 1918 beyond any possibility of erasure...there can be no more question about 1925 than there was about 1914... Looking back we can now easily see that those dates were clearly indicated in Scripture and doubtless intended by the Lord to encourage his people... (WT, 15 May 1922.)

But whether chronology is reliable or not is secondary to the fact that the WBTS's chronology, said to have been given by the unchanging Jehovah God, has been altered many times over the years. To show this we list below some of the major events with the 'evolution' that has taken place in the dating. This clearly shows that the WBTS's chronology is of man, not God, and is therefore worthless.

The absolute date

536:SS, Vol. 2, 1889, p. 80.
537: *The Kingdom Is At Hand,* 1944, p. 183.
538: WT, 1 November 1949, p. 326.
539: WT, 1 May 1952, p. 271.

6,000 years from Adam ended

1873: ZWTR, October and November 1881, p. 289.
1975: WT, 15 August 1968, p. 494.

Beginning of the Gentile Times

606: SS, Vol. 2, 1889, p. 79.
607: *Let Your Kingdom Come,* 1981, p. 137.

End of the Gentile Times

1914: ZWTR, November 1880, p. 152.
1915: ZWTR, 15 February 1892, p. 1373.
20 September 1914: WTR, 1 November 1914, p. 5566.
1 October 1914: WTR, 1 February 1916, p. 5845.
1 August 1914: WT, 1 November 1922.

Harvest time

1914 is furthest limit: ZWTR, July 1880, p. 116.
1874—1914: ZWTR, December 1880, p. 172.
1907—1914: ZWTR, 1 January 1908, p. 4110.
Began after 1919: WT, 1 August 1981, p. 23.

Resurrection of the dead

Between 1874 and 1881: ZWTR, January 1881, p. 182.
1915: ZWTR, 15 May 1893, p. 1529.

1878: ZWTR, 15 March 1902, p. 2982.
1925: *Millions Now Living Will Never Die,* 1920, pp. 88–90.
Shortly after 1925: *The Way To Paradise,* 1924, p. 224.
Any day *now: The New World,* 1942, p. 104.

Armageddon

From October 1874 to October 1914: ZWTR, 15 January 1892, p. 1355.
1914 War the beginning: *Pastor Russell's Sermons,* 1917, p. 676.
1925: WT, 15 February 1938, p. 55.
1932: WT, 15 February 1938, p. 55.
1939: 'very near': *Salvation,* p. 310.
1941: 'very near': *Children,* p. 100.
1975: *Kingdom Ministry* (USA), March 1968.

The Signs of the Times

'Tell us, When will these things be, and what will be the sign of your presence and the conclusion of the system of things?' And in answer Jesus said ... (Matt 24:3–4, NWT.)

I wonder how often these verses are read out by Jehovah's Witnesses on doorsteps. They'll go to great lengths to show that the signs Jesus related prove He returned in 1914 and that we are now living in the end times, with Armageddon just around the corner. The main public address at the Twickenham convention in 1985 asked, 'What do the signs and seasons show us about God's calendar and where we are in history?' The answer included the following statements:

Jehovah's purposes are never late or cancelled ... we are very deep into the final part of the last day ... all evidence shows that we are nearly at the end of this system of things ... earth shattering events will occur in the immediate future ... the due time has arrived to remove all religious systems and this system of things ... The signs that show this ... the frequency of wars ... famine increasing ... poverty ... crime rate.

This only repeats what the WBTS have said over and over again in their magazines and books. They quote statistics and events which seem to back up their case and certainly the average Witness is convinced. However, is there evidence which disputes their bold statements?

Let us make it clear the we believe we are living in the last days and that we are seeing an increase in the signs mentioned in Matthew 24 and other passages. But the question we seek to answer is more specific: 'Does the evidence of these signs show that Jesus Christ returned in 1914 as the WBTS claim?'

> Ridiculers may scoff, saying that there have been wars, famines, earthquakes, and so forth, repeatedly in human history. But such events take on a special significance when they all appear together... Consider these facts: The war that broke out in 1914... Following World War I came one of the greatest famines... The Spanish flu of 1918... The frequency of major earthquakes... Amid all of this... worldwide proclamation of the good news... Progressively Bible students saw unfolding before their eyes details of the composite sign... It became evident... Christ had begun to rule as King in 1914... (*Survival Into a New Earth*, 1984, pp. 22–23, 25.)

We will investigate one or two of the signs mentioned and check some of the authorities that the WBTS refer to.

Earthquakes

> From 1914 until now there have been many more major earthquakes than in other like period in recorded history. For over 1,000 years, from the year 856 CE to 1914, there were only 24 major earthquakes causing some 1,973,000 deaths. But in the 63 years from 1915 to 1978, a total of some 1,600,000 persons died in 43 great earthquakes. (*You Can Live Forever In Paradise On Earth*, 1982, p. 151.)

In 1983, after reading the above publication, I wrote to several earthquake specialists with the above quote and asked four questions:

1. According to your records, is this quotation correct?
2. Is the reason that more earthquakes are reported in recent history due to better research units such as yours?
3. According to your figures has there been an increase in earthquake activity since 1914?

4. If more people are dying today from earthquakes, is this related to the increase in world population?

Below are two sets of the replies. The first is from the Earthquake Research Unit, Tokyo University, Japan.

1. No. It is almost impossible to reply with reliable data on world earthquakes because there is no such data.
2. Yes.
3. No. Records of earthquakes have increased but we cannot say that earthquake activity has increased.
4. No answer given.

The second set of replies is from the International Seismological Centre, Newbury, Berks.

1. In general, I would not agree with the quotation...The earthquake reputed to have killed most people was in China in 1556, with 850,000 fatalities. This makes the pre-1914 figure you quote seem very small.
2. Instrumental recording was just starting around the turn of the century.
3. There is certainly no seismological evidence to make us believe that more seismic energy has been released since 1914 than in comparable periods in the past.
4. This point, regarding world population, is a very valid one. I believe that world population has grown by a factor of 100 since biblical times, and also populations have become more condensed.

If you add to this a summary of the tables found on pp. 119–41 of *Seismicity of the Earth* by Gutenberg and Richter, 1949, you find there was a 37 per cent *decrease* in earthquake activity in the eleven years after 1914 compared with the eleven years leading up to 1914. Even the WBTS must be aware of this because in ABU, p. 478, they say:

Since 1914 CE, AND ESPECIALLY SINCE 1948, there has been an increase in the number of earthquakes, especially of major ones.

Indeed, because exact seismological information has only been available for less than eighty years, I believe it can be clearly seen that the WBTS do not have proof for the facts they quote.

Frequency of Wars

In April 1983 the WT began a series, answering the question, 'Are we living in the last days?' Of course they referred to the signs as proof that we are. We find this quote concerning wars:

> So 'wars and reports of wars' would not be something new to the world... For these... to have meaning... they would have to stand out as being different... Have we seen such war? Yes, we have, and that starting with the generation of 1914... writes Quincy Wright in the book *A Study of War*. 'At least 10 per cent of deaths in modern civilization can be attributed directly or indirectly to war.' (WT, 1 April 1983, pp. 4,6.)

To the WBTS, wars and frequency of wars have clearly increased since 1914 and so become another of the signs pointing to Christ's enthronement in 1914. Do the facts bear this out? We will quote from a source who the Watchtower obviously agree with, Quincy Wright, *A Study of War*.

> Conditions relevant to war have changed more radically SINCE 1942... than in any equal period of human history... War has reached a wholly new order of potential destructiveness SINCE 1942. (pp. 1501–2.)

Taking a summary of 278 wars, starting with 1482 and ending with 1941, Wright says:

> The number of European wars had declined from over 30 a half-century in the sixteenth and seventeenth centuries to less than half that number in the nineteenth and twentieth centuries. (p. 638.)

Then listing fifteen general wars between 1600 and 1941, he comments:

This summary indicates that, with very few exceptions, ALL THE GREAT POWERS OF THE TIME PARTICIPATED IN EACH OF THESE GENERAL WARS. (p. 649.)

Wright also produces a summary on p. 651 which shows that the number of wars fought between 1800 and 1850 was forty-one, between 1850 and 1900 was forty-eight, and between 1900 and 1941 was *only* twenty-four.

A summary of these quotes, which can be backed up by many others, is as follows:

1. The turning-point regarding wars is not 1914 but 1942.
2. The frequency of wars actually decreased after 1914.
3. Although 1914 was World War I, the evidence shows that all the major powers in the world fought in general wars since 1600.

Again, there is no proof of the WBTS's claims that the frequency of war is a sign of Christ's enthronement in 1914.

Famines

While it is true that agriculture has made a lot of progress in recent years, it is also true that since 1914 mankind has witnessed numerous food shortages. (WT, 15 April 1983, p. 4.)

Here the WBTS seek to show that famine is also a sign for 1914. One book they quote a number of times in the article is *The Hungry Planet* by G. Borgstrom. But this publication says nothing specific regarding 1914 and only shows a very small increase in famines after 1914 compared with those before. However, other authorities are more specific in their comments as can be seen from the following:

PRIOR TO WORLD WAR II today's hungry nations were exporters of grain. BY THE 1950's they were importers!...UP UNTIL 1957–1959 the world as a whole was doing pretty well regarding food. It was, in fact, INCREASING its agricultural production SOMEWHAT FASTER than the number of mouths to be fed...then the increases began to falter. BY 1958 these countries had run out of land which they could farm. (*Famine—1975,* W. and P. Paddock, 1968, pp. 41,44.)

In his book *Famine*, 1981, John Robson shows on pp. 22–24 that between 1860 and 1914 there were nine major famines causing 23,850,000 deaths, and between 1915 and 1973 there were thirteen major famines but only 20,037,400 deaths. He also shows that there were NO FAMINES CAUSED BY WORLD WAR I, but two by World War II.

What does all this mean? Simply that once again the facts clearly show that 1914 is not a turning-point for famines and therefore cannot be related to any sign for that year. In fact nearly 4,000,000 more people died from famines in approximately 60 years before 1914 than in the 60 years after, and famine didn't really start destroying life on a massive scale till the late 50's.

We could examine the other signs and show clearly that although these catastrophes are going on in our days they do not point to 1914 as a special year.

What Does Scripture Say?

So far we have only looked at the statistics and practicalities of this matter. Even though these do not back up the WBTS's claims we still need to look at what Scripture teaches.

The Scripture from Matthew quoted at the beginning of the article shows that the disciples came to ask Jesus what will be *the sign* of 'your coming' and of 'the end of the age'. They only asked for one sign to cover both events. Are these separate events? The WBTS say, yes. They explain that the 'coming' is Christ's *parousia* (the Greek word used here—see p. 138), His invisible return to the throne in 1914, and that the 'end of the age' speaks of the final great battle of Armageddon, after which Christ's kingdom will be set up on earth. We are now living in the 'in-between' period.

Is this teaching Scriptural? We will make some observations.

First, nowhere in the whole of Matthew 24, or indeed in the parallel passages of Mark and Luke, do we find Jesus treating these events separately.

Second, we need to understand the shades of meaning of the different Greek words otherwise we can draw wrong conclusions. We will use the definitions of the Greek scholar W. E. Vine. *Parousia* is the word used of the coming in Matthew 24: 3,27,37,39. It 'denotes both an arrival and a consequent presence with'. *Sunteleia* is used for the end of the age in Matthew 24:3 and 'signifies a bringing to completion...the word *does not* denote a termination, but the heading up of events to the appointed climax.' *Telos* is used of the end in Matthew 24:6,13–14. It is 'the limit, at which a thing ceases to be what it was to that point'.

With these definitions in mind let us paraphrase the relevant verses in Matthew 24 and make a few comments on the WBTS's doctrine. The disciples ask, 'What will be the Sign of the arrival of your presence with us and the events that will head up to that climax?' They did not ask for the signs of His invisible presence and the conclusion of things. Jesus said (v. 6) that the signs of wars etc do not mean that the limit has been reached. In fact we need to endure to that limit (v. 13). Only after the gospel is preached everywhere will that limit be reached (v. 14).

The WBTS make no distinction between the phrase 'the conclusion' *(sunteleia)* and 'the end' *(telos)*. They say that the signs began with Christ's *parousia* in 1914 and will have their termination at 'the end'. But the Lord is showing the events that will lead up to His coming thus bringing the end. In other words, the WBTS say that these signs come *after* the parousia of Christ. But the Scriptures say that these signs come *before* His *parousia*. Who should we believe?

Matthew 24:27,37,39 are classic verses for the WBTS. They have described the Lord's 'coming' *(parousia)* of verse 3 as His invisible presence of 1914 but try to give that same definition to these verses. The Lord says His arrival will be as lightning flashing from the east to the west and like the experience of those trapped in the flood of Noah's day. Was the presence of the Lord in 1914 like this? Did anyone see it like the lightning flashing across the whole sky or like the flood waters bearing down on top of them? Those events got the immediate attention of the people but the WBTS took nearly thirty years before they said with any confidence that Christ 'came' in 1914! *Parousia* then, which must mean the same each time it is used in Scripture, cannot refer to Christ's invisible presence in 1914.

Conclusion

Having looked at both the practical events of the signs themselves, and more importantly the scriptural context, we can say that neither gives any evidence of Jesus Christ's invisible return in 1914.

SECTION 8

The New World Translation

A look at the literature of the WBTS leaves us with the impression that they believe the whole of the Bible to be God's Word and that as a Society they only teach scriptural doctrines.

The Claim

> It is of vital importance to them [Jehovah's Witnesses] that their beliefs be based on the Bible and not on mere human speculations or religious creeds. (*Jehovah's Witnesses In The Twentieth Century*, 1979, p. 3.)

> They [Jehovah's Witnesses] rely on both the Greek and the Hebrew Scriptures, and take them literally except where the expressions or settings obviously indicate that they are figurative or symbolical. (*Jehovah's Witnesses In The Twentieth Century*, 1979, p. 4.)

> If a religion really accepts the Bible as God's Word, it is not going to use certain parts of it and reject other parts...the religion that is approved by God must agree in all its details with the Bible. (*The Truth That Leads To Eternal Life*, 1968, pp. 13–14.)

> *The Kingdom Interlinear Translation* can serve as a safeguard against error in these days when many religious leaders are teaching twisted things, even twisting the written Word of God...by going to *The Kingdom Interlinear Translation of the Greek Scriptures*, a student can go to the ORIGINAL BIBLE TEXT... (WT, 15 November 1969, p. 696.)

Never forget that THE BIBLE IS OUR STANDARD and that however God-given our helps may be they are 'HELPS' AND NOT SUBSTITUTES FOR THE BIBLE. (WTR, 15 December 1909, p. 4531.)

To get understanding and other benefits, a person must approach the reading of God's Word with an OPEN MIND, THROWING ASIDE ALL PREJUDICE AND PRE-CONCEIVED OPINIONS; otherwise his understanding will be veiled. (ABU, p. 1375.)

The Reality

However, as so often with the WBTS, they do not practice what they preach. The reality is very different. Helps are put above the Word of God as the following quote shows:

... 'carefully examining' God's Word WITH THE AID of that 'slave's' publications, in order to fortify our faith ... (enemies) say that it is sufficient to read the BIBLE EXCLUSIVELY, either alone or in small groups at home. But, strangely, through such 'Bible reading', they have reverted right back to the apostate doctrines. (WT, 15 August 1981, pp. 28–29.)

We must not approach the Bible with an open mind but with the pre-conceived ideas of the Society:

The Bible is an organizational book and belongs to the Christian congregation as an organization, NOT TO INDIVIDUALS, regardless of how sincerely they may believe that they can interpret the Bible. For this reason the Bible cannot be properly understood without Jehovah's visible organization in mind. (WT, 1 October 1967, p. 587.)

However, when we do as we are bid by the Society (WT, 15 November, 1969) and check their English translation with the Greek in the KIT we see that they are the 'religious leaders teaching twisted things'. Here are a few examples of the type of changes made. The KIT literal Greek is shown first and underneath the NWT with changes in **bold type**.

1 Corinthians 10:4	was the Christ
	meant the Christ
Revelation 3:14	beginning of the creation of the God
	the beginning of the creation **by** God
1 John 4:2	the spirit of God
	inspired expression from God
John 17:3	that they may be knowing you the only true God
	their **taking in knowledge** of you the only true God
John 1:4	in him life was
	by means of him was life
John 13:31	and the God was glorified in him
	and God is glorified **in connection with** him
Hebrews 9:27	it is reserved for men once to die after but this (thing) judgement
	it is reserved for men to die once **for all** time but after this **a** judgement
Acts 10:36	Jesus Christ: this One is of all (them) Lord
	Jesus Christ: this One is Lord of all [**others**]
Hebrews 12:23	and to spirits of righteous (ones)
	and **the spiritual lives** of righteous ones

But, above all, a careful study of the NWT and especially the KIT shows that the WBTS themselves are guilty of twisting God's Word. We'll list three main examples here. (Further evidence can be found in Reachout Trust's publications, *Deliberate Deception of the New World Translation* and *Factsheets*. Also in *The Jehovah's Witness New Testament* by R. H. Countess.)

John 1:1

In this verse theos is translated 'a god'. The KIT appendix (pp. 1158–60) explains that *theos* is rendered as 'a god' because it is 'anarthrous', i.e. without the Greek definite article 'o'. This 'principle of translation' should be applied consistently. Is it?

In Mark 12:26–27 the anarthrous *theos* is rendered twice as 'God' and once as 'a God'. Note the inconsistency. Only 16 times out of 282 occurrences of the anarthrous *theos* does the NWT render it as 'god', 'a god', 'gods', or 'godly'. This means the Society made up its own rule and then broke it 94 times out of a 100. This is deception, not translation. The rule most Greek scholars accept is called 'Colrule', which says:

> A definite predicate nominative has the article when it follows the verb; it does not need the article when it precedes it.

The *theos* in John 1:1 comes before the verb 'was' and therefore does not need the definite article.

B. F. Westcott, whose Greek text it is, says clearly:

> It is necessarily without the article (*theos*, not *o theos*), inasmuch as it describes the nature of the Word and does not identify His Person. (*The Gospel According to John*, Vol. 1, 1908, p. 6.)

Colossians 1:27–28

'Union with' are two words which are added many times in the New Testament but are not in the Greek. The Society will not accept that Jesus can be 'in' us or we can be 'in Christ'. Therefore they *add* to God's Word to prevent Jehovah's Witnesses having a personal relationship with Jesus Christ. However, John 17:26 shows clearly their inconsistency of translating *en autois*.

> And I have made your name known to them and will make it known, in order that the love with which you loved me may be in them *(en autois)* and I in UNION WITH them *(en autois)*. (NWT.)

In the same verse they translate the words both 'in' and 'in union with' but the Greek is the same. We can have 'God's love' in us but not Jesus Christ. This inconsistency occurs over ninety times. The Society is guilty of inconsistency in translation because of the need to support a specific viewpoint.

John 8:58

According to the Society Jesus did not say 'I am' but 'I have been'. This is not possible according to the rules of Greek grammar as the following shows:

> The Present which indicates the CONTINUANCE of an action during the past and UP TO THE MOMENT of speaking is virtually the same as Perfective, the only difference being that the action is conceived AS STILL IN PROGRESS. (*A Grammar of New Testament Greek*, J. H. Moulton, 1963, Vol. III. p. 62.)

'I have been' does not agree with this definition of the perfective (see Appendix 4).

We have to conclude that the WBTS have gone to much trouble to twist and distort Scripture in order to make it appear that they teach biblical concepts when in fact the opposite is true.

SECTION 8A

Scholars and the New World Translation

The WBTS want us to believe that scholars approve and support their translation of the Bible. In a letter from the WBTS (London, 26 September 1985, ref: EC:SE) they give a number of quotes to prove this. We list them below. As usual the parts they left out are supplied in bold letters. The quotes are introduced in the letter as follows:

> Finally, we felt it might be of some assistance to list a few comments by various scholars concerning the New World Translation particularly highlighting the competence of its translators:
>
> Samuel Haas said of the New World Translation, **'While this work** indicates a great deal of effort and thought as well as considerable scholarship, **it is to be regretted that religious bias was allowed to colour many passages.'** (*Journal of Biblical Literature*, December 1955, p. 283.)
>
> Robert M. McCoy said: **'In not a few instances the New World Translation contains passages which must be considered as "theological translations"... John 8:58 ... On grammatical grounds alone ... cannot be justified. It cannot be called a historical present, since the words are not narrative ...** The translation of the New Testament is evidence of the presence in the movement of scholars qualified to deal intelligently with the many problems of Biblical translation.' (*Andover Newton Quarterly*, 3, 1963, pp. 29–31.)

Professor Bruce M. Metzger: 'On the whole one gains a tolerably good impression of the scholarly equipment of the translators (their names are not divulged)... **Some of the translations which are simply indefensible... The introduction of the word "Jehovah" into the New Testament... John 1:1... is not justified despite a lengthy note... the translators have not hesitated to insert four times the word "other" (totally without warrant from the Greek)... in Col[ossians] 1:16f.'** (*The Bible Translator*, Vol. 15, 1964, pp. 151–52.)

S. Maclean Gilmour, Norris Professor of New Testament: 'The New Testament translation was made by a committee whose membership has never been revealed—a committee that possessed an unusual competence in Greek... **It is clear that doctrinal considerations influenced many turns of phrase...'** (*Andover Newton Quarterly*, 1966, p. 25–26.)

Even the scholars that the WBTS quote do not support the New World Translation. But there are other scholars we should also note because of their contact with the WBTS.

Julius R. Mantey, quoted by the Society as supporting the NWT, said:

> There is no statement in our Grammar that was ever meant to imply that 'a god' was a permissible translation ... because you have been quoting me out of context, I herewith request you not quote the manual... again. (Letter to the Watchtower Society dated 11 July 1974.)

Dr A. T. Robertson, is also quoted as supporting the Society's view, but wrote:

> This is atrociously mistranslated (Romans 9:5) in the NWT... I disagree radically with this statement in the KIT. (*Word Pictures*, Vol. 4, p. 381.)

Dr William Barclay is likewise quoted as supporting the Society in the WT, 15 May 1977, pp. 319–20. This is his response:

The Watchtower article has, by judicious cutting, made me say the opposite of what I meant to say. What I was meaning to say . . . is that Jesus is . . . to put it more crudely . . . of the same stuff as God. (Letter dated 26 August 1977.)

The WBTS have not, to date, produced one biblical scholar of good reputation to support their translation, whereas many more than are quoted here have condemned it for one reason or another.

SECTION 9

Disfellowshipping

Much has been said about the unchristian teaching of the WBTS regarding the disfellowshipping or excommunicating, of its members who do not 'toe the line'. (We have used the more common spelling of 'disfellowshipping' with 'pp'. However you will note that in quotes from modern WT literature they only use 'p'.) Although it is true that they have gone beyond the letter of the law, we must say that the Bible does advocate separation for persons who deliberately and willingly go against God's commands as set forth in His Word. Sadly some churches have failed to heed this Bible counsel and have left undisciplined such unrepentant persons.

However, the WBTS have gone too far in their application of these sound biblical principles, especially with regard to those who, having committed themselves to the Society, want to leave because they've found out they've been misled. The WBTS have instilled into their membership an attitude of fear, teaching that their 'organization' is God's organization and that to turn away from them is the same as turning away from God Himself. The Governing Body, frightened that members will communicate with ex-members and find out the truth about 'the organization', forbid such communication with ex-members. Tremendous difficulties which we'll look at later arise within family relationships because of this hard attitude.

The biblical purpose of disfellowshipping is to cause the

errant Christian to repent, to remove what could be a stumbling block from the church, so that others will not be affected, to teach others to fear God's righteous judgement and to keep the church clean in the eyes of outsiders. In 1 Corinthians 5 we read of Paul's instructions to remove a Christian who was cohabiting with his stepmother. However, it is distinctly possible that this is the man who could become 'overwhelmed by excessive sorrow', and later Paul encourages the church to 'reaffirm your love for him' (see 2 Corinthians 2:6–11). Unruly Christians who would not respond to counselling were to be treated similarly, as 2 Thessalonians 3:14–15 shows. Verse 15 is particularly relevant to the WBTS.

In Matthew 18:15–18 Jesus Christ outlines three steps to take in settling difficulties, or righting the wrong. If the steps proved unsuccessful then the person was to be treated as a 'Gentile and a tax-gatherer' (Matt 18:17b). Yet despite the Jews' hatred for Gentiles and tax-gatherers they still had cause to deal with them from time to time. In all this we should also remember the heart of the Lord that He 'is not willing for any to perish but for all to come to repentance' (2 Pet 3:9). So the object of disfellowshipping should always include trying to persuade the sinner to have a repentant attitude and return to the Lord.

In any discussion of disfellowshipping, 2 John 9 and 10 must be mentioned. In the early days the church met in homes (see Romans 16:4–5; 1 Corinthians 16:19; Colossians 4:15). It would be totally out of order for these home churches to permit teachers to promote false doctrine, especially where weaker Christians who might be made to stumble would be present. So we believe that this instruction is specifically dealing with the church situation. Jesus continued to speak with all and sundry, regardless of where they stood with God. We must let our own conscience dictate whether we should allow a sinner to come into our home. Some would say that if we were to take this text too literally, then we would not be able to welcome into our home anyone who entertained different doctrines. This would include relatives, neighbours, the gasman, milkman and so on.

The WBTS have gone further than the practice of disfellowshipping unrepentant sinners, and have included in their reasons for disfellowshipping smoking, working for military establishments, working for other religious organizations, voting in elections, accepting blood transfusions and celebrating birthdays or holidays such as Christmas and Easter. Talking to other disfellowshipped ones, even if that one is a relative counts as a reason. Also, if a dissatisfied person disagrees with Watchtower teaching and discusses that disagreement with other Jehovah's Witnesses so as to promote apostasy, then that person will be disfellowshipped. Thus the organization protects itself from general discontentment and enforces unity by use of disfellowshipping.

Bill Browning knows personally of a man who became a Jehovah's Witness. After a struggle he gave up smoking. Years later he discovered his wife was having a lesbian relationship with another Witness woman. His wife left him and he began smoking again. The elders gave him six months to quit. Eventually they extended this to a year, but when he failed to break the habit they disfellowshipped him.

History

The WBTS haven't always maintained this excessively strong position.

1920

> We would not refuse to treat one as a brother because he did not believe the Society is the Lord's channel. (WT, 1 April 1920, p. 100.)

However, the Society didn't take long to change their views. By 1930 those who disagreed with President Rutherford were classed as 'evil slaves' and were called the 'man of perdition' who would be destroyed (see WT, 1930, pp. 275–81). In more recent times though their position on disfellowshipping has been solidified.

1952

The disfellowshipping arrangement was discussed in full. The conclusion concerning a disfellowshipped person was that,

> Those who are acquainted with the situation in the congregation should never say 'Hello' or 'Good-by' to him. He is not welcome in our midst, we avoid him. (WT, 1 March 1952, pp. 137–45.)

1955

Associating with a disfellowshipped person can now lead to an active Jehovah's Witness being disfellowshipped. (WT, 1 October 1955, p. 607.)

January 1972

Divorce gained on the grounds of the partner's homosexuality or bestiality was wrong and was not a divorce in God's eyes. To marry after such a divorce would cause the person to be guilty of adultery and subject to disfellowshipping. (WT, 1 January 1972, p. 32.)

December 1972

All types of illicit sexual intercourse, including homosexuality and bestiality, are now considered grounds for divorce. (WT, 15 December 1972, pp. 767–68.)

1974

Disfellowshipped ones are not to be treated with unnecessary cruelty, especially members of a Witnesses' own family or house in obvious hardship situations. They shouldn't be like the Pharisees who walked on the other side of the road. (WT, 1 August 1974, pp. 466–73.)

New rules for sexual conduct between married partners show certain acts as being *porneia*, prostitution, if one partner is not a willing participant. This would make the forceful one subject to divorce.

> Do lewd practices on the part of a married person toward that one's mate constitute a Scriptural basis for the offended mate to get a divorce? There are times when lewd practices

within the marriage arrangement would provide a basis for a
Scriptural divorce.... She could establish with the
congregation [this would include giving intimate facts to the
elders—see 1978] that the real reason for this is *porneia* and
then proceed to get a legal divorce on any truthful grounds
acceptable to the courts of the land. (WT, 15 November
1974, pp. 703–4.)

1978

Elders are not to enforce bedroom rules. Witnesses are not to
be intimidated or spied upon, though the banned practices are
still wrong. (WT, 15 February 1978, pp. 30–32.)

1981

New hard lines are to be taken with those disfellowshipped, or
those who leave, called disassociated. Even family members
are to be shunned except in the most necessary functions of life.
(WT, 15 September 1981, pp. 20–31.)

1985

Any who abandon the organization are part of the 'antichrist'
and 2 John 9–11 applies to them. They shouldn't even be
greeted. (WT, 15 July 1985, pp. 30–31.)

We can also trace the history of a number of other aspects of
disfellowhipping.

Hate

1952

Haters of God and his people are to be hated, but this does not
mean that we will take any opportunity of bringing physical hurt
to them in a spirit of malice or spite, for both malice and spite
belong to the Devil, whereas pure hatred does not. We must hate
in the truest sense, which is to regard with extreme and active
aversion, to consider as loathsome, odious, filthy, to detest.
Surely any HATERS OF GOD are not fit to live on his beautiful
earth... What do you do with anything loathsome or repugnant
that you detest and abhor? The answer is simple. You get away
from it or remove it from your presence. You do not want to have

anything at all to do with it. This must be exactly our attitude towards the haters of Jehovah.... (WT, 1 October 1952, p. 599.)

1961

When a person persists in a way of badness after knowing what is right, when the bad becomes so ingrained that it is an inseparable part of his make-up then in order to hate what is bad a Christian must hate the person with whom the badness is inseparably linked. (WT, 15 July 1961, p. 420.)

1970

So it is that enlightened Christians rightly hate those who are confirmed enemies of God, such as the Devil and his demons, as well as men who have deliberately and knowingly taken their stand against Jehovah. (WT, 15 November 1970, p. 695.)

Though strongly worded, some may see the above quotes applying to murderers or sex criminals etc. However, when we realize that any who just consistently question the Watchtower 'organization' are considered as rebelling against God Himself, the above words of hatred take on a sinister aspect.

Against the 'Organization' Means Against God

1975

Against whom was this rebellion directed? Against certain individuals in authority in the church... But the rebellion was actually against God... When anyone takes an unfaithful course, challenging Jehovah's word or arrangement, he is ranging himself up against God. (WT, 15 March 1975, p. 167.)

1980

Thus, the one who doubts to the point of becoming apostate sets himself up as a judge. He thinks he knows better... than the 'faithful and discreet slave',... He develops a *spirit of independence*... Some apostates even think they know better than God, as regards his ordering of events and outworking of his purposes. (WT, 1 August 1980, pp. 19–20.)

This attitude has not always been the policy of the WBTS. Their founding president said:

> But if ever you get from us either tract or paper which you do not find in harmony with the Scriptures, surely let us know wherein it disagrees, and do not circulate it. (ZWTR, 1 March 1894, p. 1629.)

> ... by asking questions, calling attention to what seems to be misapplications of Scripture or what not, they are to do their part in keeping the body of Christ and His teachings pure—they are to be critics ... they are ... urged to communicate, to criticize. (SS, Vol. 6, 1904, p. 263.)

Today, however, it is very different.

1952

> We should eat and digest and assimilate what is set before us, without shying away from parts of the food because it may not suit the fancy of our mental taste ... We should meekly go along with the Lord's theocratic organization and wait for further clarification, rather than balk at the first mention of a thought unpalatable to us and proceed to quibble and mouth our criticisms as though they were worth more than the slave's provision of spiritual food. (WT, 1 February 1952, pp. 79–80.)

1969

> Jehovah's organization as directed by his 'faithful and discreet slave' class should influence our every decision. (WT, 15 March 1969, p. 172.)

1983

> FIGHT AGAINST INDEPENDENT THINKING. (WT, 15 January 1983, p. 27.)

Renouncing Your Christian Standing

Not only is rebellion against 'the organization' considered to be the same as rebelling against God, but a person who says he no longer wants to be known as a Jehovah's Witness is said to be renouncing his standing as a Christian.

> One who has been a true Christian might renounce the way of the truth, stating that he no longer considers himself to be one of Jehovah's Witnesses or wants to be one. When this rare event occurs, the person is renouncing his standing as a Christian. . . . (WT, 15 September 1981, p. 23.)

The Wrongdoing of Leaving the Organization

The Bible shows that we will be judged according to our works. However, once a person has received Jesus Christ into his life as Lord and Saviour, he is neither condemned nor under judgement.

> There is therefore now no condemnation for those who are in Christ Jesus. (Rom 8:1.)

> Truly, truly, I say to you, he who hears My word, and believes Him who sent Me, has eternal life, and does not come into judgement, but has passed out of death into life. (John 5:24.)

Yet the WBTS still say:

> Persons who make themselves 'not of our sort' by deliberately rejecting the faith and beliefs of Jehovah's Witnesses should appropriately be viewed and treated as are those who have been disfellowshiped for wrongdoing. (WT, 15 September 1981, p. 23.)

> The fact is that when a Christian gives himself over to sin and has to be disfellowshiped, he forfeits . . . his approved standing with God . . . much of the association he had with Christian relatives. (WT, 15 September 1981, p. 31.)

How to View a Disfellowshipped Relative

Deliberately rejecting the faith and beliefs of Jehovah's Witnesses results in disfellowshipping and the disfellowshipped one is no longer in a position to choose to fellowship with relatives. It is therefore not the disfellowshipped person who forfeits the right of fellowship but the relatives who will not associate with him. The WBTS decide what constitutes a disfellowshipping offence and Jehovah's Witnesses accept the decision as from God Himself. So how should a Witness treat a disfellowshipped or disassociated relative?

A disfellowshiped person has been SPIRITUALLY cut off from the congregation; the former spiritual ties have been completely severed. This is true even with respect to his relatives, including those within the immediate family circle. Thus, family members—while acknowledging family ties—will no longer have any spiritual fellowship with him. (WT, 15 September 1981, p. 28.)

Prayer or Bible Study

If he [a disfellowshipped husband] wants to say a prayer, such as at mealtimes, he has a right to do so in his own home. But they [the Witness relatives] can silently offer their own prayers to God... What if a disfellowshiped person in the home wants to be present when the family read the Bible together or has a Bible study? The others might let him be present to listen if he will not try to teach them or share his religious ideas. (WT, 15 September 1981, p. 28.)

The Disfellowshipped Parent or Child who Lives Away from Home

For example, a disfellowshiped parent may be sick or no longer able to care for himself financially or physically. The Christian children have a Scriptural and moral obligation to assist... Perhaps it seems necessary to bring the parent into the home... What is done may depend on factors such as the parent's true needs, his attitude and the regard the head of the household has for the spiritual welfare of the household. This could also be true with regard to a child who had left home but is now disfellowshiped or disassociated. Sometimes Christian parents have accepted back into the home for a time a disfellowshiped child... But in each case the parents can weigh the individual circumstances... What about his morals and attitude? Will he bring 'leaven' into the home? (WT, 15 September 1981, pp. 28–29.)

Remember the WBTS are laying down rules as to how to treat one's own parents or children. They use such terms as 'moral obligation', not mentioning love; 'perhaps it seems necessary', perhaps it's not; 'may depend on factors'—though what should prevent children loving and looking after their own parents in their time of need? Then there's the son—should we let him back? Will he bring leaven into the home? It's a very cold regulation, don't you think?

Family Events

Normally, relatives are often together at meals, picnics, family reunions or other social gatherings. But when someone has unrepentantly pursued sin and has had to be disfellowshiped, he may cause difficulties for his Christian relatives in regard to such gatherings. (WT, 15 September 1981, p. 30.)

Weddings and Receptions

It should be appreciated that if a disfellowshiped person is going to be at a gathering to which non-relative Witnesses are invited, that may well affect what others do. For example, a Christian couple might be getting married at a Kingdom Hall. If a disfellowshiped relative comes to the Kingdom Hall for the wedding, obviously he could not be in the bridal party there or 'give away' the bride. What, though, if there is a wedding feast or reception? This can be a happy social occasion, as it was in Cana when Jesus attended. But will the disfellowshiped relative be allowed to come or even invited? If he was going to attend, many Christians, relatives or not, might conclude that they should not be there, to eat and associate with him, in view of Paul's directions at 1 Corinthians 5:11. Thus, sometimes Christians may not feel able to have a disfellowshiped or disassociated relative present for a gathering that normally would include family members. (WT, 15 September 1981, p. 30.)

The reason why other Jehovah's Witnesses may not wish to attend the reception when a disfellowshipped or disassociated person is present is that they are forbidden to associate or eat with such ones.

Disfellowshiping, however, implies more than ceasing to have spiritual fellowship. Paul wrote: 'Quit mixing in company...not even eating with such a man' (1 Cor 5:11). A meal is a time of relaxing and socializing. Hence, the Bible here rules out social fellowship, too, such as joining an expelled person in a picnic or party, ball game, trip to the beach or theater, or sitting down to a meal with him. (WT, 15 September 1981, p. 24.)

This is exactly what happened to Bill Browning. After leaving the Society his son was married to a lovely Witness girl. Two elders called to tell him that he would be prevented from attending either the wedding or reception. He could have enforced the law of the land and demanded to attend but decided not to spoil the wedding. So that the marriage could not be declared 'null and void' later he forfeited his legal right to attend. But it hurt very much. If his daughter gets married within the Jehovah's Witnesses he will not be allowed to be in the bridal party or give her away. What sort of organization can claim to be Christian, yet prevent a father attending the wedding of his own children?

Funeral Arrangements

The instructions of the WBTS don't end, even at death. Note carefully what they are really saying:

> Should he die while disfellowshiped, arrangements for his funeral may be a problem. His Christian relatives may like to have had a talk at the Kingdom Hall...But that would not be fitting for a person expelled from the congregation. If he had been giving evidence of repentance...such as by...attending Christian meetings, some brother's conscience might allow him to give a Bible talk at the funeral home or grave site...However, if the disfellowshiped person had still been advocating false teachings or ungodly conduct, even such a talk would not be appropriate. (WT, 15 September 1981, p. 31.)

Attitude of Relatives Not Living with the Disfellowshipped One

The second situation we need to consider is that involving a disfellowshiped or disassociated relative who is not in the immediate family circle or living at one's home ... Consequently, Christians related to such a disfellowshiped person living outside the home should strive to avoid needless association, even keeping business dealings to a minimum. (WT, 15 September 1981, p. 29.)

The disfellowshiping of a relative does not cancel out natural blood ties. However, it would be well to appreciate that only the contacts absolutely necessary in matters pertaining to family interests should be carried on ... In the case of the disfellowshiped relative who does not live in the same home, contact with him is also kept to what is absolutely necessary. As with secular employment, this contact is limited and even curtailed completely if at all possible ... If courtesies are extended, though, the Christian should make it clear that this will not be a regular practice ... The excommunicated relative should be made to realize that his visits are not now welcomed as they were previously when he was walking correctly with Jehovah ... If all family ties with an excommunicated person were kept as before, in what way could it be said that the brothers were cooperating with the disfellowshiping procedure, which is designed to keep God's visible organization clean? ... Bible principles do not support regular association with relatives who do not live in the same home with a disfellowshiped person ... We should not see how close we can get to relatives who are disfellowshiped from Jehovah's organization, but we should 'quit mixing in company' with them. (WT, 15 July 1963, pp. 443–44.)

But the disfellowshiped relative should be made to appreciate that his status has changed, that he is no longer welcome in the home nor is he a preferred companion ... He (God) also instructs Christians 'never to receive him into their home or say a greeting to him'. If normal social communion between relatives were maintained with this disfellowshiped one, a thing that is not necessary since he lives outside the home, would the Christian be obeying God? ... We must keep in clear focus the fact that the disfellowshiped one's not being able to enjoy the companionship of his Christian relatives is not their fault, as if they were treating him shoddily. They are acting according to...God's principles. The disfellowshiped one himself is responsible for his situation; he has brought it upon himself. Let the burden rest where it belongs...A disfellowshiped person who is repentant can be forgiven and reinstated into the congregation...But until that happens, faithful Christians have an obligation to uphold the disfellowshiping action by avoiding association with the disfellowshiped individual. If that one is a relative living outside the home, they will try to have no fellowship with him at all. (WT, 1 June 1970, p. 352.)

So the disfellowshipped person's relatives turn their backs on him. What of other non-related Jehovah's Witnesses?

Say Hello and You May Be Disfellowshipped

As distinct from some personal 'enemy' or worldly man in authority who opposes Christians, a disfellowshiped or disassociated person who is trying to promote or justify his apostate thinking or is continuing in his ungodly conduct is certainly not one to whom to wish 'Peace'...And we all know from our experience over the years that a simple 'Hello' to someone can be the first step that develops into a conversation and maybe even a friendship. Would we want to take that first step with a disfellowshiped person?...If the elders saw him heading in that direction by regularly keeping company with a disfellowshiped person, they would lovingly and patiently try to help him to regain God's view...But if he will not cease to fellowship with the expelled person, he...must be removed from the congregation, expelled. (WT, 15 September 1981, pp. 25–26.)

Emotional Ties

Naturally, if a close relative is disfellowshiped, human emotions can prove a major test for us. Sentiment and family ties are particularly strong between parents and their children, and they are also powerful when a marriage mate is disfellowshiped. Still we must recognize that, in the final analysis, we will not benefit anyone or please God if we allow emotion to lead us into ignoring His wise counsel and guidance. (WT, 15 September 1981, pp. 31.)

How Many?

The worldwide casualties of this policy of disfellowshipping are,
according to the WBTS's own statistics approximately 100 per
day!

> Shocking as it is, even some who have been prominent in
> Jehovah's organization have succumbed to immoral practices,
> including homosexuality, wife swapping, and child molesting. It is
> to be noted, also, that during the past year, 36,638 individuals had
> to be disfellowshiped from the Christian congregation, the
> GREATER NUMBER of them for practicing immorality. (WT,
> 1 January 1986, p. 13)

Personal Testimony

Bill Browning shares this personal testimony on the subject.

'After twenty-three years as one of Jehovah's Witnesses I
began to recognize that the WBTS had deliberately changed
their version of the Bible so that it fitted more closely to their
doctrinal position. I asked the elders to visit me and 'put me
right', for I was sure that somehow Satan was blinding my mind
(2 Cor 4:4). I had no intention of leaving but simply wanted the
truth. The elders would not look at any of my research material
but simply told me to remain loyal and obedient to Jehovah's
organization.

'I wrote to the British headquarters of the WBTS. The
replies I got didn't answer my questions and certainly didn't
satisfy me. Here are a couple of extracts:

> You will notice how important it is to resist the spirit of this world
> which is characterized by suspicion, mistrust and scepticism. It is
> imperative to watch one's deeper motives. It is equally important
> to keep a positive attitude and remember all the things Jehovah
> has done for us as well as the abundant provision of spiritual food
> made available through the 'faithful and discreet slave' class.
> (Letter from WBTS to F. W. Browning, Ref. EH:SE, dated
> 10 May 1983.)

> It has been our observation that those who promote such
> criticisms tend to ignore the massive evidence of Jehovah's

blessing and guidance, and see only the minor faults that arise because of human imperfection. In some cases they clearly do not want to see the positive side of things, and would seem to be looking for an excuse to quit serving Jehovah. (Letter from WBTS to F. W. Browning, Ref. EJ:SL, dated 20 June 1983.)

'Thus the Society were trying to dissuade me from continuing my research into them. The second letter arrived too late because I accepted the Lord Jesus into my heart as Lord and Saviour with a real 'born again' experience on 7th June 1983.

'Can you imagine being in a situation where you are totally rejected, treated as dead? The WBTS discourages association and friendship with those outside the 'organisation'. So when a person leaves they are treated as a sinner rebelling against God Himself, and not even to be greeted. There is a dramatic change in his family relationship. If all the Watchtower instructions are obeyed he would hardly, if ever, see his relatives living outside the home and much of the normal family social life would be curtailed or stopped completely.

'Under these circumstances people have committed suicide; families have broken up. Imagine the pressure on the Witness wife of the disfellowshipped one. She still loves her husband yet the instructions of the WBTS begin to drive a wedge between their loving relationship. Her husband is no longer welcome in the Witness homes she visits.

'Think of the person who has left. They were deceived for years by a false prophet and are scared to put their trust in another 'denomination'. They are desperate to experience love and kindness. If such a disfellowshipped one visits your church, how would you react?

'Let me conclude with a couple of experiences. First, the occasion I was shopping with my Witness wife in Sutton market. We literally 'bumped' into another Witness lady whom we both knew very well. My wife was still holding my arm as the lady carried on a conversation with her. Every now and again I would insert a 'How are your family?' or 'Have you managed to get everything you came for?' But though I was within two feet of her, my comments were totally ignored, and it was if I didn't exist.

'On the second occasion I was travelling in a fellow Christian's car when I saw a Witness I know. I wound down the window, said 'Hi' and waved. That evening when I returned home I found the following note:

> Bill, I am writing you this note not because I have any sympathy for you whatsoever, but just to let you know that this morning when you passed me and deliberately waved to me it was not a kind acknowledgement on my part but rather erroneously a spontaneous reflex action that you caught me off guard. Unfortunately, it was not until you had passed me that I recognized the unwelcomed face of a traitor. As far as I am concerned you did not gain a victory nor a point as it was not from my heart and Jehovah knows that, so no need for you to rejoice. Simply that at the time I was in deepest thoughts and in haste to catch the train. Please understand that as far as I'm concerned, you are an apostate and a disfellowshiped person and you have identified yourself as being one of the 'evil slave class'. As such then, I have no time for you or anything to do with you. My loyalty is for Jehovah God, Christ Jesus and his earthly organization for the past twenty-two years and will remain as such. You must realize that even when you were a brother, I did not really take to you but for God's sake I put up with you. Now that you have gone, to me you are as one of the nations, so you can hardly expect anything else. Satan has really taken you over and I only hope that I never develop a wicked heart such as yours, losing faith and deviating from the truth. But one could have seen the cut of your jib long ago, missing meetings for months, emotional and mental misbehaviour. And you had the cheek and audacity to criticise me. I hope that you understand and get my point. I am a mature and spiritual brother and witness of Jehovah God showing exactly the Bible's requirement and standards as to how to deal and treat disfellowshiped ones, which you know too. So when you catch other brothers and sisters in deep thought and when they don't expect to see you, there is no feather in your cap. I should have thought with your last humiliation and defeat with the newspapers and supposed talks on JWs you would have kept quiet, but Satan's agents never stop arguing, at least not until Armageddon. And there's no need to reply as it will only end up

in the bin and burnt as the others you have sent. Michael L.

'On the reverse of the note was the comment:

Please tell your Arian companion the contents of this letter. But being such a coward, you probably won't, or twist it to suit yourself.

'Sorry Mike, but I did tell my companion, and as you obviously don't mind me telling others, I've told the world. And to make sure that I cannot be accused of twisting, your note is quoted, in full, as received. I will make no comments as to its contents, although, 'as you must know' I would dearly love to.'

SECTION 10

Blood

Whereas the title of this section is 'blood', the heart of the matter is the WBTS's teaching on blood transfusions. But before we discuss the topic in detail let's trace its history.

History

1909

C. T. Russell, commenting on Acts 15, said:

> It was not intimated that abstinence from these things would MAKE THEM CHRISTIANS, for nothing but faith in Christ and consecration to him and endeavor to walk in his steps could constitute them Christians... The things here recommended were necessary to a preservation of the fellowship of the 'body' composed of Jews and Gentiles... A similar thought attaches to the prohibition of the use of blood. To the Jew it was forbidden... These prohibitions had never come to the Gentiles, because they had never been under the Law Covenant; but so deeply rooted were the Jewish ideas on the subject that it was necessary for the peace of the church that the Gentiles should observe this matter also. (WTR, 15 April 1909, p. 4374.)

1945

WT, 1 July, pp. 198–201, stated that blood transfusions were pagan and God-dishonouring.

1958

The injection of antibodies into the blood in a vehicle of blood serum or the use of blood fractions to create such antibodies is NOT THE SAME as taking blood, either by mouth or by transfusion, as a nutrient to build up the body's vital forces. While God did not intend for any man to contaminate his blood stream by vaccines, serums or blood fractions, doing so does not seem to be included in God's express will forbidding blood as food. It would therefore be a matter of individual judgement whether one accepted such types of medication or not. (WT, 15 September 1958, p. 575.)

1959

According to the method of handling blood prescribed by the Bible, blood when taken from a body was poured out on the ground as water and covered over with dust . . . This is because life is in the blood and such shed blood is held sacred before Jehovah God . . . Consequently, the removal of one's blood, storing it and later putting it back into the same person, would be a violation of the Scriptural principles that govern the handling of blood. (WT, 15 October 1959, p. 640.)

1961

Having a blood transfusion is now a disfellowshipping offence (WT, 15 January 1961, pp. 63–64). Donating organs (eyes) is a matter of conscience (WT, 1 August 1961, p. 480).

1963

Any fraction of blood considered as a nutrient is not to be used in medical treatment.

. . . for it is not just whole blood but anything that is derived from blood and used to sustain life or strengthen one that comes under this principle. (WT, 15 February 1963, p. 124.)

But note, just *five years before* the WBTS had made exceptions in the case of inoculations, where blood serums might be injected (see 1958 quote).

1967

Organ transplants are now considered to be a form of cannibalism and are therefore to be shunned (WT, 15 November 1967, pp. 702–4). However, just *six years before* it was a matter of conscience (see 1961 quote).

1974

Serums are now a matter of conscience but believed to be wrong.

> It can thus be seen that serums (unlike vaccines) contain a blood fraction, though minute... What then of a serum containing only a minute fraction of blood... We believe that here the conscience of each Christian must decide. Some may feel that accepting such a serum does not constitute an act of disrespect... that it does not constitute a flouting of God's expressed will... the conscience of others may call on them to reject all such serums. (WT, 1 June 1974, p. 352.)

Jehovah's Witnesses feel the need for showing 'maturity' in the congregation. Therefore even though this article implies that the decision to use, or not to use, a serum which includes a minute blood fraction is a matter of conscience, in reality the Jehovah's Witness will read that a mature person would rather die than accept something about which they are not 100 per cent certain. The phrases, 'an act of disrespect' and 'a flouting of God's expressed will' give the game away. The article concludes:

> We trust that this review of the Bible principles will be helpful... While refraining from approving or condemning in such areas where we believe the decision must be left to individual conscience, we do, nevertheless, urge all to seek to maintain their conscience clean before God, never showing deliberate disrespect for his Word.

Thus the WBTS attempts to get the person who may feel it all right to have the serum to make sure he hasn't got it wrong.

1977

Blood transfusions arc now considered as organ transplants.

> Consequently, whether having religious objections to blood
> transfusions or not, many a person might decline blood simply
> because it is essentially an organ transplant that at best is only
> partially compatible with his own blood. (*Jehovah's Witnesses and
> the Question of Blood*, 1977, p. 41.)

1978

Taking a serum injection to fight against disease is not a clear-
cut area.

> What, however, about accepting serum injections to fight against
> disease... This seems to fall into a 'gray-area'... we have taken
> the position that this question must be resolved by each individual
> on a personal basis. We urge each one to have a clear conscience
> and to be responsive to God's guidance found in his Word. (WT,
> 15 June 1978, pp. 30–31.)

1980

Organ transplants are now made a matter of conscience.

> Clearly, personal views and conscientious feelings vary on this
> issue of transplantation... there is no Biblical command pointedly
> forbidding the taking in of other human tissue. For this reason,
> each individual faced with making a decision on this matter should
> carefully and prayerfully weigh matters and then decide
> conscientiously what he or she could or could not do before God.
> (WT, 15 March 1980, p. 31.)

Only three years earlier blood transfusions were rejected on the
basis that they were organ transplants! See also 1967 quote.

1984

Bone-marrow transplant is now a matter of conscience. However, as noted before, the way the WBTS argue the matter
would lead a correctly trained conscience to say, no.

...red blood cells are formed in the marrow of certain bones...it is understandable why, in the light of the Bible's prohibition on blood, the question arises whether a Christian could accept a graft of human bone marrow...since red blood cells originate in the red bone marrow, do the Scriptures class marrow with blood? No. In fact, animal marrow is spoken of like any other flesh that could be eaten. Isaiah 25:6...'well-oiled dishes filled with marrow'... Of course, marrow used in human marrow transplants is from live donors, and the withdrawn marrow may have some blood in it. Hence, the Christian would have to resolve for himself whether— to him—the bone-marrow graft would amount to simple flesh or unbled tissue...Finally...Dr. D. E. Thomas observes that 'virtually all marrow transplant recipients will require platelet transfusions' and may be given 'packed red blood cells.'... Though a personal decision has to be made on this matter, the Bible's comments about blood and marrow should help the individual to decide. (WT, 15 May 1984, p. 31.)

Note that the WBTS are now linking the use of blood from the marrow to eating and are seeming to say that this is all right. But for years they've said that accepting blood transfusions is wrong on the basis that it's eating blood.

1977

'You must not eat the blood of any sort of flesh, because the soul of every sort of flesh is its blood. Anyone eating it will be cut off.'...By not eating the blood, but 'pouring it out' on the altar or on the ground, the Israelite was, in effect, returning the creature's life to God. For an Israelite to show disregard for life as represented by the blood was viewed as a most serious wrong. The person deliberately disregarding this law about blood was to be 'cut off', executed...A measure of guilt resulted even from eating the blood-containing flesh of an animal that died of itself or that was killed by a wild beast...Does this proper aversion to blood apply to human blood also? Yes. And that is altogether under-standable for God's law prohibited consuming 'any sort of blood', 'the blood of any sort of flesh' (Lev 17:10, 14). (*Jehovah's Witnesses and the Question of Blood*, 1977, pp. 7-10.)

These quotes concerning blood-related issues serve to show

how strongly the WBTS feel about this subject. However, they also reveal confusion on the issue of bone-marrow transplants. They imply that they are the same as eating flesh and therefore a matter of conscience, but surely that can be linked to cannibalism as the WBTS saw it in 1967.

Bill Cetnar, in his book, *Questions for Jehovah's Witnesses*, reveals yet another problem related to the blood transfusion issue that arose in the past—that is whether or not children should be permitted to have smallpox vaccinations.

1931

> Vaccination is a direct violation of the Everlasting Covenant that God made with Noah after the flood. (*Golden Age*, 4 February 1931, p. 293.)

1935

> As vaccination is a direct injection of animal matter in the blood stream vaccination is a direct violation of the law of Jehovah God. (*Golden Age*, 24 April 1935, p. 465.)

Bill Cetnar visited the Lederle laboratories where smallpox vaccine was made. He discovered that the vaccine was made by a process called 'avianization' and did not involve blood at all. The ban on smallpox vaccinations had caused terrible problems for parents because they needed a smallpox certificate before their child could start school. To obey 'God's organization', Witness parents had taken their children to sympathetic doctors who scarred their leg with acid and signed a certificate. Witness missionaries also produced a certificate from 'somewhere' in order to leave the country. Witnesses in prison as conscientious objectors faced the same problem—be vaccinated or spend your days in solitary confinement. Therefore to solitary confinement they went.

When Bill Cetnar sent a memo to the Watchtower president concerning his discovery at the laboratories it was not acknowledged. However, in a letter dated 15 April 1952 the decision to oppose smallpox vaccinations was reversed.

> The matter of vaccination is one for the individual who has to face it to decide for himself...Hence all objection to vaccination on Scriptural grounds seems to be lacking.

With this new ruling, A. H. Macmillian tried to get Witnesses in solitary confinement to have the vaccination. In his book, *Faith on the March*, he records that it took him about two hours to get the men to reverse their stand (see *Questions for Jehovah's Witnesses*, pp. 53–54 and *Faith on the March*, pp. 188–90).

Blood Transfusions

We must look now at why the WBTS are so totally against blood transfusions. They claim that their reasoning is based on the following Scriptures: Genesis 9:4—'Don't eat blood', a law given to Noah and as we all come from Noah, a law for all mankind; Leviticus 17:10—an established Israelite law which if broken warranted death; Acts 15:28–29—the law was also a Christian command.

Blood transfusion is said to be *the same as eating* but by a quicker method. (*Jehovah's Witnesses and the Question of Blood*, 1977, pp. 17–18.)

> Christians are commanded to 'abstain from blood'...the eating of blood is equated with idolatry and fornication, things that we should not want to engage in. (*Reasoning*, pp. 70–71.)

As blood transfusions are regarded as eating blood there must be no blood transfusions.

An Alternative View

Genesis 9:3–4

> Every moving thing that is alive shall be food for you; I give it all to you, as I gave the green plant. Only you shall not eat flesh with its life, that is, its blood.

A straight reading of these verses leads to the correct understanding that though they could now eat meat, it had to be dead, without life left in it. The WBTS themselves make this connection, even if accidentally.

> Jehovah God the Creator is responsible for the existence of all flesh, and for its life... Originally, vegetation and fruit, and not flesh, were given man as his diet. But after the Flood God added animal flesh, commanding, however, that 'flesh with its soul—its blood—you must not eat' Gen[esis] 9:3–4. Cannibalism, the eating of human flesh, naturally was repugnant to the human mind, was abhorred by God and his ancient covenant people Israel. (ABU, p. 587.)

The Matthew Poole Commentary, p. 23, tells us that Genesis 9:4 means, 'while it lives' and the *Jamieson, Fausset and Brown Commentary*, p. 7, says it means 'eating flesh of living animals'. The text also deals with *animal* blood, not human blood.

If this verse means that the actual blood contained life, then every time we have a nose bleed, or sustain a cut, we lose some of our life. What of the dentist who spills blood when pulling a tooth? Is he guilty of breaking God's law and deserving of death?

Leviticus 17:10

> And any man from the house of Israel, or from the aliens who sojourn among them, who eats any blood, I will set My face against that person who eats blood, and will cut him off from among his people.

The WBTS tell us they are no longer under Mosaic law, yet they continue to use that law in this instance. However, the law respecting blood states:

> It is a perpetual statute throughout your generation in all your dwellings: you shall not eat ANY FAT or any blood. (Lev 3:17.)

Do the WBTS teach no fat along with no blood? They certainly do not.

A second point to make is that 'cut off' cannot mean put to death. 1 Samuel 14:32–35 gives a clear example of this. The blood laws were broken but no one was put to death.

We need also to read Leviticus 17:11:

> FOR THE LIFE OF THE FLESH IS IN THE BLOOD, and I have given it to you on the altar to make atonement for your souls; for it is the blood by reason of the life that makes atonement.

The animals sacrificed on the altar, and especially the Passover Lamb, symbolized the coming of Jesus, 'the Lamb of God who takes away the sin of the world' (John 1:29).

Hebrews 9:20 says if there's no shed blood, there's no forgiveness. After Jesus shed His blood there were to be no more animal sacrifices on the altar, to make atonement, else we would be saying that Christ's death was not sufficient. So sacrifices passed away along with the 'pouring out of blood' (Lev 17:13).

> By this will we have been sanctified through the offering of the body of Jesus Christ once for all. And every priest stands daily ministering and offering time after time the same sacrifices, which can never take away sins; but He [Jesus Christ], having offered one sacrifice for sins for all time, sat down at the right hand of God... (Heb 10:10–12.)

Acts 15:28–29

> ... lay upon you no greater burden than these essentials: that you abstain... from blood.

Because the gospel at first was preached mainly to the Jews, the early Christians were converted Jews.

> The new Society was at first 'an Israel within Israel'. 'The prayers' (RV) were those of the Temple (Acts 3:1), which these Jewish Christians attended constantly for public devotions. They did not

cut loose from the wonted forms of Jewish piety...the atmosphere is still quite Jewish—the church would seem to be as yet merely one of those associations which from time to time arose and kept within the limits of the Hebrew religion...even very many priests becoming obedient to the faith...To their continued observance of the strict Hebrew ritual, these lower priests added belief in Jesus as 'the Christ'. The Christian church could still be thought of as a school or sect of Judaism—an error that was to have serious results. (J. Auley Steele and A. J. Campbell, *The Story of the Church*, 1934, pp. 28,31.)

The conversion of so many Gentiles soon raised serious problems as to how far these new converts ought to be bound by the laws and ceremonies of the Jewish Church. Those known as Judaizers wanted the Gentiles to be circumcised, i.e. to become Jews first; thereafter they might become Christians, but Christians with a strong Jewish tinge. (A. M. Renwick, *The Story of the Church*, 1958, p. 13.)

The above quotes give a clue as to just why the circumcision issue, as recorded in Acts 15, became a problem. It was to obtain a decision concerning circumcision that Paul and Barnabas travelled to the elders at Jerusalem. Among the elders there was James of whom it is said:

These elders at Jerusalem soon received considerable authority within the church...Beyond their authority, James, the Lord's brother, also assumed a personal prominence...In Acts 15 his voice is decisive in discussion. In Acts 21, some seven years later, he appears in a position of primacy similar to that which tradition assigns him. (*The Pickering Bible Commentary for Today*, p. 155.)

Also discussing the authorship of the Letter of James the above commentary notes:

But in the Acts and letters there is a James who stands out prominently, a pillar of the church in Jerusalem, whose position and character exactly suit the author of the letter. Though not one of the Twelve, he was the leader of judaic Christianity. (p. 1614.)

The WBTS date Galatians as written around AD 50–52 and Acts around AD 61. *The Pickering Bible Commentary for Today* dates Galatians as around AD 48 and Acts around AD 62 to 64, with the circumcision debate as AD 47 to 48. The reason we draw attention to these dates is because Paul, in his Letter to the Galatians, accused certain men from James with hypocrisy: 'they were not straightforward about the truth of the Gospel.' In fact Paul called them 'false brethren, who...spy out our liberty...[and] bring us into bondage'. The bondage was to laws, which Paul said neither saved nor justified (see Galatians 1:6–7,10–17; 2:4–16; 3:1; 5:4). This then was Paul's view of the Judaizers from Jerusalem, at the time of his visit in Acts 15. It therefore throws light upon just why 'these essentials' were laid upon the Gentiles.

To be fair, Acts 21:20 does tell us, 'How many thousands there are among the Jews of those who have believed, and they are all zealous for the Law'. Therefore it is possible that the main direction of these 'essentials' was to try to prevent division between the Judaistic Christians and the newly converted Gentiles: to seek to prevent the Jewish Christians from stumbling as a result of things that their Gentile brothers, who had never been under the law, might do.

The conflict of backgrounds is important to our understanding of 'these essentials', including the blood issue. It was the beginning of the changeover from a Jewish Christian gospel, with Jewish Christians still observing Jewish rituals, to the influx of Gentiles who surprised and shocked the Jewish Christians. The Gentiles had no interest in keeping the old rituals which had never applied to them. If we examine in sequence the way 'these essentials' came into existence, we gain further understanding of the attitudes of the Jerusalem elders and of Paul.

Acts 15:7 records the start of a great debate; in verses 13,19–21 James makes a decision; verse 22 describes what seemed a good idea; verses 23–29 record the written letter. Note that though this was the judgement of James, upheld by the rest, in verse 28 they claim the guidance of the Holy Spirit.

Acts 21:21–22 describing events some seven years later,

shows that circumcision is again the issue; in verses 23–24 Paul is told to show unity; verse 25 records that *we wrote* the letter re 'these essentials'. Note that this time there is no mention of the Holy Spirit. So isn't it possible that 'these essentials', even if given with the right motive, probably originated with the attitude of Judaistic Christians to bring the Gentiles into line, rather than being inspired of God?

What of Blood Transfusions?

Certainly the pouring out of blood is now unnecessary because that which it symbolized, the perfect sacrifice of Christ, has been made. We must not forget either that Jesus has already given a ruling concerning legalistic dietary rules:

> 'Listen to Me, all of you, and understand: there is nothing outside the man which going into him can defile him; but the things which proceed out of the man are what defile the man...' (Thus He declared all foods clean.) (Mark 7:14–19.)

As the WBTS stress that transfusing blood is the same as eating it, let's also recall Paul's words:

> But food will not commend us to God; we are neither the worse if we do not eat, nor the better if we do eat. (1 Cor 8:8.)

As in everything, we stand before Almighty God in our own conscience as to whether we believe a thing is right or wrong. Some refuse certain medicines, while others don't. Some might want to refuse blood transfusions on the grounds of contamination, but that's a free choice. Remember, however, that Genesis 9:5–6 commands us to be responsible for our own life and the lives of others. Might that not actually suggest that we use the best medical help available to save someone from dying, including blood transfusions? Certainly we can say with assurance that there is *nothing* in the Bible that forbids blood transfusions.

The WBTS judge what Jehovah's Witnesses can and cannot do. WT, 15 January 1961, p. 64, says, '...if in the future he

persists in accepting blood transfusions or in donating blood...
he must be cut off therefrom by disfellowshiping.' A sad example
of this was reported in *The Concorde Monitor*, (New
Hampshire, USA) on 8 December 1984. A terminal cancer
patient was interrogated by Jehovah's Witness elders and then
disfellowshipped on his deathbed because he accepted a blood
transfusion.

Back to the Law

The WBTS claim that their 'Governing Body' is modelled on
the one in Jerusalem. But we've seen what had happened to this
so-called 'governing body'—they went back to Judaism.

> The Jerusalem Council was a failure. It outlined a consensus but
> could not make it work in practice. Paul could not be controlled.
> Nor, presumably, could others. Nor could the 'pillars' of the
> centre party maintain their authority even in Jerusalem. They
> slipped back into Judaism. (Paul Johnson, *A History of
> Christianity*, p. 44.)

The fact that 'Paul could not be controlled' is shown in
Scripture. Paul and Barnabas went to *complain* to the elders in
Jerusalem (Acts 15:1–2) about some causing problems to
newborn Christians by preaching 'another gospel' of adherence
to the law of Moses (see Galatians 1:6; 2:4,11–14). The elders
contributed nothing to Paul (Gal 2:6) which is a very strange
way of governing! Paul and Barnabas did not take the letter
from the elders (Acts 15:22) but two men were appointed to
read it. The elders simply *requested* that Paul and Barnabas
should remember the poor (Gal 2:10).

The Letter to the Hebrews, written to Christian Jews, says
some interesting things which would not make sense unless they
were directed at Christians who had slipped back into Judaism.
Why would the writer stress that animal sacrifices were no
longer necessary unless these Christian Jews hadn't totally
accepted Christ's once for all sacrifice?

> For it was fitting that we should have such a high priest, holy,
> innocent, undefiled, separated from sinners and exalted above
> the heavens; WHO DOES NOT NEED DAILY, like those high priests, TO
> OFFER UP SACRIFICES . . . When He said, 'A new covenant', He has
> made the first obsolete . . . But when Christ appeared as a high
> priest of the good things to come, He entered through the greater
> and more perfect tabernacle . . . not through the blood of goats
> and calves, but through His own blood . . . nor was it that he should
> offer Himself often, as the high priest enters the holy place year by
> year with blood not his own . . . but He, having offered one
> sacrifice for sins for all time, sat down at the right hand of
> God . . . (verses from Hebrews 7—10.)

It is fact that some Jewish Christians continued to preach
circumcision even though it was against freedom in Christ. It is
also possible that some continued to offer sacrifices.

One thing that is certain is that the WBTS have missed the
point of the sacrifice of Jesus Christ by their insistence that
blood be poured out before meat can be eaten. The pouring out
of the blood was in respect of the coming sacrifice of Christ.

> For the law, since it has only a shadow of the good things to come
> and not the very form of things, can never by the same sacrifice
> year by year, which they offer continually, make perfect those
> who draw near. (Heb 10:1.)

It also seems clear that the 'governing body' in Jerusalem
didn't do anything to try to prevent the thousands of Jews being
'zealous for the law' (Acts 21:20). This caused Paul to say, 'You
have been severed from Christ, you are seeking to be justified
by law' (Gal 5:4).

The 'Governing Body' of the WBTS, like the 'governing
body' at Jerusalem, appear to be guilty of going back to Old
Testament law rather than preaching the sacrifice of Jesus
Christ *once for all time*. There is no salvation in adherence to
the law, only in a relationship with Christ.

> Christ . . . Himself bore our sins in His body on the cross, that we
> might die to sin and live to righteousness. (1 Pet 2:21,24.)

Come to Me, all who are weary and heavy-laden, and I will give you rest. (Matt 11:28.)

Paul asked the Galatians, 'Who has bewitched you?' (Gal 3:1). Even if the WBTS have bewitched you, the promise of Almighty God Jehovah remains:

And they will have to know that I am Jehovah when I break the bars of their yoke and I have delivered them out of the hand of those who had been using them as slaves. (Ezek 34:27, NWT.)

You will know the truth, and the truth will set you free... Therefore if the Son sets you free, you will actually be free. (John 8:32,36, NWT.)

The Cross

This article first appeared in *Bethel Ministries Newsletter,* March/April 1986, and has been reproduced with the kind permission of R. Watters. The parts included in [[ ]] have been added mainly to show the arguments found in *Reasoning*.

Did Jesus Die on a Cross?

Although the Christian church has never considered the exact method of Jesus' crucifixion or impalement a major concern, the WBTS have certainly made an issue of it. In doing so they hold true to their pattern of majoring in minor issues, often distracting their followers from the real issues. When one examines the record of the WBTS from the time of its second president (J. F. Rutherford) forward, it appears that there is a steady pattern of attempts to set themselves apart from the church systems by majoring in minors.

The WBTS consider the churches as 'unclean' for using the cross as a symbol of the death of Jesus. Although we agree that worship of the cross or any other symbol is wrong, the use of a symbol for illustrative purposes has never been wrong, either in the New or the Old Testament records. Cherubs (angels) were embroidered on the curtains of the tabernacle in Moses' time (Ex 26:1). The WBTS's use of a watch-tower as their symbol is an example. Yet the WBTS often cloud issues by stretching their point too far. In this study we will examine their claims regarding the method of Christ's death from three different perspectives: what the WBTS say, what archaeology and historical records tell us, and finally what the Bible itself says regarding the issue.

What the WBTS Has Said

Up until the late 30s the WBTS pictured Christ dying on the traditional cross. On p. 114 of *The Harp of God* (1921) Jesus is pictured as dying on a cross. Several WT magazines of the early 1900s had crosses on the front covers. [[One even told us the weight of the cross!

> When we think of THE CROSS, too, we believe that it was of no light weight . . . THE CROSS . . . must have been at least twelve to fourteen feet long, and the CROSS-BEAM must have been at least five feet . . . we would think that THE CROSS must have weighed from one hundred and fifty to two hundred pounds. (ZWTR, 15 April 1913, p. 5221.)]]

They did not consider it as an object of worship then, but rather a symbol of the death and victory of Christ over the world and the Devil. However, while later eliminating the cross as well as the name of Jesus on their front cover, they continued to use a watch-tower as their symbol.

Then in 1936 the book *Riches* stated that Jesus was not crucified on a cross but on a tree. In 1937 Rutherford began making an issue of the cross, saying that Christ died on an upright stake, and that churches were corrupt for using a 'pagan' object as a centre of attention. In the book *Enemies* he attacks the traditional story of the cross as wrong because

> The Cross was worshipped by the Pagan Celts long before the [birth] and death of Christ. (pp. 188–89.)

With no accompanying historical or archaeological evidence to support their new position, Rutherford stated his new doctrine as fact, and supported it with an irrelevant 'proof'. Actually, what pagans did with crosses before the death of

Christ has nothing to do with how the Romans crucified people. Besides, Jesus did not choose his instrument of death.

[[The WBTS continue to use this argument today. *Reasoning,* p. 90, asks, 'What were the historical origins of Christendom's cross?' Their first quote, in answer, is from the EB Vol. 6, 1946, p. 753, showing that the cross was used as a religious symbol in pre-Christian times by non-Christian peoples. They miss out the following part:

> **The death of Christ on the cross necessarily** CONFERRED A NEW SIGNIFICANCE **on the figure, which had hitherto been associated with a conception of religion not merely non-Christian but in essence often opposed to it.**]]

As years went by, 'proof' was supplied to substantiate their claim. In 1950, with the release of the NWT, the appendix (pp. 768–71) first argues that the Greek words *stauros* (Matt 10:38) and *xylon* (Acts 5:30) do not mean a cross, and that these words only mean an upright stake without a crossbeam. They said that there is no proof to the contrary. A woodcut is then presented from a sixteenth-century book, '*De Cruce Liber Primus*' (in 1984 corrected to *De Cruce Libri Tres*), by Justus Lipsius, picturing a man on an upright stake. The WBTS add immediately: 'This is the manner in which Jesus was impaled.' They then refer to an article in the Catholic *Ecclesiastical Review* of 1920 that states that the cross was not used until after AD 312 as the sign of crucifixion.

The above mentioned appendix goes on to state:

> Rather than consider the torture stake upon which Jesus was impaled a relic to be worshiped, the Jewish Christians like Simon Peter would consider it to be an abominable thing.

They then quote Paul's reference to Deuteronomy 21:22–23 at Galatians 3:13 to prove that the cross was an abomination. They continue:

> Hence the Jewish Christians would hold as accursed and hateful the stake upon which Jesus had been executed.

The WBTS make their final point in stating:

> The evidence is, therefore, completely lacking that Jesus Christ
> was crucified on two pieces of timber placed at a right angle. We
> refuse to add anything to God's written Word by inserting the
> pagan cross into the inspired Scriptures, but render *stauros* and
> *xylon* according to the simplest meanings... The passing of time
> and further archaeological discoveries will be certain to prove its
> correctness. Even now the burden rests upon all who contend for
> the religious tradition to prove that Jesus died on more than a
> simple stake.

Much the same information was contained in the appendix
of the 1969 KIT, the 1984 NWT Reference Bible and the 1985
revision of the KIT. The 1985 edition adds comments by VINE
that support the view that pagans before the time of Christ used
the symbol T representing the babylonish god Tammuz, and
that this practice apparently influenced the Catholic Church in
the issue of cross worship. Vine claims that the 'apostate' church
adapted the symbol of the cross as a hold-over from paganism.

ABU, p. 1609, adds one comment by John Denham Parsons
who wrote *The Non-Christian Cross:*

> There is not a single sentence in any of the numerous writings
> forming the New Testament, which, in the original Greek, bears
> even indirect evidence to the effect that the *stauros* used in the
> case of Jesus was other than an ordinary *stauros;* much less to the
> effect that it consisted, not of one piece of timber, but of two
> pieces nailed together in the form of a cross.

[[*Reasoning,* p. 91, also quotes from *The Non-Christian
Cross.* However, they do not add what Parsons admits on p. 17
of the same book:

> That this last named kind of *stauros* which was admittedly that to
> which Jesus was affixed, had in every case a cross-bar attached, is
> untrue; that it had in most cases, is UNLIKELY; that it had in the
> case of Jesus, is UNPROVEN.

In other words, there is *no proof* and this makes the conclusion that the WBTS reach, 'Thus the weight of evidence indicates that Jesus died on an upright stake and not on the traditional cross' (*Reasoning,* p. 90), a nonsense.]]

Considering their statements, the WBTS objections consist of four major points:

1. The biblical Greek does not suggest a cross.
2. The cross was a pagan symbol later adopted by the 'apostate' church.
3. Archaeology proves that Jesus died on an upright stake rather than a cross.
4. The cross is to be shunned rather than mentioned or displayed.

What is the scholarly response to these claims?

What the Greek Says

The Greek *stauros* has the primary meaning of a pole or stake, as the WBTS point out. What they don't mention is that the word often refers to more complex constructions, such as the cross. The Latin word *crux*, usually translated 'cross', was also at times used to refer to a mere stake. What the WBTS specifically ignore is that the Romans plainly did execute prisoners on crosses—an issue they are careful to side-step in their presentation. The horizontal bar of such crosses was called the 'patibulum', and slaves to be executed were customarily made to carry the 'patibulum' to the place of execution (*Biblical Quarterly,* Vol. 13, No. 4, p. 442).

Authoritative lexicons give the definition of *stauros* as a 'stake sunk into the earth in an upright position; a cross-piece was often attached to its upper part.' (*A Greek-English Lexicon,* Arndt and Gingrich, p. 772.) The *New International Dictionary of New Testament Theology,* which the WBTS often quote, says this about *stauros:*

Corresponding to the v[er]b *(stauroo)* which was more common, *stauros* can mean a stake which was sometimes pointed on which an executed criminal was publicly displayed in shame as further punishment. It could be used for hanging...impaling, or strangulation. *Stauros* could also be an instrument of torture, perhaps in the sense of the Lat[in] 'patibulum', a cross-beam laid on the shoulders. Finally it could be an instrument of execution in the form of a vertical stake and a cross-beam of the same length forming a cross in the narrower sense of the term. It took the form either of a T (Lat[in] *crux commissa*) or of a + *(crux immissa)*... The exact technical form and significance of execution are not conveyed by the words *stauros* and *(ana)stauroo,* without further definition. In order to determine this, it is necessary to know in what region and under what authority the execution was carried out. It is also necessary to know the standpoint of the writer who uses the term. (Vol. 1, p. 391.)

The Greek word *xylon* can mean 'wood, a piece of wood, or anything made of wood', and can refer to a cross as well, as pointed out in VINE, Vol. 4, p. 153.

Stauros and *xylon* can both be used to refer to a cross, a fact carefully side-stepped by the WBTS in their effort to prove their point. The WBTS fail to prove anything with regard to the Greek *stauros* and *xylon*. We must therefore look to the historical record for decisive proof.

Historical and Archaeological Evidence for the Cross

The WBTS have been quite deceptive over the years in their use of the woodcut illustration by Justus Lipsius. In the 1950 and 1969 editions of the NWT they reproduced one of the sixteen woodcut illustrations by Lipsius, choosing the one that pictures a man impaled on an upright stake and failing to mention that there are fifteen other illustrations, most of which picture various crucifixions on crosses. The most amazing thing of all is that they could make a statement such as 'evidence is completely lacking' that Jesus was crucified on a cross, when the very book they use as 'proof' to support their claims says Jesus died on a cross! A partial translation of the Latin text alongside a woodcut of a crucifixion on a cross is:

> In the Lord's cross there were four pieces of wood, the upright beam, the crossbar, a tree trunk (piece of wood) placed below, and the title (inscription) placed above.

The earlier (1950 and 1969) editions of the NWT, after referring to Lipsius's picture of a man on an upright stake stated, 'This is the manner on which Jesus was impaled.' They thereby attempted to convey the idea that Lipsius's book was proving their point. Since then the exposure of the WBTS's dishonesty forced them to leave this statement out of the 1984 and 1985 versions of the NWT; but they *still* use Lipsius's illustration to make their point, while failing to tell the real story! It is obvious that they are being knowingly dishonest in this matter.

Furthermore, the WBTS's reference to the *Ecclesiastical Review* is of no current value, being written in 1920, since further archaeological finds clearly contradict the Catholic statement.

This brings up another very embarrassing issue for the WBTS—that of recent archaeological finds. In the earlier editions (1950 and 1969) of the NWT they had said,

> The passing of time and further archaeological discoveries will be certain to prove its correctness. Even now the burden rests upon all who contend for the religious tradition to prove that Jesus died on more than a simple stake.

Now we will see why they have omitted this statement from the 1984 and 1985 versions of the NWT.

Buried History, Vol. 9, No. 2, p. 41, pictured a satirical graffito, dating shortly after AD 200, taken from the walls of the Roman Palatine. It depicted a crucified ass, which is intended as a mockery of a Christian prisoner who worships Christ. The Romans were no doubt amused that Christians worshipped this Jesus whom they had crucified on a cross.

In June 1968, bulldozers working north of Jerusalem accidently laid bare tombs dating from the first century BC and the first century AD. Israeli archaeologist Vasilius Tzaferis was instructed by the Israeli Department of Antiquities to carefully excavate the tombs. Subsequently one of the most exciting finds of recent times was unearthed—the first skeletal remains of a crucified man. The most significant factor is its dating to around the time of Christ. The skeleton was of a man named Yehohanan son of Chaggol, who had been crucified between the age of twenty-four and twenty-eight. Mr Tzaferis, an Israeli (not a Christian) wrote an article in the January/February 1985 issue of the secular *Biblical Archaeological Review* (BAR). Here are some of his comments regarding the method of crucifixion used in the time of Jesus:

> At the end of the first century BC, the Romans adopted crucifixion as an official punishment for non-Romans for certain limited transgressions. Initially, it was employed not as a method of execution, but only as a punishment. Moreover, only slaves convicted of certain crimes were punished for crucifixion. During this early period, a wooden beam known as a 'furca' or 'patibulum' was placed on the slave's neck and bound to his arms. The slave was then required to march through the neighbourhood proclaiming his offence. This march was intended as an expiation and humiliation. Later, the slave was also stripped and scourged, increasing both the punishment and the humiliation. Still later, instead of walking with the arms tied to the wooden beam, the slave was tied to a vertical stake... Once a defendant was found guilty and was condemned to be crucified, the execution was supervised by an official known as the Carnifix Serarum. From the tribunal hall, the victim was taken outside, stripped, bound to a column and scourged. The scourging was done with either a stick or 'flagellum', a Roman instrument with a short handle to which several long, thick thongs had been attached. On the ends of the leather thongs were lead or bone tips. Although the number of strokes imposed was not fixed, care was taken not to kill the victim. Following the beating, the horizontal beam was placed upon the condemned man's shoulders, and he began the long, gruelling march to the execution site, usually outside the city walls. A soldier at the head of the procession carried the 'titulus', an inscription written on wood, which stated the defendant's name and the crime for which he had been condemned. Later, this 'titulus' was fastened to the victim's cross. When the procession arrived at the execution site, a vertical stake was fixed into the ground.

Sometimes the victim was attached to the cross only with ropes. In such a case, the 'patibulum' or cross-beam, to which the victim's arms were already bound, was simply affixed to the vertical beam; the victim's feet were then bound to the stake with a few turns of the rope . . . If the victim was attached by nails, he was laid on the ground, with his shoulders on the cross-beam. His arms were held out and nailed to the two ends of the cross-beam, which was then raised and fixed on top of the vertical beam. The victim's feet were then nailed down against this vertical stake . . . In order to prolong the agony, Roman executioners devised two instruments that would keep the victim alive on the cross for extended periods of time. One known as a 'sedile', was a small seat attached to the front of the cross, about halfway down. This device provided some support for the victim's body and may explain the phrase used by the Romans, 'to sit on the cross'. Both Erenaeus and Justin Martyr describe the cross of Jesus as having five extremities rather than four; the fifth was probably the 'sedile'. (pp. 48–49.)

In a follow-up article on this archaeological find in the November/December issue of BAR, this statement is made on p. 21:

According to the (Roman) literary sources, those condemned to crucifixion never carried the complete cross, despite the common belief to the contrary and despite the many modern re-enactments of Jesus' walk to Golgotha. Instead, only the crossbar was carried, while the upright was set in a permanent place where it was used for subsequent executions. As the first-century Jewish historian Josephus noted, wood was so scarce in Jerusalem during the first century AD that the Romans were forced to travel ten miles from Jerusalem to secure timber for their siege machinery.

According to anthropologist Joseph Zias and Eliezer Sekeles from the Hebrew University's Hadassah Medical School, who continued research on the crucified man:

One can reasonably assume that the scarcity of wood may have been expressed in the economics of crucifixion in that the crossbar as well as the upright would be used repeatedly. (BAR, November/December 1985, p. 21.)

Similar are the details mentioned under 'Cross' in *The Dictionary of New Testament Theology* (often quoted by the WBTS):

It is certain only that the Romans practised this form of execution. But it is more likely that the *stauros* had a transverse in the form of a cross-beam. Secular sources do not permit any conclusion to be drawn as to the precise form of the cross, as to whether it was *crux immissa* + or *crux commissa* T. As it was not very common to affix a titlos (superscription, loan-word from the Latin *titulus*), it does not necessarily follow that the cross had the form of a *crux immissa*. There were two possible ways of erecting the *stauros*. The condemned man could be fastened to the cross lying on the ground at the place of execution, and so lifted up on the cross. Alternatively, it was probably usual to have the stake implanted in the ground before the execution. The victim was tied to the cross-piece, and was hoisted up with the horizontal beam and made fast to the vertical stake. As this was the simpler form of erection, and the carrying of the cross-beam *(patibulum)* was probably connected with the punishment for slaves, the *crux commissa* may be taken as the normal practice. The cross would probably have been not much higher than the height of a man...
According to Roman practice, the procedure for crucifixion would be as follows. First, there was the legal conviction. Only in extraordinary cases, such as in times of war, did this occur at the place of sentencing, the condemned man carried the *patibulum* to the spot which was usually outside the town. The expression 'to bear the cross *(stauros)*' which is a typical description of the punishment of slaves has its origin here. At the place of execution the victim was stripped and scourged. This practice was an important part of crucifixion which took place between sentencing and execution. The condemned man was tied with outstretched arms to the cross-beam which was presumably laid upon his shoulders. Nailing is testified to only in isolated instances... It is uncertain whether this was done to the feet as well as the hands. (In the post-resurrection narratives of Jesus' appearances, John 20:20,25ff. mentions Jesus' hands, and Luke 24:39 his hands and feet.) The victim was then hoisted on to the stake with the cross-beam. Death came slowly after extraordinary agony, probably through exhaustion or suffocation. The body could be left on the scaffold to rot or provide food for predatory

animals and carrion-crows. There is evidence that the body was occasionally given to relatives or acquaintances. (Vol.1, pp. 392-93.)

Extensive statements like these found in the very books that the WBTS like to quote from reveal the nature of their methods. Their Writing Department library contains one of the most extensive collections of religious books in the world. From the data base, they look high and low to find a quote that appears to agree with their position, while overlooking the mountains of evidence to the contrary in the more accepted works. They will overlook dozens of books that refute their position and quote one that agrees with them (or is made to appear in agreement), and then use an oddball reference to make their point. To the average Witness who is not aware of this technique, they appear to be presenting sound scholarship, and their conclusions are seldom if ever questioned.

Other Archaeological Finds

Aside from the most recent discoveries, there are a few others of interest we will note. Here is one involving a discovery in 1873:

In 1873 a famous French scholar, Charles Clermant-Ganneau, reported the discovery of a burial chamber or cave on the Mount of Olives. Inside were some 30 ossuaries—rectangular chests made of stone in which skeletal remains were preserved after their bodies had disintegrated...One [ossuary] had the name 'Judah' associated with a cross with the arms of equal length. Further, the name 'Jesus' occurred three times, twice in association with a cross...It would have been unlikely that Christian Jews would have been buried in that area after 135 AD since the Romans forbade Jews to enter Aelia Capitolina...after the second Jewish revolt. (*Ancient Times,* Vol. 3, No. 1, July 1958, p. 3.)

In 1939 excavations at Herculaneum, the sister city of Pompeii (destroyed in AD 78 by volcano) produced a house where a wooden cross had been nailed to the wall of a room.

Below this (cross) was a cupboard with a step in front. This was considered to be in the shape of an arc or shrine, but could well have been used as a place of prayer...If this interpretation is correct, and the excavators are strongly in favour of the Christian significance of symbol and furnishings, then we have the example of an early house church. (*Buried History,* Vol. 10, No. 1, March 1974, p. 15.)

In 1945 a family tomb was discovered in Jerusalem by Professor E. L. Sukenik of the Museum of Jewish Antiquities of the Hebrew University. Professor Sukenik is the world's leading authority on Jewish ossuaries. Note his findings:

Two of the ossuaries bear the name 'Jesus' in Greek...The second of these also has four large crosses drawn...(Professor Sukenik) concluded that the full inscriptions and the crosses were related, being expressions of grief at the crucifixion of Jesus, being written about that time...Professor Sukenik points out... [that] the cross may represent a 'pictorial expression of the crucifixion, tantamount to exclaiming "He was crucified!"' As the tomb is dated by pottery, lamps and the character of the letters used in the inscriptions—from the first century BC to not later than the middle of the first century AD—this means that the inscriptions fall within two decades of the crucifixion at the latest. (*Ancient Times,* Vol. 3, No. 1, July 1958, pp. 3–5; see also Vol. 5, No. 3, March 1961, p. 13.)

So while the WBTS have made use of obscure and long-outdated sources in an attempt to prove their point, the bulk of the historical finds as well as the most recent of excavations reveal substantial proof for the traditional crucifixion story, so long held by the churches. Yet, even though removing some of their proud claims from recent publications, the Governing Body of the WBTS have not made their followers aware of the more recent discoveries.

[[Before we pass on to the biblical aspect we should mention that in answer to the question, 'Why do Watch Tower publications show Jesus on a stake with hands over his head instead of on the traditional cross?' (*Reasoning,* p. 89) the WBTS mention another publication. Here again we add in **bold type** the part they've left out.

The Greek word rendered 'cross' in many modern Bible versions ('torture stake' in NW) is stauros...The Imperial Bible-Dictionary acknowledges this, saying: 'The Greek word for cross, [stauros], properly signified a stake, an upright pole, or piece of paling, on which anything might be hung, or which might be used in impaling [fencing in] a piece of ground. **But a modification was introduced as the dominion and usages of Rome extended themselves through Greek-speaking countries.** Even amongst the Romans the crux (from which our cross is derived) appears to have been originally an upright pole, **and always remained the more prominent part. But from the time that it began to be used as an instrument of punishment, a traverse piece of wood was commonly added... about the period of the Gospel Age crucifixion was usually accomplished by suspending the criminal on a cross piece of wood.'** (*Reasoning,* p. 89.)

Reasoning, p. 91, quotes several authorities in answer to the question, 'What were the historical origins of Christendom's cross?' They quote the opening of the book *The Cross in Ritual, Architecture, and Art* by G. S. Tyack to show that the cross was originally used in pagan worship. But they do not go on to quote:

> **In all this the Christians of the first age would have rejoiced, claiming it as a world-wide prophecy of the Cross of the Redeemer.** (p. 3.)

The Worship of the Dead, by Colonel J. Garnier, is quoted next, as saying that the cross was a pagan symbol. But on p. 225 we read:

> **Sin crucified is Salvation, but it is ONLY BY ONE CROSS that the power to do so is obtained, and that CROSS IS THE CROSS OF CHRIST.**

One final quote we'll mention is from *A Short History of Sex-Worship* by H. Cutner:

> Various figures of crosses are found everywhere on Egyptian monuments and tombs, and are considered by many authorities as symbolical either of the phallus [a representation of the male sex

organ] or of coition. **Baring-Gould is of the contrary opinion and refuses to identify the cross with the phallus**... In Egyptian tombs the crux ansata [cross with a circle or handle on top] is found side by side with the phallus. **The question of their connection is still hotly disputed. That the cross was a sacred sign long before Christ is supposed to have died upon one is conceded by Baring-Gould, for he believes that the cross 'formed a portion of that primeval religion, traces of which exist before the whole world among every people'.**]]

The Biblical Testimony of the Cross

One cannot help but notice the series of events as recorded in Matthew 27:26,31–37, Mark 15:14–26, Luke 23:26–38 and John 19:1–22 (regarding the death of Jesus) and their harmony with the method of crucifixion as described by the articles in BAR and other sources. It appears that Jesus carried the cross-beam, or patibulum, to Golgotha. There, the patibulum was affixed to an upright stake, perhaps having a seat or footpiece, and Jesus was nailed on to the whole structure. Above Him was placed the title, JESUS THE NAZARENE, THE KING OF THE JEWS.

When Jesus reappeared to His disciples in His resurrected body, He still bore the marks left by the nails in His hands. The disciples were afraid that this was a spirit form rather than their Lord in the flesh. Luke 24:37 tells us that 'they were startled and frightened as though they were seeing a spirit.' Jesus spoke up:

Why are you troubled, and why do you have doubts arise in your hearts? See My hands and My feet, that it is I Myself; touch Me and see, for a spirit does not have flesh and bones as you see I have. (Luke 24:38–39.)

The WBTS, incidentally, would have us believe that Jesus *was* a spirit at that time and actually *did* just materialize a body so as to comfort them. They thereby infer that Jesus was lying to them just to soothe their fears! How much better to believe the Word for what it says, that it *was* Jesus, and his hands still had the marks of the nails.

This brings up the most conclusive passage of all which reveals that Christ was not crucified as the Governing Body portray in their publications. The apostle John tells us that Thomas, who was not there when Jesus first appeared to the rest, would not believe it was actually Jesus (he thought it must have been a spirit too!). He told the others:

> Unless I see in His HANDS the imprint of THE NAILS, and put my finger in the place of THE NAILS, and put my hand into His side, I will not believe. (John 20:25.)

Note that Thomas knew there was *more than one nail* that punctured Jesus' hands. Yet, the WBTS always picture Jesus as having *one nail* through both hands! When Jesus reappeared for the sake of Thomas, He showed Him His hands so that Thomas could see and believe (John 20:26–27).

Apparently feeling that they needed to respond to this challenge, the Governing Body wrote an article for the 'Questions From The Readers' in WT, 1 April 1984, p. 31. They cloud the issue with a partial quote from *The Cyclopaedia of Biblical, Theological, and Ecclesiastical Literature* (which doesn't support their claim) in an effort to make it appear as a 'waste of time' to speculate on how many nails Jesus was affixed with. (They are right: we don't know; but we do know that there were at least two in His hands!) Then they try to imply that Thomas was sloppy in his speech, saying that even though Thomas only mentions the nail holes in his hands, he might have been referring to the nails in Jesus' feet as well. The article concludes with the statement:

> Thus, it is just not possible at this point to state with certainty how many nails were used. Any drawing of Jesus on the stake should be understood as artists' productions that offer merely a representation based on the limited facts that we have. Debate over such an insignificant detail should not be permitted to becloud the all-important truth that 'we became reconciled to God through the death of his Son' (Rom 5:10).

It appears that now, since the evidence has swung against them in this manner, they are resorting to the old technique of accusing the opposition of what they themselves are guilty of. They are the ones that have made statements such as:

> The evidence is, therefore, completely lacking that Jesus Christ was crucified on two pieces of timber placed at a right angle. We refuse to add anything to God's written Word... The passing of time and further archaeological discoveries will be certain to prove its correctness. Even now the burden rests upon all who contend for the religious tradition to prove that Jesus died on more than a simple stake.

Now they have to eat their own words, and as usual, they shift the blame to cover themselves. Remember, they are the ones to accuse people of 'false worship' for using the symbol of the cross. As far as Christians are concerned, the exact method of crucifixion is not a big issue. Rather, the manner in which the Bible presents the cross is the real issue.

Paul's Testimony on the Cross

It is true that the Jews viewed execution by the cross as an accursed way to die, for it meant shame and, at least in some cases, no hope for a resurrection. Similarly, the WBTS view the concept of Christ dying on a stake in a negative light. Note these statements:

> How would you feel if one of your dearest friends was executed on false charges? Would you make a replica of the instrument of execution, say a hangman's noose or an electric chair? Would you kiss that replica, burn candles before it or wear it around your neck as an ornament? 'Of course not,' you may say... To the Jews and the Romans the manner in which Jesus died was humiliating and shameful. He was executed like a criminal of the lowest sort, like the wrongdoers impaled alongside him (Luke 23:32). His death therefore misrepresented him in the worst way possible. To Christians the instrument of execution itself would therefore have been something very repulsive. Venerating it would have meant

glorifying the wrong deed committed on it—the murder of Jesus Christ. (*Awake!*, 8 November 1972, p. 27.)

The WBTS are here confusing the issue by classing those who 'venerate' or worship a cross with those who consider the cross as a symbol of Christianity. Certainly there is no justification for worshipping before the cross or kissing it; but there *is* justification for considering the cross as a symbol of Christianity. While the Jews may have considered the cross a shameful thing, the apostle Paul *boasted* of the cross of Christ. In Galatians 6:14 he says:

> But may it never be that I should boast, except in the cross of our Lord Jesus Christ, through which the world has been crucified to me, and I to the world.

The Greek word translated as 'boast' is *kauchomai,* which is translated to boast or glory over something. Paul plainly gloried in the symbol of the cross; it was a sign of victory, not defeat. In 1 Corinthians 1:17–18 he tells us that Christ sent him to preach the message of the *cross*, and that people would stand or fall according to their response to such a simple message! He goes on to say that some (like the Jews and JWs) would stumble over the cross (because of its significance in their minds), while others would consider it foolishness (1 Cor 1:21–23). But to Christians the cross meant the power and wisdom of God! He says that this is because God deliberately chose the weak, foolish and despised things of the world to make His point, so that His children could *glory* in what others consider despised!

Paul tells the Corinthians that he had decided to use the message of the cross of Christ as his main emphasis (1 Cor 2:2), even to the point of avoiding more scholarly arguments or fine points. Why? Because of God's ability to weed out those with wrong motives through using a humble message. He did not want to attract people to Christianity by giving them material or intellectual hopes, but he desired to reach those who realized the degree of sin in the world and who would see the great wisdom in Jesus dying for their sins.

This has been the message of the church throughout the centuries—that Jesus died on the cross for our sins, and is alive and can live through us (1 Cor 15:1–3; Luke 24:45–47). This message only seems to appeal to certain people; often the lowly and simple (1 Cor 1:26–29). Accordingly, counterfeit groups could be expected to use certain types of intellectual persuasion and material hopes as the main emphasis or as their 'gospel'. Missing from such would be the convicting work of the Holy Spirit and supernatural regeneration (the new birth). Note these promises in John 14–16:

> ...He will give you another Helper, that He may be with you forever; that is, the Spirit of truth, whom the world cannot receive, because it does not behold Him or know Him, but you know Him because He abides with you, and will be in you. (John 14:16–17; compare John 3:3,5,7.)

> And [the Holy Spirit], when He comes, will convict the world concerning sin, and righteousness, and judgment...(John 16:8.)

Paul also uses the cross as a symbol for the cause of Christianity, as well as the death of the old nature. He tells us that some have become 'enemies of the cross' (Phil 3:18). He talks about the old nature and the Law as being 'nailed to the cross' (Col 2:14). He picks up on the theme of Jesus regarding the cross (Matt 10:38; 16:24; Luke 9:23; 14:27) and talks about 'crucifying the old nature' (Gal 2:20; 5:24). Over and over, Paul considers the cross a sign of victory, not defeat! He boasted in the cross!

Christians are not afraid of the cross nor do they worship it. It is simply a symbol—representing the greatest act of love in the universe! May we, too, grasp the great significance of Jesus' death on the cross. May we preach the simple gospel of the death, burial and resurrection of Jesus (1 Cor 15:3–4) rather than any material hope or an 'invisible presence of Christ' since 1914, 'lest the cross of Christ should be made of no effect' (1 Cor 1:17, KJV).

Summary

First, the WBTS's arguments concerning the Greek words *stauros* and *xylon* offer no proof for their point.

Second, whatever usage of the cross existed before or after the time of Christ is irrelevant to the issue, as there is no conclusive evidence that first-century Jews or Christians looked upon the crucifixion as a specifically pagan symbol. It was a means to an end—the punishment or death of a criminal. Symbols mean different things at different times. At any rate, Jesus did not choose the instrument of death. Also, the cross appears in excavations much earlier than the WBTS's claim of fourth century (*Awake!*, 8 November 1972, p. 27).

Third, archaeological evidence, if anything, proves Jesus died on the traditional cross. There is little or no contention on this point among modern scholars.

Finally, while Jews of Paul's day may not have used visual symbols (including watch-towers) due to their extreme view of pictorial representations, the cross nevertheless became the symbol of the Christian faith. Though objects or symbols are not to be worshipped, the apostle Paul gloried in the cross as the Christian sign of victory!

SECTION 12

Children

A number of you will have been shocked to find a very young child with an adult on your doorstep who appears to be able to recite the 'Witness patter' very well. Some, for the days we are living in, will be even more shocked to find two young children together.

We have received, in the months that this manual has been in preparation, several calls enquiring about the position of the WBTS regarding children. Usually these are to do with custody cases etc going through the courts.

As we've shown in Section 9 on disfellowshipping, children will suffer emotional hardships in the break up of families. But what of the child who is put with the Witness partner in a custody case; or even a Witness child in a united family; are there wrong pressures placed on them?

Duane Magnani has produced an excellent study on this subject called *Saleskids*. For any who want an in depth study those volumes are well worth obtaining (see order form at back of book). Here we just give a 'flavour' by quoting a number of WBTS sources in order to show the problems faced by children in the Society. We hope this will give you an understanding of the plight of a Jehovah's Witness child.

Who Can Children Associate With?

It would follow, then, that ANY RECREATION YOU TAKE outside of school should NOT BE WITH WORLDLY YOUTHS...(WT, 1 September 1964, p. 535.)

The ideal situation is for parents to have such a fine program outlined for their children that LITTLE OR NO TIME REMAINS FOR OUTSIDE ASSOCIATION. (WT, 1 February 1974, p. 93.)

To keep separate from the world while in school, young Witnesses should consider THE DANGERS OF BECOMING INVOLVED IN EXTRACURRICULAR ACTIVITIES. (*Organized to Accomplish Our Ministry*, 1983, p. 133.)

So Witness parents encourage their children to use after-school hours principally to pursue spiritual interests, rather than to excel in some sport. Participation in organized sports, we believe, would expose Witness youths to UNWHOLESOME ASSOCIATIONS. (*School and Jehovah's Witnesses, 1983, p. 23.*)

Which Recreations are Banned?

Much time is wasted that could be better spent in learning profitable matters or in preaching activity. SPORTS AS ORGANIZED TODAY are conducive to hero worship, which is dangerous and unchristian. (WT, 15 January 1952, p. 46.)

The extreme fascination of CHESS can result in its consuming large amounts of one's time . . . even developing hostility toward another . . . (*Awake!*, 22 March 1973, p. 14.)

And do you show empathy when you imprison us in your zoos in restricting cages to be gawked at? How do you think we feel? Would you like to change places with us? (*Awake!*, 5 August 1973, p. 18.)

The Field Service

Do you engage in field service regularly, TAKING YOUR CHILDREN along? Do THEY observe you in door-to-door work, back-call work and home Bible study work, hearing you make effective presentations. (WT, 15 January 1954, pp. 50–51.)

Parents who love their children and who want TO SEE THEM ALIVE in God's new world will encourage and guide them toward goals of increased service and responsibility. (WT, 15 March 1962, p. 179.)

Activity in the Christian ministry cannot be confined to adults. It is a privilege of service that you children can Scripturally participate in and SHOULD ENGAGE IN. If you want to obey Jehovah you will ENGAGE REGULARLY . . . serve your Creator EVERY DAY during vacation periods . . . do you OBEY HIM by zealously engaging in it regularly? (WT, 15 August 1962, p. 493.)

Be a regular publisher by sharing in the field ministry. Then when SECULAR SCHOOL is out, be a VACATION PIONEER . . . with the goal of later entering into the full-time service as a PERMANENT CAREER. (*Qualified To Be Ministers*, 1967, p. 258.)

Children should be trained at a VERY EARLY AGE to accompany their parents in the field Ministry. (*Our Kingdom Ministry*, June 1982, p. 4.)

Loyalty to Jehovah and his organization is necessary if we are to gain everlasting life. At this time of testing, how can Christian youths maintain integrity? . . . Increasing numbers of young ones are rejecting high-paying jobs or higher education in favor of a CAREER IN THE MINISTRY. They humbly accept counsel and direction from older ones that will ENABLE THEM TO CONTINUE IN LOYAL SACRED SERVICE. (*Our Kingdom Ministry*, August 1982, pp. 1,3.)

It would hardly be consistent for such a youth, of his own choice, to PURSUE EXTENSIVE SECULAR STUDIES beyond what is required BY THE LAW or BY HIS PARENTS. (WT, 1 September 1975, p. 543.)

However, as the WBTS became more automated they found they lacked necessary skills amongst Witnesses. But it was the parents who had second thoughts, not the WBTS!

It is no shame for a person to learn a trade and work with his hands. Indeed, these days it is getting to be the practical thing to do. That is another reason why SOME PARENTS NOW have second thoughts about the matter of a college education. (*Awake!*, 8 June 1971, p. 8.)

Pressure!

ALL MEMBERS OF THE FAMILY . . . should be interested in furthering pioneer activity and willing to make sacrifices to that end. (WT, 15 March 1975, p. 187.)

If you would like to get to know your children better, what they are really thinking... ascertaining how much they really love Jehovah, arrange TIME TO TAKE THEM with you in the FIELD SERVICE. (*Our Kingdom Service*, June 1976, p. 4.)

Are you young publishers showing a willingness to study with your parents and accompany them in the field service? You can be sure Jehovah is pleased with you when you do. Yes, both PARENTS AND CHILDREN ARE CALLED UPON TO SHOW APPRECIATION FOR THE FAMILY ARRANGEMENT. (*Our Kingdom Service*, December 1977, p. 4.)

Parents, of course, have the ADDITIONAL RESPONSIBILITY of helping their children to be ACTIVE in spiritual things... WORK OUT A REASONABLE SCHEDULE of theocratic activity... Thus, they show a personal interest in their *CHILDREN'S* WELFARE... (*Our Kingdom Ministry*, December 1982, p. 2.)

Being Used

Children can often create a favourable impression in the minds of householders who have not shown much interest in the Bible. (*1964 Yearbook of Jehovah's Witnesses*, p. 161.)

She [4 year old] is my help during times of opposition. When I find a householder opposing I ask my daughter to give the sermon. (*1965 Yearbook of Jehovah's Witnesses*, p. 223.)

Adult publishers are often glad to have young ministers along... Sometimes people will not open their doors to a man alone... but will be inclined to... listen when a you.igster publisher is along. (*Our Kingdom Ministry*, October 1972, p. 7.)

Children are often the center of attention... Some casual statement or incident might prompt the children to speak up in an appealing way that touches the heart of other family members. (*Our Kingdom Ministry*, December 1983, p. 4.)

Correction and Disfellowshipping

In the case of where a father or mother or son or daughter is disfellowshiped, how should such a person be treated by members of the family... The parent must by laws of God and of man fulfil his parental obligations to the child or children as long as they are dependent minors, and the child or children must render filial submission to the parent as long as legally underage . . . Of course, if the children are of age, then there can be a departing and BREAKING OF FAMILY TIES . . . If children are of age and continue to associate with a disfellowshiped parent because of receiving material support . . . they must consider how far their spiritual interests are being endangered . . . and whether they can arrange to support themselves, LIVING APART FROM THE FALLEN-AWAY PARENT. (WT, 15 November 1952, p. 703.)

A baptized child's being a minor does not shield him from REPROOF BEFORE THE CONGREGATION by the elders, or DISFELLOWSHIPING, if he commits serious wrongdoing. (*Organization for Kingdom-Preaching and Disciple-Making*, 1972, p. 175.)

Are Your Children in Danger?

If, for example, a twelve-year-old boy answers the door, what is your reaction? . . . has the boy ever heard the good news of the Kingdom . . . most young people these days have a little money and it may be possible to place a . . . book . . . (*Our Kingdom Ministry*, February 1973, p. 8.)

We should not feel that we must always ask to speak to their parents . . . Where can we find young people? . . . search them out . . . at summer camps, in the vicinity of summer schools or in recreational areas. (*Our Kingdom Service*, August 1977, p. 4.)

Who are 'Wishy-Washy' Christians?

It is a serious matter to represent God and Christ in one way, then find that our understanding of the major doctrines of the Scriptures was in error, and then after that, to go back to the very doctrines that, by years of study, we had thoroughly determined to be in error. CHRISTIANS CANNOT BE VACILLATING— 'WISHY-WASHY'—ABOUT SUCH FUNDAMENTAL TEACHINGS. WHAT CONFIDENCE CAN ONE PUT IN THE SINCERITY OR JUDGEMENT OF SUCH PERSONS? (WT, 15 May 1976, p. 293.)

This is the definition of the WBTS on who is 'wishy-washy'. At the same time it shows what their attitude should be to such 'wishy-washy' people. Below we simply investigate some aspects of the teaching of WBTS to find out where they stand in this matter.

The Powers (Romans 13:1)

Evil as these Gentile governments have been, they were permitted or 'ordained of God' for a wise purpose (Rom 13:1). (SS, Vol. 3, 1886, p. 250.)

... the Scriptural exposition of Romans chapter 13. It showed that Jehovah God and Christ Jesus, rather than worldly rulers and governors are 'The Higher Powers' ... (*The Truth Shall Make You Free*, 1943, p. 199.)

So the 'superior authorities' have their setting logically in the world outside the congregation. (WT, 15 November 1962, p. 683.)

The Sower

JESUS CHRIST, with his prophetic foresight, could foreknow the outcome for the symbolic mustard grain that HE PLANTED in the first century. (WT, 1 October 1975, p. 600.)

In the parable, the 'man' that sowed the mustard grain pictures the 'WICKED ONE,' SATAN THE DEVIL. (*Man's Salvation Out Of World Distress At Hand*, 1975, p. 208.)

Which is correct... JESUS is to be considered as THE PLANTER referred to in this parable. (*Our Kingdom Ministry*, November 1975, p. 4.)

Leaven

LEAVEN REPRESENTS CORRUPTION throughout the Scriptures: in every other instance... it is represented as evil and impurity, something that is defiling ... Jesus refers to leaven as a corruption... (ZWTR, 15 May 1900, p. 2635.)

The LEAVEN OF RIGHTEOUSNESS of this God-approved nucleus... (Matt 13:33). (WT, 1 April 1962, p. 204.)

Accordingly, the parable of the leaven... is on the negative side... leaven... is used THROUGHOUT SCRIPTURE in an unfavorable sense... (WT, 1 October 1975, pp. 592,603.)

Heaven or Earth?

But while we still would urge *justified believers*... we cannot hold out as a hope, the *heavenly* prize. We point such to... future EARTHLY blessings. (ZWTR, July 1882, p. 377.)

Though BOTH COMPANIES WILL BE SPIRITUAL BEINGS... the 'great company' [great crowd] will be the companions of the Bride... there will be a very great difference in the DEGREES OF GLORY. (ZWTR, March 1883, p. 458.)

Do those of the 'great crowd'... also go to heaven?... The description... indicates, not necessarily a location but an approved condition... The expression 'before the throne'... does not require that they be in heaven... Great Crowd, earthly hope. (*Reasoning*, pp. 167,441.)

Organ Transplants

> The question of placing one's body or parts of one's body at the disposal of men of science or doctors . . . it does not seem that any Scriptural principle or law is involved. It therefore is something that EACH INDIVIDUAL MUST DECIDE FOR HIMSELF. (WT, 1 August 1961, p. 480.)

> Baptized Christians have dedicated their lives, bodies included, to do the will of Jehovah their Creator. In view of this, CAN SUCH A PERSON DONATE HIS BODY OR PART OF IT for unrestricted use by doctors or others? (WT, 15 November 1967, p. 703.)

> Regarding the transplantation of human tissue or bone . . . this is a matter for conscientious decision by each one of Jehovah's Witnesses . . . THERE IS NO BIBLICAL COMMAND POINTEDLY FORBIDDING the taking in of other human tissue. (WT, 15 March 1980, p. 31.)

Conclusion

A look at these few subjects shows us clearly that according to their own definition the WBTS are 'wishy-washy'. Therefore we must also note their conclusion concerning themselves . . . 'What confidence can one put in the sincerity or judgement of such persons?'

SECTION 14

A Bible Study

The following study designed especially for Jehovah's Witnesses leaves them to find the answers from the Scriptures themselves, instead of being told from the publications! Separate copies are available from Reachout Trust.

Introduction

Leaving the WBTS is usually a traumatic experience. You will sever contact with many friends and have restricted contact with close family.

Another cause for concern might be your eternal security. You've been taught that the only way to escape God's judgement is to belong to the WBTS and if you leave you wonder if you will forfeit this right. We want you to know that there are those who understand what you are going through.

Some will find the questions adequate in themselves whereas others will want personal help. If you are one of these, please contact us and we'll try to put you in touch with someone locally. Failing a personal contact we'll certainly arrange for someone to write to you.

The aim of these questions is to show scriptural answers to the errors that you have been taught in the past. We will try not to force preconceived ideas on you but simply ask questions and allow you to dig the answers from the Bible.

Up until now you have been dependent on the WBTS as

'the servant giving food in due season', and we do not want to replace them with another man or society. The Bible shows that the main source of 'spiritual food' is a personal relationship with the Lord which is supplemented and indeed safeguarded by the corporate meetings of the church.

We recommend, because of mistranslations in the New World Translation, that you use a modern version such as the New American Standard Bible. This is readily available from Christian bookshops or some larger bookstores.

Lesson 1: The Open Book

Acts 17:11

1. What did the Bereans study to check Paul's teaching?
2. What should we study to check the teaching we hear?

2 Timothy 3:16–17

3. Who is made adequate and equipped for every good work?
4. Does this description only apply to a few of God's people?
5. What are the Scriptures profitable for?

1 Corinthians 2:9–16

6. Who, according to verse 9, will receive things that have been hidden up until now?
7. Is this you?
8. How does God reveal things to us?
9. Who, according to verses 14 and 15, can receive God's Words?
10. What makes a man or woman spiritual? Does belonging to a particular society? Doing good works? Receiving God's Holy Spirit?

1 Timothy 2:4

11. Who does God desire to come to the knowledge of the truth?

Summary questions

A. Who can understand the Bible?

B.   How can we understand the Bible?

C.   Has God restricted the understanding of the Bible to just a few?

Lesson 2: Receiving Food

Joshua 1:8

1.   What was Joshua to do?

2.   What does it mean to meditate?

3.   Was Joshua to meditate on God's Word or a book about God's Word?

4.   What was the result of meditating?

1 Corinthians 10:3,11 and Exodus 16:4–36

5.   Should we learn from the mistakes they made in the Old Testament?

6.   Did the children of Israel get their food from Moses?

7.   Did Jehovah show any favouritism as to who should get the most?

8.   Did God's supply to the people ever run out?

9.   According to Exodus 16:4 what did the people need to do?

Colossians 3:16

10.   Whose Word should dwell within us?

11.   In what measure?

12.   Does the Word affect just our minds?

13.   What should I read often to fulfil this verse?

Summary questions

A.   Who do we receive our food from?

B.   Should we receive our food weekly, daily, or when?

C.   Which part of us should be full of God's Word?

Lesson 3: The Kingdom and its Gospel

Ephesians 1:18–23

1.   When was Christ enthroned in heaven?

2. Is there a gap between His ascension and His enthronement?

John 18:36–37

3. Is Christ's kingdom like other kingdoms of this world?
4. Was Jesus already King of His kingdom at this time?

Colossians 1:13

5. What had Paul been delivered from?
6. What had Paul been delivered into?
7. Can this be our experience?

Revelation 21:23–26 and 22:4

8. Is the New Jerusalem, the 'capital' city of the kingdom?
9. Will others be going into the city, besides those who live there?
10. Will they see the Lord Jesus?
11. Does this mean that the New Heavens and the New Earth are blended together?

1 Corinthians 15:1–4

12. Do these verses summarize the gospel of the kingdom that Paul preached?
13. What are the three main aspects of this gospel?

Colossians 1:25–29

14. What was Paul's God-given task?
15. Was this for a few people or all people?
16. Can you benefit from this same preaching today?

Summary questions

A. When was Christ enthroned as King?
B. Is the kingdom for all or a few?
C. How can I live in the good of Christ's kingdom reign?

Lesson 4: Born Again

John 10:15–16

1. Who does Christ lay down His life for?

2.   Remembering who Jesus is talking to, who do you think the 'other sheep' are?
3.   How many flocks (classes) do we end up with?
4.   Do we all have the same experience of the Lord?

1 John 5:1

5.   Who is born of God?
6.   Is this restricted to a certain number?

2 Corinthians 5:17

7.   What happens to our past when we experience this new life in Christ?

John 14:23

8.   Who does Jesus say will live with us in our new life?
9.   Is this a physical or spiritual dwelling with us?

John 3:3

10.   What needs to happen to us if we want to see Christ's kingdom?
11.   According to the following Scriptures what must I do to be born again?
Romans 3:23—What must I realize?
Romans 6:23—What must I realize?
1 John 5:11–13 and John 1:12
Romans 10:9–10

Summary questions

A.   Is being born again an experience for just a few people?
B.   Can I be born again?
C.   How can I be born again?

Lesson 5: Death and Judgement

1 Thessalonians 5:23

1.   How many parts is man made up from?
2.   Will all of them be preserved at the Lord's coming?

Hebrews 12:22–23

3. Where were the spirits of these men who had died?
4. Does everyone's 'spirit' go to heaven at death?

Matthew 10:28

5. Can a natural man kill the soul as well as the body?
6. Who alone has the ability to destroy the soul?
7. Are the body and the soul made and destroyed in the same way?

2 Corinthians 5:6–9

8. For Paul would there be any waiting to be with the Lord when he left the body?
9. When he was at home with the Lord was he absent from body, soul and spirit; body and soul, or body?

Hebrews 9:27–28

10. When does our judgement come?
11. Does this verse (or indeed any other) teach that we have a second chance after death?
12. When Christ returns will He still be dealing with the sins of His people?

Summary questions

A. According to the Bible does the soul return to dust?
B. According to the Bible does our spirit go straight to heaven when we die?
C. According to the Bible do we have a 'second chance' to pass God's judgement after we have died?

Lesson 6: Jehovah — Jesus — Holy Spirit

Deuteronomy 6:4

1. How many 'Gods' are there?
2. Why do you think the Hebrew word for God is the plural word *Elohim*? Compare Deuteronomy 4:31: 'the Lord your God (plural—*Elohim*) is a compassionate God (singular—*El*).

John 6:27

3. Who is God according to this verse?

John 20:28

4. Who is God according to this verse?

Acts 5:3–4

5. Who did Ananias lie to according to verse 3?
6. Who did Ananias lie to according to verse 4?
7. Therefore who is God according to these verses?
8. The Bible says there is only *one* God. But it also declares that *three* people are that God. How can this be explained?

Galatians 1:1

9. Who raised Jesus from the dead?
10. Now read John 2:19–21. Who raised Jesus from the dead here?
11. Then read Romans 8:11. Who raised Jesus from the dead here?
12. Can three separate people raise Jesus from the dead? If not what is the explanation?

Summary questions

A. Does the Bible teach that there is more than one God?
B. Does the Bible teach that Jehovah is God?
C. Does the Bible teach that Jesus is God?
D. Does the Bible teach that the Holy Spirit is God?
E. Overall then, what does *the Bible* teach concerning Jehovah, Jesus and the Holy Spirit?

Lesson 7: Faith and Works

Ephesians 2:8–10

1. How are we saved?
2. Are good works essential for our salvation?
3. Why does God not allow works to count towards our salvation?

4.   Are the good works that we do of our own choosing?

Romans 4:1–5

5.   How was Abraham justified?
6.   In the light of verse 4, can we work to receive the reward of eternal life?
7.   Why, according to verse 5, is it more important to have faith than works?

John 6:28–29

8.   What is the most important work for us to do?

James 2:14–26

 9.   According to verses 14 and 15 who is James talking to?
10.   In the light of Ephesians 2:8–9 is James talking about initial salvation, i.e. being born again, or our continual growth into the fullness of our salvation?
11.   In the light of Romans 4:1–5 is James talking about initial salvation, i.e. being born again, or our continual growth into the fullness of our salvation?
12.   Can we be a growing Christian and not display God's works that He has prepared?
13.   What are the works that God prepared for you to do?

Summary questions

A.   Are works necessary for us to be born again?
B.   How does the Bible teach us we can be saved (born again)?
C.   As the Bible does not contradict itself, how do you explain James 2:14–26 in the light of Ephesians 2:8–9?

APPENDIX 1

Is Jehovah a Correct Pronunciation?

Here are just a few of the many quotations on this subject. However, these are enough to show the clear agreement that there is amongst scholars on whether we can pronounce YHWH as Jehovah.

> The form Jehovah arose out of a misunderstanding which in turn arose out of the reluctance of pious Jews to pronounce the Divine Name...Instead they uttered the *adonay*, my Lord. In the M[asoretic] T[ext] the Divine Name was written with the consonants of YHWH and the vowels of *adonay*...THE FORM JEHOVAH IS THUS A MALFORMATION giving what is virtually a transliteration of a word which is in the text of the Heb[rew] O[ld] T[estament], but which was never actually used as a word. (*New International Dictionary of New Testament Theology*, Vol. 2, 1976, p. 69.)

> To give the name JHVH the vowels of the word for Lord (Hebrew Adonai) and pronounce it *Jehovah*, is about as hybrid a combination as it would be to spell the name *Germany* with the vowels in the name *Portugal*—viz., *Gormuna*. THE MONSTROUS COMBINATION *Jehovah* is not older that about 1520 AD (J. B. Rotherham, *The Emphasized Bible*, p. 21.)

> JEHOVAH: A mispronunciation (introduced by Christian theologians but almost entirely disregarded by the Jews) of the Hebrew 'YHWH', the (ineffable) name of God...THIS PRONUNCIATION IS GRAMMATICALLY IMPOSSIBLE; it arose through pronouncing the vowels of...'Adonay' with the consonants of...

'YHWH'... 'Jehovah' is generally held to have been the invention of Pope Leo X's confessor, Peter Galatin. (*The Jewish Encyclopedia*. Vol. 7, pp. 87–88.)

In the Hebrew we have four consonants that are placed together, denoting the name of God. They are Y H V H. We do not have the letter 'J' in the Hebrew alphabet. The name 'Jonah' that you know in Hebrew is 'Yonah'. When the translators saw this name, they could not pronounce it. No Hebrew can pronounce it today. The way we pronounce it is 'ADONAI', meaning Lord. Here is what is done. The Y was changed to J being we don't have a J letter. Then we inserted vowels e, o and an a and came up with 'Jehovah'. *But there is no such name*. The Lord said to Moses when he asked who shall I say sent me, say 'I AM' has sent me. 'I Am What I Am', 'I Shall Be What I Shall Be'. 'I Will Be What I Will Be'. *THERE IS NO SUCH NAME AS JEHOVAH*. (Rabbi Michael Esses, *Letters*.)

Jehovah... repr[esenting] Heb[rew] YHWH (given the vowels of *adonai* 'my lord' to indicate substitution of latter word in reading, *HENCE ERRON[EOUS]*. (*The Concise Oxford Dictionary*, 1981, p. 538.)

Jehovah is a Christian transliteration of the tetragrammaton long assumed by many Christians to be the authentic reproduction of the Hebrew sacred name for God but now recognized to be a LATE HYBRID FORM NEVER USED BY THE JEWS. *(Webster's Third New International Dictionary.)*

John 1:1

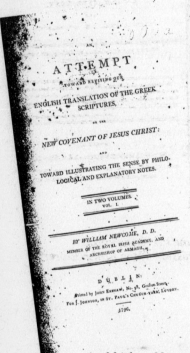

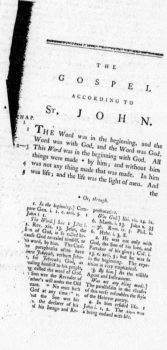

AN

ATTEMPT
TOWARD REVISING OUR

ENGLISH TRANSLATION OF THE GREEK
SCRIPTURES,

OR THE

NEW COVENANT OF JESUS CHRIST:

AND

TOWARD ILLUSTRATING THE SENSE BY PHILO-
LOGICAL AND EXPLANATORY NOTES.

IN TWO VOLUMES.
VOL. I.

BY WILLIAM NEWCOME, D. D.
MEMBER OF THE ROYAL IRISH ACADEMY, AND
ARCHBISHOP OF ARMAGH.

DUBLIN:
Printed by JOHN EXSHAW, No. 98, Grafton-Street,
For J. JOHNSON, IN ST. PAUL'S CHURCH-YARD, LONDON.
1796.

THE

GOSPEL
ACCORDING TO

St. JOHN.

CHAP. I.

1 THE Word was in the beginning, and the Word was with God, and the Word was God. 2-3 This *Word* was in the beginning with God. All things were made • by him; and without him 4 was not any thing made that was made. In him 5 was life; and the life was the light of men. And the

• Or, *through.*

*Archbishop Newcome's original version
Reproduced by kind permission of the British Library.*

248

LUKE XXIV. JOHN I.

38 posed that they beheld a spirit. And he said unto them,
" Why are ye troubled? and why do thoughts arise in your
39 hearts? see my hands and my feet, that it is I myself;
handle me, and see me: for a spirit hath not flesh and
40 bones, as ye behold that I have," And when he had thus
41 spoken, he showed them *his* hands and *his* feet, And while
they still believed not through joy, and wondered, he said
42 unto them, " Have ye here any food?" And they gave
43 him a piece of a broiled fish, and of a honey-comb. And
he took and ate *of them* in their presence.
44 And he said unto them, " These *are* the words which I
spake unto you, while I was yet with you; That all things
must be fulfilled which were written in the law of Moses,
and in the prophets, and in the psalms, concerning me."
45 Then he opened their mind, that they might understand
46 the scriptures; and said unto them, " Thus it is written,
and thus the Christ ought to suffer, and to rise again from
47 the dead the third day: and repentance and remission of
sins *ought* to be preached in his name among all the na-
48 tions, having begun from Jerusalem. And ye are witnesses
49 of these things. And, behold, I *will* send upon you the
promise *made* by my Father: but stay ye * in the city of
50 *Jerusalem*, until ye be endued with power from on high."
And he led them out to Bethany; and lifted up his
51 hands, and blessed them, And it came to pass that, while
he blessed them, he was parted from them, and carried up
52 into heaven. And they did him obeisance, and returned
53 to Jerusalem with great joy: and were continually in the
temple, praising and blessing God.

THE GOSPEL ACCORDING TO ST. JOHN.

CHAPTER I,

1 THE Word was in the beginning, and the word was †
2 God, and the word was a god, This *Word* was in the be-
3 ginning with God. All things were done by him;
without him was not any thing done that hath been †
4 By him was life; and the life was the light of men.
5 the light shone in darkness; and the darkness overcame
it not †.
6 There was a man sent from God, whose name was

* So W. dwell, N.   † " Its lustre was not impaired
darkness which surrounded it," Newcome, Or, " the
ness admitted it not,"

THE

NEW TESTAMENT,

IN

AN IMPROVED VERSION,

UPON THE BASIS OF

ARCHBISHOP NEWCOME'S NEW TRANSLATION:

WITH

A CORRECTED TEXT,

AND

NOTES CRITICAL AND EXPLANATORY.

PUBLISHED BY A SOCIETY FOR PROMOTING CHRISTIAN KNOW-
LEDGE AND THE PRACTICE OF VIRTUE, BY THE
DISTRIBUTION OF BOOKS.

No offence can justly be taken for this new labour; nothing prejudicing
any other man's judgement by this doing; nor yet professing this so absolute a translation, as that hereafter might follow no other who might see
that which as yet was not understood.

Archbishop Parker's Preface to the Bishops' Bible.

London:

Printed by Richard Taylor and Co. Shoe Lane.

SOLD BY J. JOHNSON, ST. PAUL'S CHURCH-YARD; AND LONGMAN,
HURST, REES, AND ORME, PATERNOSTER ROW.

1808.

*[ΕΥΑΓΓΕΛΙΟΝ] ΚΑΤΑ ΙΩΑΝΝΗΝ.
(GLAD TIDINGS)   BY   JOHN.
*ACCORDING TO JOHN.

*Benjamin Wilson's
Emphatic Diaglott*

ΚΕΦ. α'. 1.

CHAPTER I.

Der Prolog: 1, 1-18

¹ Im Anfang war das Wort,
und das Wort war bei dem Gott,
und ein Gott (oder: Gott von Art) war das Wort.
² Dieses war im Anfang bei dem Gott.
³ Durch dasselbe ist alles geworden,
und ohne dasselbe wurde gar nichts,
was geworden ist.
⁴ In ihm war Leben,
und das Leben war das Licht der Menschen.
⁵ Und das Licht scheint in der Finsternis,
aber die Finsternis hat es nicht ergriffen.
⁶ Ein Mensch trat auf, von Gott gesandt, mit Namen Johannes. ⁷ Dieser kam zum Zeugnis, um Zeugnis zu geben für das Licht, damit alle durch ihn zum Glauben kämen. ⁸ Jener war nicht das Licht, sondern er wollte (nur) Zeugnis geben für das Licht. ⁹ Jener wahre Licht, das jeden Menschen erleuchtet, der in die Welt kam. ⁹ Es war das ⁱ⁰ Es war in der Welt,
und die Welt ist durch es geworden,
aber die Welt wollte von ihm nichts wissen.
¹¹ Es kam in das Seine,
aber die Seinen nahmen es nicht auf.
¹² So viele es jedoch aufnahmen,
ihnen gab es Vollmacht,
Gottes Kinder zu werden,
ihnen, die an seinen Namen glauben, ¹³ welche nicht aus dem Blut noch aus dem Willen des Fleisches noch aus dem Willen des Mannes, sondern aus Gott gezeugt sind. ¹⁴ Und das Wort ward Fleisch und zeltete unter uns, und wir schauten seine Herrlichkeit, eine Herrlichkeit, wie sie der Einzigerzeugte vom Vater hat, voller Gnade und Wahrheit. ¹⁵ Johannes zeugt von ihm und ruft: Dieser war es, von dem ich sagte: Der nach mir kommt, ist vor mir gewesen, denn er war eher als ich. ¹⁶ Denn aus seiner Fülle haben wir alle empfangen, und zwar Gnade um Gnade. ¹⁷ Denn das Gesetz wurde durch Mose gegeben, die Gnade und die Wahrheit (aber) kamen durch Jesus Christus. ¹⁸ Niemand hat Gott je gesehen. Der einzigerzeugte Sohn (nach anderen Textzeugen: Gott), der im Schoß des Vaters ist, der hat (von ihm) Kunde gebracht.

Die ersten 18 Verse des Johannesevangeliums haben vor allem in den letzten Jahrzehnten der Forschung viel Mühe bereitet. Der Abschnitt wird herkömmlicherweise als „Prolog" bezeichnet. Diese Bezeichnung ist aber alles andere als eindeutig, und man hat auch bald erkannt, daß sie nicht viel weiterführt. Zweck dieses Prologs? Er ist sicher keine literarische Vorrede für Gebildete, wie Lk. 1, 1-4, aber auch keine Themaangabe im Sinne von 1.Joh. 1, 1-4. Der Prolog stellt auch keine pädagogische Hinführung für den damaligen Leser dar, es wird in diesem Abschnitt auch nicht die heilsgeschichtliche Anfang des vierten Evangeliums markiert und schließlich auch kein Summarium des folgenden Evangeliums gegeben. Viel näher läge es, im Prolog den regelrechten Anfang des Evangeliums zu sehen. Aber 1, 19 ff. mit seiner Folge von Perikopen im Erzählungsstil setzt nicht

1,1–18

*Das Evangelium
nach Johannes
—Siegfrid Schulz*

I. Der Prolog 1, 1–18

1 Am Anfang war der Logos,
und der Logos war bei dem Gott,
und ein Gott war der Logos.

2 Dieser war am Anfang bei dem Gott.

3 Alles ist durch ihn geworden,
und ohne ihn ist nichts geworden.

Das Evangelium nach Johannes—Jurgen Becker

The Faithful and Discreet Slave

Today the Society use the phrase 'faithful and discreet slave', taken from their NWT. But originally they used the term 'faithful and wise servant'. Both mean the same—the only mouthpiece of God upon earth, who alone is distributing the true food to other servants.

> From this it is clearly seen that the editor and publisher of *Zion's Watch Tower* [Charles Taze Russell] DISAVOWED ANY CLAIM to being individually, in his person, that 'faithful and wise servant'. He never did claim to be such. (*God's Kingdom of a Thousand Years Has Approached*, 1973, p. 346.)

That seems very conclusive! But let's investigate. Are today's 'faithful and wise servant' class lying in order to hide something?

> We believe . . . that Brother Russell faithfully filled THE OFFICE OF SPECIAL SERVANT OF THE LORD; and that he was made ruler over all the Lord's goods . . . Often when asked by others, Who is that faithful and wise servant? Brother Russell would reply: 'Some say I am; while others say the Society is.' BOTH STATEMENTS WERE TRUE; for Brother Russell was in fact the Society in a most absolute sense . . . (WT, 1 March 1923, p. 68.)

> . . . during the Lord's *presence* . . . our Lord . . . will make choice of ONE CHANNEL for dispensing the meat in due season, though other channels or 'FELLOW-SERVANTS' will be used . . . (SS, Vol. 4, 1897, p. 613.)

Clearly at that time the WBTS taught that the faithful and wise servant was *an individual*, not a group, and that the individual was C. T. Russell.

Finally, let's look at the Biography of Pastor Russell.

> Thousands of the readers of Pastor Russell's writings believe that he filled the office of 'that faithful and wise servant', and that his great work was giving the household of faith meat in due season. His modesty and humility precluded him from openly claiming the title, but HE ADMITTED *AS MUCH IN PRIVATE CONVERSATION* (SS, Vol. 1, 1924, p. 7.)

Russell claimed he was the 'faithful and wise servant', the WBTS taught that he was the 'faithful and wise servant'. But the present-day 'faithful and wise servant' deny it and tell lies to cover up the change they have made from one man to the Society. (Further, more detailed evidence of this matter can be found in *Who Is The Faithful And Wise Servant* by Duane Magnani.)

APPENDIX 4

John 8:58

Here are a few quotes from various scholars about John 8:58. Can it be translated 'I have been' or must it be 'I am'?

> The Present which indicates the CONTINUANCE of an action during the past and UP TO THE MOMENT of speaking is virtually the same as Perfective, the only difference being that the action is conceived AS STILL IN PROGRESS. (*Moulton's Grammar of New Testament Greek,* Vol. III p. 62.)

('I have been' does not agree with this definition of the Perfective.)

> The Witnesses reject the trinity and believe that Jesus Christ was the first creation of God. Thus the translation of John 8:58...On grammatical grounds alone, the rendering cannot be justified, since the tense of *eimi* is present. It cannot be called a historical present, since the words are not narrative, but a part of Jesus' statement. To express the meaning 'I have been', John would have used the imperfect *en.* (R. M. Mcoy, 'Jehovah's Witnesses and Their New Testament', *Anderson Newton Quarterly,* 3, 1963, p. 29.)

> The difference between the two verbs applied to Abraham and Himself, in this great saying, is to be carefully observed. 'Before Abraham was *brought into being,* I exist. The statement, therefore, is not that *Christ came into existence before Abraham did* as Arians affirm is the meaning: it is that He never *came into*

253

being at all, but *existed* before Abraham had a being. (Jamieson, Fausset and Brown, *Bible Commentary*, Vol. 3, 1976, p. 406.)

His claim is not that he is the greatest of the prophets, or even greater than Abraham himself. He belongs to A DIFFERENT ORDER OF BEING. The verb *genesthai* [came to exist] is not applicable to the Son of God at all. He stands outside the range of temporal relations. He can say EGO EIMI. (C. H. Dodd, *The Interpretation Of The Fourth Gospel*, 1953, p. 261.)

There can be no doubt as to the meaning of the final answer... *Verily, verily, I say unto you, Before Abraham was...I am*. The phrase marks a timeless existence. In this connexion 'I was' would have expressed simple priority. Thus there is in the phrase the contrast between the created and the uncreated, and the temporal and the eternal. (B. F. Westcott, *The Gospel According to St. John*, p. 140.)

The references to the grammars, given in the article [WT, 15 February 1957], prove nothing concerning the question at hand because they describe situations not applicable to John 8:58... From John 8:42 to 9:12 the verb 'to be' occurs twenty-one times. The New World Translation renders the tense twenty of the twenty-one times by the correct tense in English. THE SINGLE INSTANCE OF INCORRECT RENDERING of the tense of the verb 'to be'... IS the present tense of EIMI IN JOHN 8:58... the second argument used... the claim that the rendering has 'wide support by recognized scholarship'... it should be pointed out that these renderings are not literal translations of EIMI as a 'historical present', but are interpretative renderings attempting to wrestle with the momentous statement...'Before Abraham...I AM'. (Dr H. A. Sturz, *The Bible Collector*, July—December 1971, pp. 27–28.)

Was, I am...It is important to observe the distinction between the two verbs. Abraham's life was under the conditions of time, and therefore had a temporal beginning. Hence, Abraham *came into being*, or *was born*...Jesus' life was from eternity. Hence the formula for *absolute, timeless* existence, *I am*. (M. R. Vincent, *Word Studies In The New Testament*, Vol. 2, 1980, p. 181.)

Postage & Packing – Up to £5 add 25%
                      Between £5 & £10 add 20%
                      Between £10 & £20 add 15%
                      Over £20 add £3.00

Cheques payable to "Reachout Trust".
Allow 14 days for delivery
Send completed form to: Reachout Trust
                         PO Box 43
                         Twickenham TW2 7EG
                         England

* * * * * * * * * * *

Please send me further information (tick as required) on the
following:

Information sheet about **REACHOUT TRUST**

Organizing a training **SEMINAR** in our church

Reachout's **QUARTERLY NEWSLETTER**

Reachout's annual **SET FREE IN CHRIST CONVENTION**

Full literature/tape/video **PRICE LIST**

How I could **HELP IN THE WORK** in my area

The 16mm film and video of **WITNESSES OF JEHOVAH**

Details of how I can **GIVE** to Reachout

ORDER FORM

Below is a list of publications, mentioned in this book, available from Reachout Trust. Prices are correct at the time of going to press but are subject to change without notice.

PUBLICATION	COST £	NO. REQUIRED	TOTAL
The Alternative View Reachout Trust	1.50		
Crisis of Conscience—h/b Ray Franz—p/b	9.00 7.50		
Deliberate Deception In The NWT Reachout Trust	0.15		
Gentile Times Reconsidered Carl Olof Jonsonn	7.00		
Jehovah's Witness Bible Study Reachout Trust	0.65		
Jehovah's Witness Factsheets Reachout Trust	0.65		
Jehovah's Witness New Testament Robert Contess	7.00		
Jehovah's Witness Pack—Special Reachout/Various	2.00		
Saleskids—2 vols Duane Magnani	13.00		
The Truth Revealed Reachout Trust	0.50		
Watch Out—Warning Tracts Reachout Trust (per 100)	4.00		
Where Is Michael? Duane Magnani	4.00		
Who Is The Faithful and Wise Servant? Duane Magnani	4.00		
Witnesses of Jehovah—video. Excellent documentary	45.00		
SUB TOTAL			
P. & P. (see over)			
TOTAL ENCLOSED			